# *It's* About TIME

## Planning Interventions and Extensions
## in Secondary School

# Mike Mattos    Austin Buffum

Jack Baldermann | Luis F. Cruz | Joe Doyle | Darin L. Fahrney
Paul Goldberg | Aaron Hansen | Dennis King
Regina Stephens Owens | Steve Pearce | Rich Rodriguez
Bob Sonju | Timothy S. Stuart | Jane Wagmeister

*Foreword by Richard DuFour*

Solution Tree | Press

*a division of*
Solution Tree

555 North Morton Street
Bloomington, IN 47404
800.733.6786 (toll free) / 812.336.7700
FAX: 812.336.7790

email: info@solution-tree.com
solution-tree.com

Printed in the United States of America

Visit **go.solution-tree.com/rtiatwork** to download the reproducibles in this book.

18 17 16 15 14     1 2 3 4 5

Library of Congress Cataloging-in-Publication Data

Mattos, Mike (Mike William)
   It's about time : planning interventions and extensions in secondary school / Mike Mattos and Austin Buffum, editors [and others] ; foreword by Richard DuFour.
      pages cm
   Includes bibliographical references and index.
   ISBN 978-1-936763-05-4 (perfect bound)  1.  Remedial teaching.  2.  Response to intervention (Learning disabled children) 3.  Learning disabled children--Education. 4.  Learning disabilities--Diagnosis.  5.  Middle school teaching.  6.  High school teaching. I. Buffum, Austin G. II. Title.
   LB1029.R4M365 2015
   371.102--dc23
                              2014028789

**Solution Tree**
Jeffrey C. Jones, CEO
Edmund M. Ackerman, President

**Solution Tree Press**
*President:* Douglas M. Rife
*Associate Acquisitions Editor:* Kari Gillesse
*Editorial Director:* Lesley Bolton
*Managing Production Editor:* Caroline Weiss
*Senior Production Editor:* Edward M. Levy
*Proofreader:* Ashante Thomas
*Text and Cover Designer:* Laura Kagemann
*Compositor:* Rachel Smith

I dedicate this book to the exceptional educators and support staff of Pioneer Middle School in Tustin, California. Most of what I know about creating a great secondary school is due to what we learned together by doing the work. I am forever grateful for the privilege of serving as principal of this outstanding school.

—Mike Mattos

This book is dedicated to the brave group of professionals at San Clemente High School who sought to create a professional learning community at that school. A special word of thanks goes to Charles Hinman and George Knights, who invested so much of their own passion into the effort.

—Austin Buffum

# Acknowledgments

Bringing this anthology from concept to completion was truly a collaborative effort, beginning with the outstanding professionals at Solution Tree. Guided by the leadership of CEO Jeffrey C. Jones and Solution Tree Press president Douglas M. Rife, Solution Tree has become the premier educational publishing and staff development company in the world. Specifically, we would like to thank Lesley Bolton for her efforts to coordinate this project, as well as Edward Levy and Kari Gillesse for their superb editing. We hope that this book moves Solution Tree one step closer to achieving its vision of transforming education worldwide.

This book would not have been possible without the contributing authors: Jack Baldermann, Luis F. Cruz, Joe Doyle, Darin L. Fahrney, Paul Goldberg, Aaron Hansen, Dennis King, Regina Stephens Owens, Steve Pearce, Rich Rodriguez, Bob Sonju, Timothy S. Stuart, and Jane Wagmeister. These individuals do not make their living as writers—they are exceptional educators, working primarily as site-, district-, and county-level administrators. We have tremendous empathy and appreciation for their efforts, as we know what it's like to try to find time to write after working as an educator all day. Their prose has brought the journey of each school to life.

We thank the exceptional schools that are featured in this book: Westlawn Middle School, White Pine Middle School, Baldwin Park High School, Robert Frost Junior High School, Fossil Ridge Intermediate School, Bloomington High School South, Jane Addams Junior High School, Riverside Brookfield High School, TeWinkle Middle School, Singapore American School, Gateway Community School, and the Virtual School and Early College Academy. These schools did not wait for the perfect conditions to begin restructuring to better serve their students. Instead, they got started, made mistakes, tried again, stayed focused, and most importantly, achieved! The lessons they learned from doing the work have blazed a trail for others to follow. We applaud their collective courage and dedication to ensure that every student succeeds on their campuses.

We would also like to acknowledge and thank the outstanding educators of Adlai E. Stevenson High School, both past and present. While no chapter in this anthology focuses specifically on Stevenson, that school has directly and indirectly influenced almost every other school mentioned. Over twenty years ago, the Stevenson staff started the journey of becoming a professional learning community (PLC), causing them to rethink every traditional secondary policy, procedure, and schedule. As a four-time National Blue Ribbon School, Stevenson continues to serve as a model of success for schools across the world.

Finally, while the schools described here represent a wide range of locations and demographics, they all share one underlying trait—each functions as a professional learning community. Richard DuFour, Robert Eaker, and Rebecca DuFour have dedicated their lives to developing, articulating, promoting, supporting, and living the Professional Learning Communities at Work™ process. Generously giving of their time and expertise, they have personally mentored almost every contributor to this anthology. We are forever grateful for their support, wisdom, and friendship.

> Visit **go.solution-tree.com/rtiatwork** to download the reproducibles in and access materials related to this book.

# Table of Contents

# Chapter 2

**Co-Teaching the RTI and PLC Way** . . . . . . . . . . . . . . . . . . . . . . . . . .**35**
*By Aaron Hansen*

# Chapter 3

**The Most Effective Intervention Is Prevention** . . . . . . . . . . . . . . . . . .**57**
*By Luis F. Cruz*

# Chapter 4

**Three Doses of Intervention and Acceleration** . . . . . . . . . . . . . . . . . . **79**
*By Paul Goldberg*

# Chapter 5

# Chapter 6

# Chapter 7

## Chapter 8

**Building and Sustaining a Culture That Supports Learning for All** ...................................................**167**
*By Jack Baldermann*

## Chapter 9

**The Power to Change Lives: Creating a Secondary Intensive Reading Intervention Model** .......................... **199**
*By Rich Rodriguez*

## Chapter 10

**Maximizing Student Learning Through a Compassionate Response to Intervention Model** ............................... **219**
*By Darin L. Fahrney and Timothy S. Stuart*

# Chapter 11

**From a Last Resort to a Model School of Choice**. . . . . . . . . . . . . . .**251**

*By Jane Wagmeister*

# Chapter 12

**Personalizing Learning Through Online Interventions**. . . . . . . . . . **291**

*By Regina Stephens Owens*

# About the Editors

 **Mike Mattos** is an internationally recognized author, presenter, and practitioner who specializes in uniting teachers, administrators, and support staff to transform schools by implementing response to intervention (RTI) and professional learning communities (PLCs). Mike co-created the RTI at Work™ model, which builds on the foundation of the PLC at Work™ process by using team structures and a focus on learning, collaboration, and results to drive successful outcomes.

Mike is former principal of Marjorie Veeh Elementary School and Pioneer Middle School in California. At both schools, Mike helped create powerful PLCs, improving learning for all students. In 2004, Marjorie Veeh, an elementary school with a large population of youth at risk, was named a California Distinguished School and won the Title I Academic Achievement Award.

A National Blue Ribbon School, Pioneer is among only thirteen schools in the United States selected by the GE Foundation as a Best-Practice Partner and is one of eight schools chosen by Richard DuFour to be featured in the video series *The Power of Professional Learning Communities at Work: Bringing the Big Ideas to Life*. Based on standardized test scores, Pioneer ranks among the top 1 percent of California secondary schools and, in 2009 and 2011, was named Orange County's top middle school. For his leadership, Mike was named the Orange County Middle School Administrator of the Year by the Association of California School Administrators.

**Austin Buffum, EdD,** has thirty-eight years of experience in public schools. His many roles include serving as former senior deputy superintendent of California's Capistrano Unified School District. Austin has presented in over five hundred school districts throughout the country and around the world. He delivers trainings and presentations on the RTI at Work model. This tiered approach to RTI is centered on PLC at Work concepts and strategies to ensure every student receives the time and support necessary to succeed. Austin also delivers workshops and presentations that provide the tools educators need to build and sustain PLCs.

Austin was selected 2006 Curriculum and Instruction Administrator of the Year by the Association of California School Administrators. He attended the Principals' Center at the Harvard Graduate School of Education and was greatly inspired by its founder, Roland Barth, an early advocate of the collaborative culture that defines PLCs today. He later led Capistrano's K–12 instructional program on an increasingly collaborative path toward operating as a PLC. During this process, thirty-seven of the district's schools were designated California Distinguished Schools and eleven received National Blue Ribbon recognition.

Austin is coauthor with Suzette Lovely of *Generations at School: Building an Age-Friendly Learning Community*.

A graduate of the University of Southern California, Austin earned a bachelor of music degree and received a master of education with honors. He holds a doctor of education from Nova Southeastern University.

To book Mike Mattos or Austin Buffum for professional development, contact pd@solution-tree.com.

# Foreword

Richard DuFour

Over many years, I have had the privilege to work with more than a quarter of a million educators in workshops and institutes. At each event, the moment arises when I poll the group on the following: "How many of you agree that virtually all of the mission statements our schools and districts develop are based on the premise that the fundamental purpose of the school is to help all students learn, that most educators would sincerely like to help all the students learn, and that if all students are to learn, some will need more time and support for learning than others?" The response to this question has always been a resounding, "Yes, we agree."

Then, I pose a final question, "Do you work in a school in which students are guaranteed additional time and support for learning when they struggle?" If schools were rational organizations, the only possible answer to this question would be, "Yes, of course, our students are ensured extra time and support for learning." Invariably, however, the overwhelming majority of the audience answers, "No, we don't guarantee students receive additional time and support."

When I press educators on why they answer in the negative, they point to the same obstacle: "The schedule won't let us." This response puzzles me, so I ask, "Who is this schedule, and why is he being so mean to you? Why won't he let you do what you know must be done?" I then ask, "Have any of you ever worked in a school that has changed its schedule?" Almost all attendees indicate that they have. So, we have educators who declare that some students need extra time and support to become proficient in essential knowledge and skills and acknowledge that in their own experience schedules can be changed, yet they assert their current schedule won't allow them to do what must be done. The answer to this dilemma is obvious: change the schedule so that it *supports* rather than *undermines* your priorities.

As a former high school principal responsible for building the master schedule, I recognize that schools do not have total license in this area. They must address certain givens. For example, there is typically little flexibility regarding when students arrive on and leave campus, because the bus schedules that drive those decisions are carved in stone. The schedule must also account for enough instructional minutes to comply with state standards. Lastly, no principal would ever think of depriving a teacher of lunch: teachers are *entitled* to a duty-free lunch period.

The editors and authors of *It's About Time: Planning Interventions and Extensions in Secondary School* make the compelling case that a school with a mission to help *all* students learn must recognize that when students struggle, they are *entitled* to extra time and support. They assert that the real test of a school's commitment to learning for all students is not the eloquence of its mission statement but rather what happens in the school when students don't learn.

## More Than Time

The first key to supporting all students is to ensure that the schedule provides educators with access to the students who need them most during the school day. While addressing that key is absolutely essential, it is not sufficient. Educators must also ensure that they use the extra time for learning in the right way and for the right purpose. No one has provided greater clarity on the critical conditions for effective intervention and extension than the editors of this book, Mike Mattos and Austin Buffum.

They have presented a clear and compelling picture of what effective systems of intervention and extension will look like in the real world of schools. I urge you to read carefully the section High Levels of Learning for All (page 5) in their introduction. Then, read the chapters to see how each school has used evidence to ensure that students who struggle receive additional time and support in a way that is timely, directive, diagnostic, tiered, and systematic. In these schools, what happens when students struggle is not left only to the teacher to whom they are assigned. Students are guaranteed additional time because the entire *school* responds in a way that provides assistance, without removing the student from new direct instruction or lowering curriculum standards. Furthermore, accompanying the focus on intervention is a commitment to extend the learning for students who are highly proficient. In chapter after chapter, the authors describe how the commitment to help all students learn at high levels has increased the percentage of students moving from proficiency to advanced levels of learning.

# Common Themes

The editors showcase a variety of schools. Despite the differences among them, several common themes emerge as each school's story unfolds.

## Linking Systematic Intervention and Enrichment to the Professional Learning Communities at Work™ Process

In every chapter, readers will hear consistent advice: systematic intervention and enrichment must occur in the larger context of a professional learning community (PLC). Unless the three big ideas of a PLC—(1) a commitment to help *all* students learn at high levels, (2) a collaborative and collective effort to foster that commitment, and (3) a focus on results to meet students' individual needs and to inform and improve individual and collective professional practice—are driving the school's work, time and structures to support intervention will have little impact. In fact, in the wrong school culture, teachers may view intervention as one more reason they are not responsible for student learning. If teachers assume, "I taught it, they didn't learn it, so let the intervention system deal with it," they will accomplish little.

Mattos and Buffum insist that schools must first embrace the culture of a PLC before moving to the question of intervention. It is evident that the authors in this book have taken their message to heart. In their own schools, these educators avoided the common tendency to regard systematic intervention and enrichment as a program to add to their existing structure and culture. They engaged in dialogue to shape the assumptions, beliefs, and expectations that constitute school culture. They went beyond writing mission statements about learning for all students to address the four questions that bring that mission to life (DuFour, Eaker, & DuFour, 2008).

1. What knowledge, skills, and dispositions do we want students to learn?

2. How will we know when each student has learned?

3. How will we respond when some students don't learn?

4. How will we respond when some students are already proficient?

## Engaging Staff in Dialogue Throughout the Implementation Process

Leaders must engage all staff in dialogue regarding their assumptions about the school, the rationale for creating systematic intervention, and ways to overcome the inevitable difficulties that occur throughout implementation. Shaping culture requires conversations rather than presentations and dialogue, not monologue. School leaders in these chapters didn't make a PowerPoint presentation on systematic intervention and extension before plunging ahead. They linked the idea to a larger purpose, stressed why the system was needed before delving into how it would operate, and encouraged feedback from the staff. They built shared ownership to ensure that the system was not an administrative mandate but a collective decision all staff embraced.

### Persevering in the Face of Setbacks

No chapters will describe how a school's initial implementation of systematic intervention and enrichment worked flawlessly and has continued without difficulty. Initial efforts often led to new problems and unanticipated consequences. Rather than abandoning their efforts in the face of challenges, the educators began again more intelligently. When one approach failed to bring about the desired results, they tried another, and another, and another. As Darin L. Fahrney and Timothy S. Stuart write in chapter 10, "Our administrative team and teacher leaders had to practice what we preach to students: grit, perseverance, and problem solving" (page 222). This message rings through all of the chapters. Their commitment to continuous improvement led these educators to search constantly for better practice.

The best strategy to ensure that people sustain a collective effort over time is to remove obstacles to progress and provide the resources and support that enable them to feel successful in the work they are being asked to do (Amabile & Kramer, 2011). The school leaders featured in this book were constantly seeking feedback about problems that were occurring and then engaging the entire staff in finding solutions. They did not assume they had all the answers to every issue. They recognized, however, the importance of calling the attention of people throughout the organization to an obstacle to progress and then enlisting their help in seeking ways to remove the obstacle. They also created a sense of momentum by calling attention to small, incremental progress as soon as it occurred.

### Focusing on Results

Each author demonstrates an awareness that the effectiveness of his or her school's systems of intervention and enrichment must be determined by concrete results rather than noble intentions. The authors appeal to the moral imperative of providing greater individual support to meet the needs of each student. Some authors provide anecdotal accounts of how individual students benefitted. Some share staff members' positive perceptions about their school's journey to develop effective interventions. In the final analysis, however, true to the PLC process, they recognize the need to answer the question, "How do we know our students are learning?" Each contributor then provides compelling evidence of the significant impact systematic intervention and extension had in his or her school on higher levels of learning for students.

I am certain that many people who purchase this book will be looking for an intervention and extension schedule to copy for their school. However, no schedule has the power to change the culture of a school. It is the thinking behind the schedule—the assumptions, beliefs, and expectations that led to its creation—that makes a schedule so powerful. Building an effective system of intervention and extension is a natural outgrowth of a faculty's recognition that its professed mission to help all students learn will never be more than words on paper until they take specific actions. Most importantly, staff must clarify what students are to learn in every unit of instruction; establish an ongoing process of gathering evidence of student learning; provide individual students with additional time and support for learning in a timely, directive, diagnostic, and systematic way; and use evidence of student learning to inform and improve instruction.

How many secondary schools would you need to see to be convinced that educators *can* provide students with extra time and support for learning? Is it five; is it ten? Thanks to their tireless work in supporting educators, the editors of this book can point you to the website www.allthingsplc.info, where hundreds of educators have solved the riddle of time. It is imperative that educators acknowledge that they are not the victims but the masters of time. As the title of this wonderful volume makes clear, *it's about time* that educators respond to the question, "Do you work in a school where students are guaranteed additional time and support for learning when they struggle" with the only plausible answer: "Of course! How else can we ensure all students will learn?"

# References

Amabile, T., & Kramer, S. (2011). *The progress principle: Using small wins to ignite joy, engagement, and creativity at work.* Boston: Harvard Business Press.

DuFour, R., Eaker, R., & DuFour, R. (2008). *Revisiting professional learning communities at work: New insights for improving schools.* Bloomington, IN: Solution Tree Press.

# Introduction: Harnessing the Power of Time

## Mike Mattos and Austin Buffum

Time. It waits for no one, flies when you are having fun, and heals all wounds. Just a stitch of it saves nine. It can be raced against, borrowed, wasted, and served. It may be ripe, due, on your hands, and on your side. You can have a whale of it, yet when you have much to do, have so little.

In the world of education, these common idioms about time hold true. In the United States, the average student spends thirteen years and approximately fifteen thousand hours of time at school from kindergarten through high school—a boatload of time. Yet, with the staggering amount of required curriculum that must be taught each year, teachers are faced with a daunting reality: so much to teach, so little time.

At the secondary level, this time crunch is multiplied exponentially by the expectation that schools not only teach mandatory curriculum but also offer college coursework for students who are accelerating, remediation work for skills that students should have already mastered, and enrichment through extracurricular opportunities in athletics, the arts, community service, clubs, and social activities—a seemingly infinite number of demands expected in a finite amount of time. Because adequate time is an essential variable in the formula of learning, this dilemma has a profound impact on both students and educators.

## The Importance of Time to Student Learning

It is commonly said that in this world, nothing can be certain except for death and taxes. In the education world, we have our own two universal truths.

1. **Every student does not learn the same way:** Every student has unique learning needs, based on his or her prior knowledge and

experiences, cultural values, learning styles, and aptitudes. Due to these differences, no matter how well a teacher teaches a concept, we know some students won't get it the first time, because the best way to teach a concept to one student might fail miserably with another in the same class.

2. **Every student does not develop at the same speed:** We know that there are spans of time in which students mature, both physically and intellectually. Some of these developmental spans, such as the period in which students start to show the physical changes of puberty, can be quite significant—it is not uncommon for a high school classroom to have a boy still waiting for his growth spurt sitting next to a fellow classmate who is a foot taller and already shaving. Less visible to the eye, but just as age-appropriate and extreme, are the differences in which adolescents develop intellectually and socially. Just as a group of boys won't develop the need to shave at the same speed or on the same day, secondary school students will not acquire the ability to solve abstract equations or display empathy at the same speed.

If we condense these two universal truths into a simple formula to ensure student learning, the equation would look like this (Bloom, 1968; Buffum, Mattos, & Weber, 2012; Guskey & Pigott, 1988):

$$\text{Targeted Instruction} + \text{Time} = \text{Learning}$$

If a school can make both teaching and time variables in this equation and target them to meet each student's individual learning and developmental needs, the school is more likely to achieve high levels of learning for every student.

For any school dedicated to ensuring that all students learn at high levels, making the time to meet each student's varying learning needs is a critical consideration. Achieving this goal would be much easier if the U.S. education system was purposely designed around this outcome. Unfortunately, our traditional secondary model of education is not only misaligned to this goal but purposefully designed to make time a rigid constant for all students, since the goal was not high levels of learning for all students but success for a select few.

## The Original Purpose of Secondary Education

We should hardly be surprised that our traditional secondary school practices fail to make teaching and time variables, as the original purpose of secondary education in America was for only a small number of students to attend and for even fewer to graduate. High schools were established in the late 1800s as selective institutions, "catering to the relatively few students who had the interest and the means to attend school after the primary grades" (Rumberger, 2011, p. 21). As stated by Harvard University president Charles Eliot in 1893:

> The main function (of high school) is to prepare for the duties of life that small proportion of all the children in the country—a proportion small in number, but very important to the welfare of the nation—who show themselves able to profit by an education prolonged to the eighteenth year, and whose parents are able to support them while they remain in school so long. (Dorn, 1996, p. 36)

This philosophy became a reality. In 1900, only 14 percent of children fourteen to seventeen years old attended high school (Rumberger, 2011).

While the percentage of America's youth attending high school increased dramatically throughout the first half of the 20th century, the predominant view of secondary school as a selective process remained. In his widely cited 1959 book *The American High School Today*, former Harvard president James Bryant Conant argued for all students to attend high school but proposed the curriculum be differentiated to prepare students for diverse futures—some for advanced schooling and some for the workplace (Rumberger, 2011). In such a system, students are sorted into tracks based primarily on their perceived ability and prior academic success. Students deemed to have greater academic potential are placed in higher tracks designed to prepare them for college, while students placed in lower tracks prepare to immediately enter a vocational trade after high school. If a student struggled in the higher track, the solution in most cases was not to provide additional time and support but instead to lower the student's academic expectations and demote him or her to a lower track.

While some might argue that this selective approach to secondary education was partially driven to maintain class elitism, there was an undeniable economic reality to this design. A vast majority of Americans either farmed or worked in factories throughout the 20th century—careers that rarely required a high school diploma or college degree. If we were still preparing a majority of students for the labor-driven professions of the 20th century, this traditional model would be ideal. But time stands still for no one.

## The Brutal Facts

Drastic economic changes driven by global competition and technological advances require us to rethink and revise our fundamental purpose and practices in secondary education. Consider the following characteristics of the 21st century U.S. economy.

- Less than 1 percent of the population directly farms for a living, and less than 10 percent work in factories (Hagenbaugh, 2002; U.S. Department of Agriculture, Utah State University Extension, & LetterPress Software, n.d.).

- According to the U.S. Department of Labor, nearly two-thirds of the new jobs created between 2006 and 2016 will be in occupations that require postsecondary education or considerable on-the-job training, while jobs requiring routine manual tasks will continue to decrease (Chao, 2008).

- Among traditional blue-collar trades, higher levels of academic preparation will be a prerequisite for employment. For example, the nonprofit organization ACT (2006) examines the mathematics and reading skills required for electricians, construction workers, upholsterers, and plumbers and concludes they match what's necessary to do well in a first-year college course.

- Wages for careers that require higher levels of education and training will outpace nondegreed jobs, with the average college graduate earning 77 percent more than the typical high school graduate (Bureau of Labor Statistics, 2008).

Educators commonly say that it is our job to prepare students for the real world. Well, the stats we've just listed are the real world. In our current global economy, there is virtually no pathway to the middle class that does not require a postsecondary education—anything less is a one-way ticket to poverty. As the American Diploma Project (2004) states:

> Successful preparation for both postsecondary education and employment requires learning the same rigorous English and mathematics content and skills. No longer do students planning to work after high school need a different and less rigorous curriculum than those planning to go to college. In fact, nearly all students will require some postsecondary education, including on-the-job training, after completing high school. Therefore, a college and workplace readiness curriculum should be a graduation requirement, not an option, for all high school students. (pp. 8–9)

Restructuring education to meet 21st century needs has been the driving force behind many educational reform initiatives. From block scheduling and advisory periods to starting the school year earlier so there is more instructional time prior to the high-stakes tests given each spring, a majority of reforms have focused primarily on revising the secondary master schedule and calendar. While these reforms have reallocated instructional time, they have failed to realize significant gains in student achievement, primarily because most schools continue the practice of tracking.

As Jeannie Oakes (2005) finds in her landmark study, *Keeping Track: How Schools Structure Inequality (second edition),*

> the deep structure of tracking remains uncannily robust. Most middle and high schools still sort students into classes at different levels based on judgments of student "ability." This sorting continues to disadvantage those in lower track classes. Such students have less access to high-status knowledge, fewer opportunities to engage in stimulating learning activities, and classroom relationships less likely to foster engagement with teachers, peers, and learning. (p. 4)

At a time when we need all students to have access to postsecondary education, the current conduit connecting elementary school and college is designed like a sieve—sifting students out of advanced tracks until the precious few deemed most capable remain. Rearranging the number or length of periods in the school day will not solve this problem.

## High Levels of Learning for All

To achieve high levels of learning for every student, schools must restructure their assumptions and practices around the following essential outcomes.

- All students will leave high school with the skills, knowledge, and dispositions necessary to succeed in postsecondary education, so all students must have access to college-readiness coursework. Schools will remove tracks of core instruction focused exclusively on below-grade-level expectations.

- Because all students do not learn the same way, develop at the same speed, enter school with the same prior knowledge, or have the same academic supports at home, students will be provided additional time and support to achieve these rigorous expectations.

- Because a single teacher could not possibly meet the diverse needs of all his or her students, schools will create a systematic intervention process to ensure that struggling students are guaranteed to receive additional time and support for learning that goes beyond what an individual classroom teacher can provide. Achieving this goal will require staff members to work collaboratively and take collective responsibility for each student's success.

- Some students will need a little extra support from time to time, while others will enter school with profound gaps in their foundational skills. To meet this diverse range of needs, schools will provide both supplemental (Tier 2) and intensive (Tier 3) interventions.

- Intervention will be provided in addition to core instruction, not in place of it. Students will not miss new essential core instruction to get extra help.

- Extra support will be available to all students who demonstrate the need. Because some students cannot come to school early or stay late, schools will embed this help during the school day, when students are required to be at school and all staff members are available to assist.

- Some students will not choose to voluntarily take advantage of this additional support. This should be expected, as some will lack the maturity, self-motivation, parental support, or vision of what is necessary to succeed as an adult. Because success or failure in school is life altering, students will not be given the option of failing. Interventions, when necessary, will be directive.

- Some students will enter school already meeting grade-level expectations. Additional time and support will not come at the expense of these students. Just as schools establish extra assistance to help at-risk students reach grade-level expectations, they will also provide all students with additional time and support to help them succeed in the most rigorous coursework.

Achieving these outcomes for every student will require more than a new bell schedule. To use an analogy, if reforming secondary education were likened to re-modeling a house, we need more than new flooring and some fresh paint; we need to take the house down to the foundation and rebuild. This level of change is difficult, messy, and full of unexpected obstacles. If you have ever taken on the task of a major home remodel, you quickly learn that the devil is in the details.

## The Real Problem

Creating a systematic process to provide students with additional support, offered in addition to grade-level core instruction, will undoubtedly require significant revisions to a school's schedule. Most schools assume that the biggest obstacle to this goal is determining how to manipulate the minutes within the school's current bell schedule to make interventions possible during the school day. In reality, this is often the easiest part of the process. There is not a secondary school in the United

States that does not create special schedules throughout the year—for assemblies, fine arts events, testing, and so on. Creating these unique schedules comes down to basic mathematics. For example, if a school wants thirty minutes for a pep rally, the administrative team shaves minutes off of periods and transition times throughout the day to total thirty and then adds these borrowed minutes together and inserts them back into the schedule. Completing this task does not require a task force to study the problem. Creating the time needed for secondary supplemental intervention periods would follow the same process.

The real obstacles begin when a school considers the logistics of having potentially hundreds of students transitioning to specific interventions. Critical questions arise, such as:

- How do we successfully use this time to support student learning?
- How do we determine what interventions to offer?
- How do we assign staff?
- How do we transition students to the correct help sessions?
- How do we hold students accountable to attend?
- How do we move beyond a study hall approach and actually provide targeted instruction?
- How do we efficiently monitor student progress?
- What do we do with students who don't need extra help?
- How do we provide intensive interventions to students who lack the foundational skills of reading, writing, number sense, or the English language and still give them access to grade-level curriculum?
- What if students need help in multiple academic areas?
- What if a student's needs are not academic, but instead the student lacks the motivation to try?
- How do we keep the process from becoming a paperwork nightmare?
- If we shave minutes off regular classes, how will teachers be able to cover the required curriculum?
- How can we achieve these outcomes within our current resources and without asking teachers to work beyond their contractual obligations?
- Where does special education fit into this process?

These are all legitimate and difficult logistical questions that can stall a school's efforts to provide students additional time for learning. Fortunately, there are secondary schools across North America and beyond that have grappled with these questions, overcome the obstacles, and seen significant and sustained improvement in student achievement. Having some of these schools share specific, proven solutions is the purpose of this anthology.

## Proven Solutions From Real-Life Schools

There is an old Chinese proverb that says, "To understand the road ahead, ask those coming back." The contributors to this anthology work on the frontlines of education. They have rolled up their sleeves, worked collaboratively, and addressed the obstacles that hinder a school's ability to provide students with systematic, timely, targeted, and directive interventions during the school day.

We have purposely selected a wide variety of schools for this anthology, including:

- K–8, middle, junior high, and high schools
- Smaller and larger schools
- Traditional and alternative schools and a virtual school
- Public and private schools
- Schools whose demographics range from majority at risk to extremely affluent
- Schools in locations that range from Alabama to Singapore
- Schools whose master schedules contain from four to ten periods a day

While the specific demographics and schedules vary from school to school, the essential outcomes are the same: each of these schools created the time and processes necessary to ensure that all students had access to both rigorous college-prep core instruction *and* the extra individualized support needed to achieve these outcomes.

Equally important, educators at each of the contributing schools realized that a new schedule alone would not be enough. Success with this goal requires creating a school culture focused on student learning and collaborative structures. To this end, these schools implemented Professional Learning Community (PLC) at Work™ practices. The solutions we offer in each of the following chapters are by-products of the collective efforts of all staff members working together to answer the four critical questions of a PLC (DuFour, DuFour, Eaker, & Many, 2010).

1. What do we expect students to learn?

2. How do we know they are learning it?

3. How do we respond when they do not learn?

4. How do we respond when they have already learned?

Finally, we specifically selected model schools that created time and effective interventions without receiving additional funding, staffing, or concessions to lengthen their school day. It would hardly be replicable if one of our contributing schools started its story with the narrative, "We received a two-million-dollar school-improvement grant, which funded paying our staff a stipend to lengthen the school day." Almost every example in this book was achieved within the school's existing resources, in accordance with teacher contractual agreements, and in compliance with district, state, and federal regulations.

## An Overview of This Anthology

The goal of each chapter is to provide more than a broad explanation of how a particular school created time for interventions; instead, the text digs deeper into exactly how the school used time for interventions and extensions and provides the reader with actual schedules, tools, and examples. At the beginning of each chapter, we provide a short commentary to emphasize the critical considerations that led to the school's success. The chapters themselves address the unexpected obstacles that came up during implementation, showing how the school successfully overcame these hurdles and providing evidence that the school's efforts significantly improved student learning.

It is not necessary to read each chapter in order; in fact, depending on the current needs of your school or district, some chapters might be more relevant and helpful to your journey. However, while each chapter can be read independently, the chapter order represents a continuum of intensity, starting with interventions that will best support student success in Tier 1 core instruction and ending with interventions more directly focused on students who need intensive remediation in foundational skills and behavior.

To assist, the following is a brief overview of each chapter:

- In chapter 1, Dennis King discusses how Westlawn Middle School in Huntsville, Alabama, created time for interventions during initial teaching by identifying essential learning outcomes, using formative assessments to monitor student progress in real time, and using multiple instructional practices to embed preteaching and reteaching during core instruction.

- In chapter 2, Aaron Hansen describes how White Pine Middle School in Ely, Nevada, created flexible time for intervention during Tier 1 core instruction through the use of team teaching.

- In chapter 3, Luis F. Cruz details how Baldwin Park High School in Southern California created a proactive intervention support class for incoming at-risk freshmen to support their immediate success in core classes.

- In chapter 4, Paul Goldberg explains how Robert Frost Junior High School in Schaumburg, Illinois, created three "doses" of intervention time to support learning for all students.

- In chapter 5, Bob Sonju explains how Fossil Ridge Intermediate School in St. George, Utah, created a supplemental intervention period to provide targeted interventions and extension during the school day.

- In chapter 6, Joe Doyle demonstrates how Bloomington High School South in Bloomington, Indiana, created a supplemental intervention period utilizing the school's existing student management software to track intervention offerings and student participation.

- In chapter 7, Steve Pearce shares how Jane Addams Junior High School in Schaumburg, Illinois, created a flex period to provide interventions and how this program evolved into multiple schedules to target different types of student needs.

- In chapter 8, Jack Baldermann offers multiple ways that Riverside Brookfield High School, outside of Chicago, provided intensive support for incoming at-risk students through the use of pre-identification, summer school, and an intensive intervention support class.

- In chapter 9, Rich Rodriguez outlines how TeWinkle Middle School in Costa Mesa, California, created an intensive reading intervention program that still provides all students access to grade-level English language arts standards.

- In chapter 10, Darin L. Fahrney and Timothy S. Stuart describe how Singapore American School created a "compassionate RTI" process that focuses on both the academic and social needs of students requiring additional time and support.

- In chapter 11, Jane Wagmeister details how Gateway Community School, an alternative high school serving extremely at-risk youth in Camarillo, California, transformed its campus from a place of despair to a school of success through the use of a schoolwide behavior intervention program.

- In chapter 12, Regina Stephens Owens describes how Spring Independent School District in Houston, Texas, created the Virtual School and Early College Academy, an online school that provided students additional time and support primarily through the use of technology and social media.

In closing, a point of caution: Richard DuFour often says, "Embrace the forest; don't fall in love with a tree." While the goal of this book is to provide educators with detailed examples of exactly how real-life schools created time to implement specific interventions, there will undoubtedly be aspects in every example that do not perfectly match your school's current resources and reality. Our bigger goal is not only to reveal detailed examples of specific interventions but more importantly the larger guiding priorities and collaborative processes that created them.

The model schools in this anthology did not look to buy an intervention "program" to improve their school; rather they focused on an ongoing, collaborative process of improvement. While you may not be able to re-create the exact interventions described in each chapter, you can re-create the process, tailoring these examples to your students' unique needs and building on the specific talents and resources available at your school and within your own local, state, or provincial guidelines.

Keeping this important caution in mind, a forest awaits!

# References

ACT. (2006). *Ready for college and ready for work: Same or different?* Iowa City, IA: Author.

American Diploma Project. (2004). *Ready or not: Creating a high school diploma that counts.* Washington, DC: Achieve. Accessed at www.achieve.org/files/ReadyorNot.pdf on March 5, 2014.

Bloom, B. S. (1968). Learning for mastery. *Evaluation Comment, 1*(2), 1–12. (ERIC Document Reproduction No. ED053419).

Buffum, A., Mattos, M., & Weber, C. (2012). *Simplifying response to intervention: Four essential guiding principles.* Bloomington, IN: Solution Tree Press.

Bureau of Labor Statistics. (2008, February). *Occupational projections and training data: 2008–9 edition.* Washington, DC: U.S. Department of Labor.

Chao, E. L. (2008, June 23). *Remarks prepared for delivery by U.S. Secretary of Labor Elaine L. Chao to the Greater Louisville Inc. Metro Chamber of Commerce.* Washington, DC: U.S. Department of Labor. Accessed at www.dol.gov/_sec/media/speeches/20080623_COC .htm on March 5, 2014.

Dorn, S. (1996). *Creating the dropout: An institutional and social history of school failure.* Westport, CT: Praeger.

DuFour, R., DuFour, R., Eaker, R., & Many, T. W. (2010). *Learning by doing: A handbook for professional learning communities at work* (2nd ed.). Bloomington, IN: Solution Tree Press.

Guskey, T. R., & Pigott, T. D. (1988). Research on group-based mastery learning programs: A meta-analysis. *Journal of Educational Research, 81*(4), 197–216.

Hagenbaugh, B. (2002, December 12). U.S. manufacturing jobs fading away fast. *USA Today.* Accessed at www.usatoday.com/money/economy/2002-12-12-manufacture_x.htm on July 8, 2011.

Oakes, J. (2005). *Keeping track: How schools structure inequality* (2nd ed.). New Haven, CT: Yale University Press.

Rumberger, R. W. (2011). *Dropping out: Why students drop out of high school and what can be done about it.* Cambridge, MA: Harvard University Press.

U.S. Department of Agriculture, Utah State University Extension, & LetterPress Software. (n.d.). *Growing a nation: The story of American agriculture.* Accessed at www.agclassroom .org/gan/classroom/pdf/embed1_seeds.pdf on July 8, 2011.

**Dennis King, DEd**, has focused throughout his career on school improvement, first as a practicing school administrator and now as an education consultant. His experience as a high school science teacher, assistant principal, high school principal, executive director, and assistant superintendent for school improvement created the foundation for his becoming a Solution Tree associate supporting professional learning communities, formative assessment, and response to intervention. Since 2003, Dennis has worked with hundreds of schools across the United States to strengthen their school improvement processes and supply research-based strategies to support students during their learning. In addition to working as a consultant, he is an assistant professor at Baker University in Overland Park, Kansas, in the Educational Leadership Program for aspiring district leaders.

To book Dennis King for professional development, contact pd@solution-tree.com.

# Making Time for Interventions During Core Instruction

Dennis King

We often think of interventions as the additional time and support provided after core instruction to assist struggling students. As the story of Westlawn demonstrates, however, the key to an effective system of interventions begins with making sure that most students succeed in initial instruction. When more students "get it" during core instruction, less time and fewer resources are needed for reteaching, thus saving both.

*Editors' Note*

We would like to highlight three highly successful strategies that Westlawn used schoolwide to create time through more effective core instruction.

1. Essential standards were broken down into specific student learning targets. Using the Alabama state curriculum, teacher teams not only identified a doable number of essential learning outcomes that they ensured all students would master for each unit of study, but they also broke these standards down into the specific skills and knowledge that students would need to learn in each lesson to ultimately master the larger goal. By taking this additional step, teachers could target short formative assessments and activities during the unit to see how students were doing along the way. Think about it: if a student struggles on the first learning target needed in a sequence of skills necessary to master a larger goal but the teacher does not find this out until the end-of-unit assessment, then for this student the time between the first learning target and the end-of-unit assessment is wasted.

2. The essential standards and criteria for proficiency were shared with the students at the start of the unit. While this might seem like common sense, this is rarely the reality at most secondary schools. Think back to when you were in

school. Prior to a high-stakes assessment, how often did a teacher or professor show you exactly what you needed to know? Yet, our failure to do so makes students guess what they are expected to learn. Invariably, some students guess poorly, which then will require extra time for interventions. When learning targets are explicitly provided to students up front, we exponentially increase the chance that they will be mastered during core instruction, thus saving time later. In the end, what it takes to succeed in a unit, class, or secondary school should not be a mystery.

3. Students were provided formative opportunities and feedback prior to summative assessments. In a drama class, the teacher has the cast rehearse numerous times before the big performance, allowing actors to make mistakes, learn, and improve. Likewise, a football coach has his team scrimmage for days and weeks prior to the first game, allowing players to learn from their errors and improve. Sadly, students are rarely provided opportunities to practice and receive coaching prior to a big academic performance. Providing students with opportunities to rehearse prior to an end-of-unit assessment, then providing corrective feedback to each student on areas of need, is a highly effective intervention.

We suspect that some educators might read this chapter and conclude that they don't have the class time needed to give formative assessments and provide student feedback. In response to this concern, we offer this suggestion: Don't begin by trying to implement this process on every unit and lesson. Instead, identify one or two critical learning targets that every student needs to master in your next unit of study. Then, apply this process. As teachers and students get efficient at these practices, you will find that you don't have the time to *not* do these practices.

---

Westlawn Middle School, located in southwestern Huntsville, Alabama, is an urban Title I school serving grades 6–8. The student body is very diverse, with a racial and ethnic breakdown consisting of 52 percent Black, 26 percent Hispanic, 16 percent Caucasian, 4 percent multiracial, 1.3 percent Asian, 0.5 percent Pacific Islander, and 0.2 percent American Indian / Alaska Native. Approximately 11 percent (59 out of 549) of the student population qualifies for special education service, 12.8 percent (70 out of 549) of the students qualify as English learners (ELs), and approximately 98.4 percent of the school enrollment qualifies for free or reduced lunch. Ninety-one percent of the teachers at Westlawn Middle School are highly qualified in their content area and are in compliance with the guidelines outlined in No Child Left Behind (NCLB, 2002).

The desire to enhance learning for all students has driven both districts and schools to implement formal testing programs to identify the skill deficiencies of their students. Correctly identifying these deficits and then providing targeted instruction to address them are necessary steps in ensuring that students gain the skills they need to compete in a global marketplace. These screening and benchmark assessments identify students who have already fallen behind (Tier 3), but these assessment data do not measure items like student motivation, engagement, or a culture of failing, and when too many students are failing at core instruction, these assessment data come too late. Additionally, many schools are finding it difficult to create additional intervention time to address Tier 3 concerns. If schools focus on skill development only quarterly, biannually, or annually by investigating benchmark assessments, schools using standardized universal screening methods will struggle to address their overall intervention problem—the failure of students to master the core curriculum. The previous Westlawn Middle School practice of test, monitor, intervene, and test was not a proactive strategy to reduce the intervention needs over the long term. The sense of urgency was at an all-time high as the Westlawn faculty faced immediate concerns not only from eight years of low achievement but also from students' lack of ownership, demonstrated in both achievement and behavior. In essence, too many students were failing in the core instruction. A more proactive approach was needed.

Addressing the immediate instructional needs of students during core instruction provided the foundation for strong Tier 1 support. Westlawn started a process of ongoing assessment, feedback, and intervention, creating additional time within the classroom to master essential skills and standards. Formalizing the instructional process of monitoring students during the instructional block required teachers to work within their content teams to first identify essential learning outcomes and then develop specific learning targets to reach them. This was a new process for Westlawn teachers, who were not accustomed to working collaboratively to create specific products for Tier 1 instruction. Teachers reinforced the concentrated instruction process through "identifying the essential knowledge and skills that all students must master to learn at high levels, and determining the specific learning needs for each child to get there" (Buffum, Mattos, & Weber, 2012, p. 45). This process of allowing students to experience success early in the instructional unit and track their own progress engaged students in their own learning. This focus on strong Tier 1 support created an instructional model that allowed teachers to focus on the curriculum for those students who lack both the will and skill to master the essentials in sixth, seventh, and eighth grades.

## Learning What Works

The Westlawn staff based their Tier 1 intervention plan on several powerful, research-based instructional practices. Research has shown that formative assessment coupled with student feedback results in a tremendous increase in student achievement and engagement (Hattie, 2009; Hattie & Timperley, 2007; Marzano, Pickering, & Heflebower, 2011; Stiggins, Arter, Chappius, & Chappius, 2004). In *What Works in Schools: Translating Research Into Action*, Robert J. Marzano (2003) explores how highly effective schools overcome the effects of student backgrounds. Marzano's top effect for improving student achievement is the guaranteed and viable curriculum, which creates a student-friendly environment. In this model, each collaborative team deconstructs the curriculum standards into student-friendly learning targets. The deconstruction of the standards provides the viability for teaching all components of the standard.

As learning targets are developed, two major factors with a high probability of ensuring student learning are *alignment* and *time*. Alignment refers to aligning all facets of instruction (standards, benchmarks, frameworks, instruction, and assessment) and provides students with equal opportunities to learn the content standards. Time refers to teachers having adequate instructional time during the day and over the course of the academic year to engage students in activities that support their learning.

As teacher content-based teams clarify the essential skills in the curriculum standard, they provide the foundation for both teachers and students to monitor learning based on the learning targets the teacher teams have identified for each standard (Wiliam, 2011). This enables them to also effectively develop common formative assessment during Tier 1 instruction. Strengthening Tier 1 support cannot be done effectively without the information provided by common formative assessments to guide the process (Buffum et al., 2012). The formative assessment process drives both the curriculum (identifying what we want students to learn) and interventions (effective student support) during instruction. As Dylan Wiliam (2011) writes, "When implemented well, formative assessments can effectively double the speed of student learning" (pp. 36–37). Additionally, meta-analysis studies by John Hattie (2009) find that student self-reporting of grades (students tracking their progress) yields a 1.44 effect-size gain, almost one and a half years of growth in a one-year period of time. Additionally, the use of corrective feedback to guide students accelerates their achievement during the assessment process. Effective Tier 1 intervention incorporates each of these findings to strengthen instruction for students. Allowing students to know what they need to learn (where I am going), in comparison to what they know (where I am now) and how to close the gap, is an effective visualization of the intervention journey in Tier 1 (Sadler, 1989).

Formative assessment makes the curriculum viable for students. It gives them time to learn the essential standards. However, the surge of formative assessment has created murky waters when it comes to clarity of both purpose and implementation. Shepard and colleagues (2005) define formative assessment as a tool to strengthen the assessment process, leading to improved teaching and learning. However, Dylan Wiliam (2011) notes, "trying to make the term formative assessment apply to a thing (the assessment itself) just doesn't work" (p. 38). When the formative assessment is referred to as a specific tool (thing or event), the use may have multiple interpretations, the least of which is to provide the necessary feedback supporting students in their learning. Formative assessment includes items such as district benchmark assessments or standardized assessments given quarterly within the system. Unfortunately, these assessments have little or no instructional value as they lack opportunities to engage students during instruction. The need to shift formative assessment from an event or specific tool to a process is a critical distinction for consideration. The Assessment Reform Group in the United Kingdom argues that using assessment as a process to improve learning requires five elements to be in place.

1.  The provision of effective feedback to students

2.  The active involvement of students in their own learning

3.  The adjustment of teaching to take into account the results of assessment

4.  The recognition of the profound influence assessment has on the motivation and self-esteem of students, both of which are crucial influences in learning, and

5.  The need for students to be able to assess themselves and understand how to improve (Wiliam, 2011, p. 39)

Effective use of assessment as a promoter of learning—as opposed to a way to document learning that offers little or no feedback to students—is an important step in Tier 1 instruction. Effective use of intervention monitoring in Tier 1 must be based on the targeted support formatively assessed during the student's learning (Buffum et al., 2012).

Feedback from formative assessment is effective when it is timely, descriptive of the work, positively geared toward the learning journey, clear and specific, and differentiated by the student (Brookhart, 2008). Hattie (2009) finds that providing students with descriptive feedback can result in a desired effect-size gain of 0.40 to 0.73 on summative exams.

# Identifying and Overcoming Obstacles

With the start of a new school year, the mindset from eight years of poor academic performance permeated Westlawn's student body. With a new administrative team and a few new teachers, the task was to shift that mindset from one of academic failure to academic success, from low achievement and apathy to achievement and engagement—a difficult task laced with many obstacles. The ongoing sense of academic failure created a sense of school rejection. Carol Dweck (2006) reminds us that "rejection does not mean you're not smart or talented. It means you are not fulfilling your potential" (p. 19). The ongoing sense of academic failure created a sense of school rejection. When a school is labeled as failing due to low achievement scores, that school can often become paralyzed. At Westlawn, the golem effect (where low expectations lead to a decrease in performance) was evidently stopping all progress, including research-based core instruction.

To restore the focus on learning and reverse the golem effect, we shifted the focus toward development of a school leadership team. Identifying key teacher leaders who would focus on both school culture and collaboration was a critical first step. The leadership team, along with the teaching faculty, collaboratively developed vision statements to guide the direction for improvement. Using a collaborative process, they asked staff members to define the type of school they wanted Westlawn to become in the next three years and carefully recorded each response on chart paper. The responses were then collected under the following six categories.

1. Academic achievement

2. Parent involvement

3. Professional development

4. Culture and safety

5. Technology

6. Student involvement

Next, we established collective commitments for each vision statement, in order to shape behaviors for both students and staff. For example, the collective commitment of teachers to high levels of academic achievement was to:

- Implement explicit, strategic teaching strategies in every class

- Implement higher-order thinking skills through open-ended questions

- Implement the Alabama Course of Study (ALCOS) for standards-based instruction and assessment

For students, the commitment to high levels of academic achievement meant that they would:

- Be actively involved in the learning by talking, writing, investigating, reading, and listening during instructional time

- Actively participate in state and district assessments within the time frame outlined by the district

- Be engaged and invested in monthly formative assessments that determine students' academic progress

- Take ownership

These commitments are a set of behaviors determined and agreed on by faculty and students to guide the focus of their work. These combined commitments become the foundation for successful implementation of Tier 1 support.

## Making Time in the Schedule

Buffum and colleagues (2012) define concentrated instruction as the systematic process of identifying the essential knowledge and skills that all students must master to learn at high levels and determining the specific learning needs for each child to get there. At Westlawn, content grade-level teams identified the essential learning from the Alabama Course of Study for the core content areas of math, English language arts, social studies, and science. As illustrated in figure 1.1 (page 22), the resources necessary to support each question originated from team products associated with the four critical questions (see page 9) of collaborative teams in a professional learning community (DuFour & Eaker, 1998).

The process begins with teams identifying the resource to answer question 1 of a collaborative team in a PLC, What do we want students to learn? The resource or curriculum standard is then unpacked into learning targets to become the products produced by teams to support the standard. Question 2 of collaborative teams in a PLC utilizes the products from question 1 (learning targets) to produce common formative assessments. The answer to question 3, What will we do when students don't learn?, is driven from the data produced for effective interventions from the common formative assessment. Question 4, What will we do when students have learned?, is also based upon the formative assessment data produced from the common formative assessment. Teams can use this data to determine enrichment strategies or as a means for differentiated instruction. Establishing a specific time allotment to create these products occurred through the use of release time during the first quarter. As the year progressed, collaborative time was created on a weekly basis.

| Critical Question | Product | Resource |
|---|---|---|
| 1. What do we want students to learn? | Learning targets | Essential learnings, state standards, Common Core State Standards |
| 2. How will we know students have learned? | Common formative assessments | Learning targets |
| 3. What do we do when students don't learn? | Interventions | Data from the common formative assessments |
| 4. What do we do when students have learned? | Enrichment or differentiated instruction strategies | Data from the common formative assessments |

Figure 1.1: Products and resources related to the four critical questions.

The creation of team products allowed the essential learning to be taken directly to the student through the use of formative assessments, student data notebooks, interventions, and enrichment activities (discussed later in this chapter). As teachers became clear about specific learning targets, they implemented a variety of teaching strategies in all classrooms. This use of strategic instruction allowed teachers to assess learning targets before, during, and after they delivered the instructional component. *Before* activities act as quick formative assessments measuring learning targets from the previous lesson. Based on before assessments, teachers provided additional time for students to grasp the material. These activities included:

- Quick write—connecting new concept to previous concept
- ABC brainstorm/summary—activating prior knowledge with associated words
- Preview and predict—making predictions from previous knowledge
- Think-aloud—monitoring of reading comprehension and direct thinking
- Table talk—having a group discussion on topic or content
- Carousel brainstorm—allowing students to share previous learning
- Thinking maps—using graphic organizers to represent thinking

To maximize instructional time *during* the lesson, focused strategies allowed students to reflect on the new content. These included:

- Carousel—sharing of learning as new targets are presented
- Placemat—using this cooperative learning strategy to allow students to think about, share, and record their learning in groups

- Coding—coding the text during reading
- QUAD—working with questions, answers, and details
- Margin notes—engaging with the text
- Venn diagram—comparing and contrasting concepts

*After* strategies allowed students to reflect on the learning and reinforce the new content for both student and teacher. These included:

- 3–2–1—three things you found out, two interesting things, one question
- Quick write—asking students to respond to specific questions
- SIP—summarizing, imaging, predicting
- Group/paired summary—allowing pairs to summarize content from reading of the lesson
- Exit slips—summarizing key learning of the target

A new intervention schedule was not created for Tier 1 support. Rather, the use of flexible groups, teacher tables, and small-group instruction during the instruction block allowed students to receive additional time and support to master the learning targets from each standard.

Traditional schools present the standards in large chunks of information without learning targets. Under these circumstances, assessing a student's learning at the end of a unit using a test does not give either the student or teacher a mechanism to diagnose the cause of the student's struggle. This leaves students with a sense of frustration, disengagement, and in some cases failure. If the standard contains too much information for the students to master, an ineffective process for Tier 1 support occurs. Figure 1.2 illustrates the frequency of assessment based upon the curriculum standard or learning targets. In this case, the common assessment is administered at the end of the five-week unit, providing little or no feedback to the student during instruction.

Standard for the unit

Week 1 ├────────────────────────────────────────────┤ Week 5

Frequency of assessment of unit standard per learning target

Figure 1.2: Frequency of assessment based on learning target.

Instead, at Westlawn, small targets were created to contain manageable segments or chunks of content (learning targets) based on the standard to allow for frequent assessment and feedback during instruction. Figure 1.3 illustrates a more frequent approach to assessment within the five-week unit. The vertical lines represent the frequency of assessment based upon the learning targets created from the curricular standard. The increased frequency allows teachers to assess, provide feedback, and intervene based upon smaller concepts found within the standard itself, therefore strengthening Tier 1 support during the learning process for students.

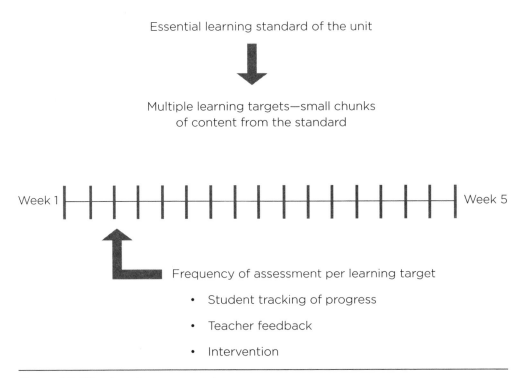

Figure 1.3: Westlawn's assessment process.

This process was extremely effective for all students, especially low-achieving students. Students must be able to see the target we expect them to learn. If the target is too large or the assessment too frequent, they become confused, lost, and disengaged from the classroom and learning process.

As teachers collaborated to unpack the standards, they also determined the proficiency level that defined mastery for each target. This allowed students to set goals and seek additional help to meet the desired level of mastery. Learning targets containing verbs identified basic knowledge (what we want students to learn) using either Webb's Depth of Knowledge (DOK), Marzano's taxonomy, or Bloom's taxonomy (table 1.1). The basic knowledge taxonomy allows teachers to scaffold the student learning based upon the verb association identified in table 1.1. The verb levels are identified within the standards teams focused on or the basic knowledge students will need to know to comprehend the complexity of higher-level verbs. The basic knowledge verbs require students to master the content at a proficiency level of 100 percent, compared to higher levels of knowledge that may require 70 to 80 percent proficiency, as determined by the team. As they mastered each small chunk of information within the standard, students were able to track their progress and experience success during their learning. Moreover, teachers were able to offer effective feedback based on these small learning targets.

**Table 1.1: Learning Target Verbs Per Bloom's and Marzano's Taxonomies and Webb's DOK**

| Bloom's (Revised) Taxonomy | Marzano's Taxonomy | Webb's DOK |
|---|---|---|
| Remember/ Understand | Retrieval | Recall and Reproduction (DOK 1) |
| Apply | Comprehension | Skills and Concepts (DOK 2) |
| Analyze | Analysis | Strategic Thinking (DOK 3) |
| Evaluate/Create | Knowledge Utilization | Extended Thinking (DOK 4) |

Figure 1.4 (page 26) illustrates how an eighth-grade math team identified the key essential learning supporting the Alabama Course of Study and created the learning targets and proficiency levels for pre-algebra.

## Monitoring Student Progress

At Westlawn, Tier 1 intervention during instruction was the focus of all teachers. The desire to visualize learning for each student through student data trackers provided a vehicle to address the learning needs, based upon specific learning targets from the curricular standard, through convergent assessment. As Buffum, Mattos, and Weber (2012) note, "Convergent assessment is an ongoing process of collectively analyzing targeted evidence to determine the specific learning needs of each child and the effectiveness of the instruction the child receives in meeting these needs" (p. 77). Tier 1 intervention monitoring is based on student progress toward specific learning targets from both formative assessments during instruction and summative assessments at the end of the instructional units. A teacher-developed tool called a student data tracker allowed students to become users of their data. Figure 1.5 (page 27) shows an example of a student data tracker using the pre-algebra learning targets and proficiency levels.

| Our goal is at least 80% mastery of all content standards. | **ALCOS 9 [8-EE7]:** Solve linear equations in one variable.<br>**(a)** Give examples of linear equations in one variable with one solution, infinitely many solutions, or no solutions. Show which of these possibilities is the case by successively transforming the given equations into simpler forms until an equivalent equation of the form x = a, a = a, or a = b results (where a and b are different numbers).<br>**(b)** Solve linear equations with rational number coefficients, including equations whose solutions require expanding expressions, using the distributive property, and collecting like terms. | | | | | | |
|---|---|---|---|---|---|---|---|
| | **Vocabulary** | **8-EE7** | | **8-EE7a** | **8-EE7b** | | |
| | Learning Target | Learning Targets | | Learning Target | Learning Targets | | |
| | I can define: *equation, linear equation, coefficients, variables, like terms, and distributive property.* | I can solve one-step equations. | I can solve two-step equations. | I can solve linear equations with one solution, infinitely many solutions, or no solutions. | I can solve linear equations with variables on both sides. | I can solve linear equations by using the distributive property. | I can solve linear equations by collecting like terms. |
| **Proficiency Level** | 100% | 80% | | 80% | 80% | 80% | 80% |

*Source: Westlawn Middle School.*

Figure 1.4: Pre-algebra learning targets and proficiency levels for solving one-variable equations.

| Learning Targets | Where am I now? | | | |
|---|---|---|---|---|
| | I need lots of help. | I still need help. | I'm almost there. | I've got this. |
| A. I can define: *equation*, *linear equation*, *coefficients*, *variables*, *terms*, *like terms*, and *distributive property*. | | | | |
| B. I can solve one-step equations. | | | | |
| C. I can solve two-step equations. | | | | |
| D. I can solve linear equations with one solution, infinitely many solutions, or no solutions. | | | | |
| E. I can solve linear equations with variables on both sides. | | | | |
| F. I can solve linear equations by using the distributive property. | | | | |
| G. I can solve linear equations by collecting like terms. | | | | |

*Source: Westlawn Middle School.*

Figure 1.5: Student data tracker using pre-algebra learning targets and proficiency levels.

*Visit **go.solution-tree.com/rtiatwork** for a reproducible version of this figure.*

The student data tracker creates an opportunity for each student to reflect and identify where he or she is in the learning process, using questions like the following:

- What did I do in this unit to achieve success, or what could I have done better to raise my grade?
- What is my biggest strength in the class?
- What is my biggest weakness in the class?
- What can I do during the next unit to ensure that I do my best?
- What can my teacher do to help me get there?

As students visually tracked their own progress, additional time for focused interventions from each learning target was created during the instructional block. This allowed both the student and teacher to identify where students needed additional support prior to the next lesson or class period. These team-developed student trackers are maintained within the classroom with the aid of a student data notebook (see figure 1.6).

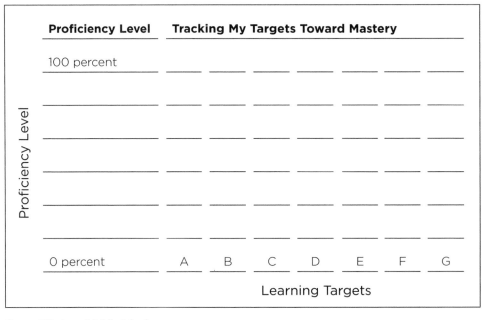

Source: Westlawn Middle School.

Figure 1.6: Student data notebook.

Visit **go.solution-tree.com/rtiatwork** for a reproducible version of this figure.

Student use of the formative assessment data with the student data tracker created a sense of ownership and inspired goal setting in students. Hattie (2009) finds through meta-analysis that when students track their learning progress based on the expected proficiency level, the effect size gain is 1.44 (1.0 = 1 standard deviation of one year's growth). The tracked data at the learning-target level shifted the focus from teacher to students. The students became users of data, allowing monitoring and feedback to occur with both the student and teacher. Students became proactive as their engagement increased. Interventions were developed, allowing the students to experience success *during* their learning. Interventions, based on the students' needs for each target, were embedded in the instructional block and given immediately. Classrooms are interactive, as teachers are using flexible groups, teacher tables (small-group, teacher-guided instruction), and one-to-one instruction based on small chunks of information (learning targets) that are critical to acquiring the essential learning within the curricular unit.

## Meeting the Needs of Students Who Don't Need Interventions

The ability of students to track their progress based on the learning target creates an effective basis for differentiated instruction in Tier 1. As teachers unpack the standards, key concepts for students to master become evident. Extension activities are structured in the same fashion as Tier 1 interventions: if teachers administer a preassessment with learning targets identified, they can focus on small-group instruction or teacher tables, or center activities on the next depth-of-knowledge level based on Webb's DOK. For example, if the learning target requires students to know at the recall level (DOK 1), such as recalling elements and details of story structure, including sequence of events, character, plot, and setting from an English language arts (ELA) standard, the students are able to extend to DOK 2. This allows students to apply the information gained from DOK 1 by identifying and summarizing the major events of the narrative. The extension activities are able to take place within the instructional block so students can expand on information previously learned.

## Learning Along the Way

After one year of offering strategic teaching through the use of concentrated instruction and convergent assessment to determine which students need additional support during instruction, student engagement and achievement are reaching new heights at Westlawn. In essence, Westlawn is not participating in the implementation dip—the typical decline in achievement after one year of implementation, as the entire school is focused on achievement.

As the school moves forward, the focus is on refinement, celebration, and capacity building. The school continues to refine and improve the Tier 1 intervention process. Teams of teachers delve deeper into instruction through the use of common assessment data, as opposed to simply adding new programs. These teams continue to strengthen the collaborative process by developing targeted support based on team-developed common assessments. Principal Lynette Alexander has maintained the focus by both expanding the leadership capacity within the school and celebrating and recognizing students.

One obstacle is the adherence to a district pacing guide. As teacher teams unpack the pacing guide to identify what is required of students, we must remember that students do not learn at the same pace. While the school is implementing the guide, teachers allow additional time for students to master the learning targets while fulfilling the pacing of the essential learning throughout each quarter. (The pacing guide is, it should be noted, a general guideline rather than a strict requirement.) Time can be adjusted for students to learn the required target based on each student's needs, while still fulfilling the spirit of the mandated curriculum.

After one year of implementing concentrated instruction and convergent assessment to guide effective intervention strategies, Westlawn has maintained its focus and is moving forward. The selection and development of a new teacher leadership team is a crucial step in this process. The original teacher leadership team (cohort 1) remains intact. Both cohort 1 and the new leadership team, cohort 2, are undergoing capacity building. Additionally, professional development with cohort 2 is based on the same professional development offered to cohort 1 the previous year. Now, two groups of key teacher leaders are working in tandem to strengthen the school's intervention and assessment process. Both groups working together with the same information (designing products to answer the four critical questions of a team) not only strengthens the process but also reduces opportunities for implementation dip challenges in the future.

Student celebrations provide additional reinforcement to enhance learning in the classroom. The use of Edmodo, an interactive social media platform for students and teachers, in the Westlawn school community led to the creation of an electronic bulletin board for student recognition. As students achieve mastery on the specific learning targets, teachers publicly recognize their achievement and celebrate their work. Additional celebrations aligned to student achievement include ice cream and chicken-wing parties and student-incentive prizes such as candy, limousine rides, and school dances. Celebration has encouraged students to maintain momentum on learning within each course.

Interventions within the classroom are continually refined as students and teachers organize time within the instructional block. As students receive the necessary support to learn during instruction, the implementation dip is rejected. Mastery of the content within the classroom through research-based instruction has allowed the school to reach tremendous growth on summative measures such as the Standardized Testing and Reporting (STAR) program and on state assessments, reducing the need for Tier 3 interventions.

## Meeting and Exceeding Standards

While Westlawn's demographics remained consistent, tremendous growth occurred schoolwide during the 2012–2013 school year. The STAR student data show an increase in schoolwide STAR reading proficiency levels when comparing fall to spring data. The number of schoolwide STAR students reading at or above benchmark grade level increased by 13 percent, from 23 percent on the spring 2012 benchmark assessment to 36 percent on the spring 2013 benchmark assessment. These results are consistent with the findings of the Alabama Reading and Mathematics Test (ARMT+) reading end-of-year data, which show seventh grade as 73 percent meeting or exceeding standards in reading, a 19 percent increase from the previous school year. Eighth-grade end-of-year data show 61 percent meeting or exceeding standards in reading, a 16 percent increase from the previous school year.

Student performance in math demonstrated outstanding growth as well. The STAR data from the 2012–2013 school year reported an increase in schoolwide STAR math proficiency levels when comparing fall to spring data. The schoolwide STAR students performed at or above benchmark grade-level percentage, increasing 29 percent, from 19 percent on the spring 2012 benchmark assessment to 48 percent on the spring 2013 benchmark assessment. These results are consistent with the findings of the ARMT+ math end-of-year data, indicating that 59 percent of sixth-grade students met or exceeded standards in math, a 9 percent increase from the previous year. In addition to the outstanding growth on these summative measures, the number of students requiring Tier 3 support for 2013–2014 was reduced. Students have regained a sense of pride in their school, and teachers report that student apathy has decreased.

Once a source of failure, Westlawn became a home for success within one year. The focus of staff and students on achievement during instruction (Tier 1) has reversed the culture of low achievement and replaced it with a culture of high achievement and pride.

## References and Resources

Brookhart, S. M. (2008). *How to give effective feedback to your students.* Alexandria, VA: Association for Supervision and Curriculum Development.

Buffum, A., Mattos, M., & Weber, C. (2012). *Simplifying response to intervention: Four essential guiding principles.* Bloomington, IN: Solution Tree Press.

DuFour, R., & Eaker, R. (1998). *Professional learning communities at work: Best practices for enhancing student achievement.* Bloomington, IN: Solution Tree Press.

Dweck, C. (2006). *Mindset: The new psychology of success.* New York: Random House.

Hattie, J. A. C. (2009). *Visible learning: A synthesis of over 800 meta-analyses relating to achievement.* New York: Routledge.

Hattie, J., & Timperley, H. (2007). The power of feedback. *Review of Educational Research, 77*(1), 81–112.

Marzano, R. J. (2003). *What works in schools: Translating research into action.* Alexandria, VA: Association for Supervision and Curriculum Development.

Marzano, R. J., Pickering, D., & Heflelbower, T. (2011). *The highly engaged classroom.* Bloomington, IN: Marzano Research Laboratory.

Sadler, R. D. (1989). Formative assessments and the design of instructional systems. *Instructional Science, 18*(2), 119–144.

Shepard, L. A., Hammerness, K., Darling-Hammond, L., & Rust, F. (2005). Assessment. In L. Darling-Hammond & J. Bransford (Eds.), *Preparing teachers for a changing world: What teachers should learn and be able to do* (pp. 275–326). San Francisco: Jossey-Bass.

Stiggins, R., Arter, J., Chappius, J., & Chappius, S. (2004). *Classroom assessment for student learning: Doing it right, using it well.* Portland, OR: Assessment Training Institute.

Tomlinson, C. A., & Moon, T. R. (2013). *Assessment and student success in a differentiated classroom.* Alexandria, VA: Association for Supervision and Curriculum Development.

Wiliam, D. (2007). Changing classroom practice. *Educational Leadership, 65*(4), 36–42.

Wiliam, D. (2011). *Embedded formative assessment.* Bloomington, IN: Solution Tree Press.

**Aaron Hansen** is a leadership consultant with the Northeastern Nevada Regional Professional Development Program and a Solution Tree associate. Previously, he led the transformation of White Pine Middle School (WPMS) into a nationally recognized high-achieving school in Nevada. Under Aaron's leadership, WPMS was named a National Model School (2009–2012) and the only middle school in the country to earn the title School of Distinction by the International Center for Leadership in Education in 2010. WPMS is listed on www.allthingsplc.info as a model of effectiveness. The school was also named a Nevada Title I Distinguished School and has received many other awards, recognitions, and honors. Aaron has been featured on ABC's *World News With Charles Gibson*, CNN's *American Morning*, Fox Network's *Fox and Friends*, and in a BBC documentary about effective anti-bullying programs and building positive school cultures. Aaron was named Nevada's Innovative Educator of the Year in 2009. He has worked with numerous schools and districts across the United States, helping them improve their processes in PLCs, RTI, teacher and leader improvement, and positive culture transformation.

You can follow Aaron on Twitter @AaronHansen77.

To book Aaron Hansen for professional development, contact pd@solution-tree .com.

# Co-Teaching the RTI and PLC Way

Aaron Hansen

**Editors' Note**

When a teacher presents new content in class, not every student is going to grasp it by the end of the lesson. If the learning targets are essential to a student's future academic success, then the problem the teacher faces is this: "What do I do with the students who don't need reteaching while I provide help to the students who do? There's only one of me!" White Pine Middle School's example demonstrates how a school addressed this dilemma by providing an extra teacher in almost every core class without hiring any extra staff. Class sizes were increased by about five students per class to achieve this goal, but with the additional teacher available, the teacher-to-student ratio in each class was actually lowered—an outcome that most teachers would welcome. Even if a school cannot revise its current faculty assignments to create a co-teacher position, the concept of having a pair or team of teachers regroup students for reteaching and "stretch" projects within a given class period can be replicated by virtually any school that has more than one staff member.

Equally important, at White Pine teachers did not give students who did not need reteaching busywork but instead gave them meaningful stretch projects that extended their learning. (Many of the stretch goals described in this chapter could be aligned to the higher-level thinking skills required by the Common Core State Standards.) This is critical, as creating flexible time for interventions should not come at the cost of students who don't require extra help.

White Pine Middle School is located in the rural high desert mountains of northeastern Nevada in a town called Ely. It's a blue-collar community with the largest employers an open-pit copper mine and a maximum-security state prison.

Working for either of these employers requires tough people who are willing to do dangerous jobs and work swing shifts. White Pine serves about 300 students, grades 6–8, about half of whom receive free or reduced-priced lunch. About 70 percent of students are Caucasian, 20 percent are Hispanic, 5 percent are Native American, and 2 percent are African American. After some difficult conversations about where the school was headed, in the summer of 2006, the staff made a commitment to become a professional learning community and since then has seen rapid improvement. White Pine Middle School has been recognized throughout the state and country and highlighted in numerous journal articles and news stories as a model for transformational change.

## Framing the Challenge

White Pine Middle School had been very successful for a few years in implementing the professional learning community (PLC) process and had gained considerable attention for turning its culture around. However, internally, the staff struggled with what steps to take next to ensure that it did not plateau but would actually reach its collective vision of meeting *every* student's learning needs. The school had found that, with its at-risk middle school adolescents, impeccable classroom management and intense planning were required to provide effective intervention, while simultaneously ensuring meaningful enrichment of those who were proficient. A few teachers who were truly exceptional and put forth exceptional efforts could meet this challenge. However, most teachers struggled with the enormous task of providing for the diversity of needs while simultaneously managing a middle school classroom. Teachers were frustrated! They knew they needed to address individual needs to reach their vision but found they lacked a practical approach for actually doing it on a regular basis.

Differentiating instruction to meet the needs of thirty diverse learners is a challenge, to say the least. Differentiating for a classroom of thirty diverse middle school learners, more than half of whom are not proficient in prerequisite skills, is asking more than what is reasonable of the average individual teacher.

Then the challenge became even more acute. Intense budgetary shortfalls due to an economic recession led to the cutting of programs and teachers throughout the district. Prior to the cuts, 50 percent of White Pine's sixth graders were coming to the school lacking proficiency in grade-level standards. Now that grew to nearly two-thirds. In addition to students' growing needs, a large number of the staff had turned over due to staff reductions and forced placements. White Pine now had plenty of elementary-trained teachers with no previous experience managing an at-risk middle school classroom, but it lacked content specialists. When we honestly discussed our situation as a staff, we came to the conclusion that it was not reasonable to expect that teachers would be able to differentiate their instruction to meet the needs of our increasingly challenging demographic on their own, even with the support of our strong PLC structures and current interventions. If we were going to reach our vision of meeting individual student needs, we had to change some of our existing structures.

# Returning to Our PLC Roots

Recognizing that the PLC process had taken us this far, we returned to it and asked the question, "How can we restructure our school so that we can better answer the four fundamental questions on a *daily* basis for each of our students?" Those four fundamental PLC questions are:

1. What is it we expect students to learn?

2. How will we know if they have learned it?

3. How will we respond when they don't learn?

4. How will we respond when they have learned? (DuFour, DuFour, Eaker, & Many, 2010)

## Creating Time

The guiding coalition (a leadership team composed of teacher leaders and administrators) reworked the schedule to find more time for core classes so that teachers could formatively assess and intervene daily. The coalition started by adding twenty minutes to the instructional day by maximizing the amount of student contact time allowed by the teacher contract. The lunch period was also shortened to what was permissible by the contract, picking up another four minutes. Although it had been implemented previous to co-teaching, a contributing factor for garnering minutes was the shortening of passing times by one minute, saving a total of seven minutes per day. These schedule changes would allow teachers the time, in a class period, to deliver a lesson (PLC question 1), formatively assess (PLC question 2), and still have about twenty to twenty-five minutes of time left for intervention and enrichment (PLC questions 3 and 4).

## Arranging Co-Teaching

Like many other small schools, ours had no full-time elective teachers. Elective and intervention classes were taught by our core teachers one or two periods a day. For example, a teacher might teach three seventh-grade language arts classes and Spanish I and Spanish II for his or her electives. Interventions were not always provided by the regular subject-area teacher. Another might teach three sixth-grade math classes and teach math intervention (sixth to eighth grades) for two periods. (Math intervention, a Tier 3 intervention, was designed by need, not by grade level.) So, for example, the eighth-grade language arts teacher might be the language arts intervention teacher for a seventh-grade student. Another teacher might teach three sections of eighth-grade science and then teach journalism and art as electives.

With no full-time elective teachers, it was possible to move all of the elective and intervention classes to the same times during the day. By doing so, it was possible to reduce elective class periods by five minutes and add these minutes to the core classes. Twenty minutes were taken from an advisory period and shifted to Cougar Academic Time (CAT Time) which is flexible Tier 2 intervention time directed by grade-level PLC teams. Using the minutes gathered, core classes, as mentioned, were extended to seventy minutes per day—plenty of time to assess, intervene, and enrich daily! Tables 2.1 and 2.2 (pages 40–42) show the old and new schedules, respectively.

| Teacher | First Period 59 min. | Second Period 58 min. | Third Period 58 min. | Fourth Period 58 min. | Lunch 38 min. | Fifth Period 58 min. | Sixth Period 58 min. | Advisory 45 min. |
|---|---|---|---|---|---|---|---|---|
| **Caramella** | Math 7 | Ma th 6 | Math 8 | Math 8 | | Math 6 | Math 7 | |
| **Lawrence** | Math 6 | Math 8 | Math 7 | Math 8 | | Math 6 | Math 6 | |
| **Walker J.** | Math 6 | Math 8 | Math 7 | Math 8 | | Math 6 | Math 7 | |
| **Haslem P.** | Phys. Science | Gen. Science | Phys. Science | Life Science | | Life Science | Leadership | |
| **Solari** | Phys. Science | Gen. Science | Phys. Science | Gen. Science | | Life Science | Life Science | |
| **Ernest** | Read 180 7 | | Read 180 6 | | | Humanities 7 | Humanities 6 | |
| **Petersen** | Reading 180 7 | | Read 180 6 | | | | | |
| **Speakman** | Humanities 8 | | Humanities 7 | | | Humanities 6 | | |
| **Tokerud** | Humanities 8 | | Humanities 7 | | | Humanities 8 | | |
| **Walker M.** | Humanities7 | | Humanities 6 | | | Humanities 8 | | |
| **Gubler** | Elective | | | | | Elective | Elective | |
| **Smith** | PE 6 | PE 7/8 | PE | PE | | Humanities 7 | Humanities 6 | |
| **Walker H.** | Band 7 | Band 6 | Band 8 | | | | | |
| **Plenger** | | | | | | Elective | Elective | |
| **Siber** | | | | | | HS Algebra | HS Algebra | |
| **Haslem K.** | Petersen | | Reading | Reading | | Walker J. | Walker J. | |
| **Jensen** | RTI/Data | Lawrence | Caramella | Walker J. | | Lawrence | Lawrence | |
| **Nicholes** | Life Skills | Halsem P. | Lawrence | Haslem P. | | Life Skills | Life Skills | |
| **Backus** | Haslem P. | Gubler | Solari | Walker J./Lunch | | Locke/Walker J. | Walker M. | |

*Source: White Pine Middle School.*

Figure 2.1: Previous schedule and teacher assignments.

Continued on next page ↓

| Coble | Lawrence | Ernest | Petersen | Petersen/Lunch | Lawrence | Plenger |
|---|---|---|---|---|---|---|
| **Garcia** | Petersen | Petersen | Ind. Study | PE | Lawrence | Walker J. |
| **Hunt** | Walker J. | Walker H. | Haslem K. | Haslem P. | Haslem P. | Nicholes |
| **Leavitt** | Nicholes | PE | Haslem P. | Haslem K. | Lunch/Smith | Smith |
| **Van Camp** | PE | PE | PE | PE | Lunch/RTI | RTI |

|  | First Period | Second Period | Third Period | Fourth Period | Nutrition Break. | Fifth Period | Lunch | Sixth Period | Seventh Period | Eighth Period | Ninth Period |
|---|---|---|---|---|---|---|---|---|---|---|---|
|  | 8:03–8:06 3 min. | 8:09–8:39 30 min. | 8:42–9:52 70 min. | 9:55–11:05 70 min. | 11:05–11:10—5 min. | 11:10–12:20 70 min. |  | 12:56–1:46 50 min. | 1:49–3:39 50 min. | 2:42–3:22 40 min. | 3:25–3:35 10 min. |
| **Smith** | Advisory | CAT | Science 8 | Science 8 |  | Science 8 |  | Weights 8 | Leadership | Explore | Advisory |
| **Speakman** | Advisory | CAT | Humanities 8 | Humanities 8 |  | Humanities 8 |  | Spanish 6 | Spanish 6 | Explore | Advisory |
| **Tokerud** | Advisory | CAT | Math 8 | Math 8 |  | Math 8 |  | Math Intervention | Math Intervention | Explore | Advisory |
| **Nicholes** | Advisory | CAT | Humanities 8 | Science 8 |  | Math 8 |  | Math Intervention | Math Intervention | Life Skills | Advisory |
| **Leyba** | Advisory | CAT | Math 8 | Humanities 8 |  | Science 8 |  | PE 8 | PE 7/8 | Explore | Advisory |
| **Gray** | Advisory | CAT | Science 7 | Science 7 |  | Science 7 |  | Math Intervention | Math Intervention | Explore | Advisory |

*Source: White Pine Middle School.*

Figure 2.2: New schedule and teacher assignments.

| | | | | | | | | | | |
|---|---|---|---|---|---|---|---|---|---|---|
| **Ernest** | Advisory | Explore | Seventh Read 180 | Seventh Read 180 | Humanities 7 | | Humanities 7 | Humanities 7 | CAT | Advisory |
| **Walker, J.** | Advisory | Explore | Math Intervention | Math Intervention | Math 7 | | Math 7 | Math 7 | CAT | Advisory |
| **Haslem** | Advisory | Explore | System 44 | Eighth Read 180 | Math 7 | | Science 7 | Humanities | CAT | Advisory |
| **Gubler** | Advisory | Explore | NV Studies 7 | NV Studies 7 | Science 7 | | Humanities 7 | Math 7 | CAT | Advisory |
| **Johnson** | Advisory | Explore | Eighth Read 180 | Math Intervention | Science 6 | | Science 6 | Science 6 | CAT | Advisory |
| **Petersen** | Advisory | Explore | Eighth Read 180 | Sixth Read 180 | Humanities 6 | | Humanities 6 | Humanities 6 | CAT | Advisory |
| **Laity** | Advisory | Explore | | PE 6/7 | Math 6 | | Math 6 | Math 6 | CAT | Advisory |
| **Paty** | Advisory | Explore | | Drawing 8 | Math 6 | | Science 6 | Humanities 6 | CAT | Advisory |
| **Bybee** | Advisory | Explore | | Math Intervention | Science 6 | | Humanities 6 | Math 6 | CAT | Advisory |
| **Hall** | Advisory | Combined Band (yr) | Beginning Band | Advanced Band | | | | | | |
| **Plenger** | Advisory | Explore | Technology 6 | Technology 6/7 | | | | | | |
| **Whited** | Advisory | Explore | Mind-storms (Yr.) | Mind-storms 6 (Qtr.) | | | | | | |
| **Hill** | Nicholes | Speakman | Band | PE | Ind. Study | | Ind. Study | Ind. Study | Ind. Study | Nicholes |

Continued on next page →

| Kaamasee | Advisory | Ind. Study | Ind. Study Nick | Ind. Study Nick | | Math Intervention | Math Intervention | Gym | Advisory |
|---|---|---|---|---|---|---|---|---|---|
| **Jackson** | Advisory | Johnson | Petersen | Johnson | | Band | PE | Explore | Advisory |
| **Ciceu** | Allen/ Jensen | Smith | Humanities 8 | Science 8 | Math 8 | Reading Intervention | Reading Intervention | Explore | Allen/ Jensen |
| **Wall** | Pay | Petersen | Petersen | Johnson | | Nicholes | Haslem | Nicholes | Pay |
| **Locke** | Advisory | SWS | SWS | SWS | SWS | SWS | SWS | SWS | Advisory |

However, changing the schedule to provide more time wasn't enough. To effective-ly meet individual student needs, we had to provide teachers with the support to be able to use the extra time. That support came in the form of having co-teachers in as many classrooms as possible. We increased average class size, which was twenty-six, by about five students and reduced the number of core class sections offered in the schedule. By eliminating sections, we were able to free up teachers for co-teaching. Existing inclusion teachers were strategically placed, making it possible to have two-thirds of all core classes co-taught by two certified teachers. Paraprofessionals were also strategically placed so that almost all core classes had a second adult in the room. This allowed less-than-superhuman teachers to formatively assess, form flex-ible groups, and provide meaningful intervention and enrichment every day.

Our desired outcomes were simple. We wanted to better answer the four funda-mental PLC questions in order to be more responsive to individual student needs on the Tier 1 level *every* day. And given the diverse learning needs of our incoming students, we wanted to design a system that was nimble, that could respond on de-mand in real time to the needs of struggling students without holding up those who were proficient. Co-teaching the PLC and RTI way was born! By having the extra time and two adults to help manage the classroom, it was possible to answer PLC questions 2, 3, and 4 on a daily basis.

## Initial Concerns

Foreseen potential challenges were personality or style conflicts and differing opin-ions among teachers. The staff discussed these issues before implementation and developed a collective commitment to be kind yet truly honest with each other. Relying heavily on the PLC culture, teachers were able to overcome minor differ-ences that arose as they kept their vision of better serving students as their greatest priority.

Another concern that the staff had was the increase in class size. However, through multiple conversations, staff members came to a consensus that, although class sizes would increase, the new structure would be better for meeting individual student needs.

As a result of its previous positive change, the school had generated a high degree of community support. We thus experienced little to no community resistance for the new changes being proposed.

## Daily Assessment

With a schedule in place that gave more time and adult support to help differ-entiate instruction and intervention, teachers were able to formatively assess daily and to truly achieve what Buffum, Mattos, and Weber (2012) term "*convergent assessment*—an ongoing process of collectively analyzing targeted evidence to determine the specific learning needs of each child and the effectiveness of the instruction the child receives in meeting these needs" (p. 10). Teachers became more acutely aware of assessing student learning and observing the progress of their students for the purpose of later grouping them according to their needs. In math, they administered short pencil-and-paper formative assessments each day. These were usually one to three questions and were typically used to confirm what teachers had observed about individual student learning. Teachers took a few minutes to review the assessments in class and group students according to their needs. A sample sixth-grade lesson might be planned as follows.

**Overarching Standard:** Understanding ratio concepts and using ratio reasoning to solve problems, 6.RP.A.1, 6.RP.A.2, 6.RP.A.3

**Explain Daily Learning Target and Bell Work (5 min.):** "I will be able to solve simple unit-rate problems."

**Direct Instruction and Practice (33 min.)**

**Formative Assessment (5 min.)**

**Example:**

1.  If it took 7 hours to mow 4 lawns, then at that rate, how many lawns could be mowed in 35 hours?

2.  At what rate were lawns being mowed? (National Governors Association Center for Best Practices & Council of Chief State School Officers, 2010)

**Review Assessment (7 min.):** Teachers quickly review assessments and group students according to their needs.

**Intervention (20 min.):** Small-group intervention provided by the most qualified adult for those students who are struggling with the concept to help them clarify errors in their thinking.

**Enrichment (20 min.):** With guidance from the adult not providing intervention, students work on their interdisciplinary "stretch project"—design your own restaurant.

**Example:**

Using rates and ratios, adapt recipes of the items on your restaurant's menu to single portions or large-group portions and build a weekly budget. (More detail will follow about how the interdisciplinary stretch project works.)

In subjects like science or language arts, where it is a little more difficult to give pencil-and-paper assessments every day, teachers "unobtrusively" assessed where their students were in relation to the specific learning targets based on assignments students worked on or during conferencing (Marzano, 2010). In a language arts class, for example, co-teachers kept a clipboard with the learning targets to be learned over the course of the week in order to reach the broader mastery of a writing standard. As teachers circulated and conferenced with individual students, giving them feedback, they would record each student's progress on the learning targets for the week. In this way, whenever there was independent work, students could be grouped according to their needs and given coaching and support targeted to their specific needs. With so many of our students coming to us deficient in various skills, it was necessary to formatively assess constantly if our instruction was going to be responsive to the many and varied needs that existed.

## Enrichment

Those needing intervention were quickly grouped together according to need, and those who "got it" worked on their interdisciplinary stretch projects, which were designed to extend students' learning and push them to apply more deeply the concepts they were learning to real-life problem solving. For the "design your own restaurant" project, students might be challenged to work in teams and eventually present their proposal in front of "investors"—parents, teachers, and other students—during CAT Time. Teachers could develop the criteria in ways that deepen learning in any standard. In the restaurant example, students might reinforce the math standards they were learning by developing menus and budgeting the costs of furniture. The project might reinforce science standards that were being learned by having students improve their research skills and apply strict nutrition guidelines imposed by the science teacher. The language arts standards might focus on persuasion and writing to an audience, asking students to write persuasive proposals to investors and to develop advertisements. A final multimedia presentation might culminate in a presentation during which items from the menu could be sampled and students' learning celebrated by the investors.

The stretch projects offered students an opportunity to extend their learning and to demonstrate not just proficiency but mastery of the standards they were learning in class by connecting them to real-life problem solving. In the WPMS gradebook, "mastery" equated to reaching the score of 4 in the standard, while "proficiency" equated to earning a 3. In this system, it was essential that a student demonstrated proficiency in essential standards, but although highly encouraged, it was not considered essential that the students demonstrate mastery. In other words, students were not required to complete the stretch project to pass the class.

Grade-level teacher teams developed rubrics to determine whether students had indeed demonstrated mastery of the content standards through their stretch projects. Every student was given access to the stretch project, but students were given time to work on these projects in class, sometimes multiple times per day, if they demonstrated proficiency in the daily learning target. After teachers formatively assessed students' progress on the daily learning target, students were grouped for intervention or allowed time and given support for working on their stretch projects. An ancillary benefit was that some students became highly motivated to demonstrate daily proficiency in order to have time for their stretch projects. If a student struggled with a concept in a content area, that student received immediate help and could return to the project as soon as he or she demonstrated proficiency in that skill—sometimes within the same period.

A typical issue with interdisciplinary projects is that students often struggle to make the connection from one subject to the next, and teachers struggle to build a continuity of expectations from one subject to the next. Often, these projects become isolated assignments that don't end up meshing together very well and don't help students establish the relevance that they are intended to show. Our experience is that when a co-teacher was part of each of the core classes, much greater clarity was achieved among students, because the co-teacher was able to help students connect how the individual subject expectations fit into the vision of the final product.

### Diagnosing the Need and Tracking the Data in Real Time

Since the groups were formed each day based on student performance, they were naturally tailored to the needs of the day. Teachers started with who got it and who didn't, but became more adept over time at targeting the intervention more precisely. For example, the language arts team realized that embedded in the essential standard "I will cite textual evidence to support a claim through writing" were multiple learning targets. Co-teachers started tracking what specific skills or targets students were struggling with on data trackers (figure 2.3). On their ever-present clipboards, co-teachers had the overarching standard of citing textual evidence, but they also had the subtargets: Can the student identify a claim? Can the student find valid evidence? Can the student use appropriate conventions while quoting from the text? During conferences, teachers would determine exactly what the student was struggling with. Comparing notes, the teacher team would make a quick determination of what need was most imperative for each student. The most qualified adult (as determined by the co-teaching team) would provide the most pressing intervention.

Highlight the names of students who are not on progress to proficiency and need additional intervention in CAT Time and note which learning targets they are struggling with. Bring your list with specific student needs to your grade-level PLC meeting.

| Student Names | Learning Target 1.a—Student can make a logical claim that's connected to the text. | Target 1.b—Student can find relevant evidence in a text to back up a claim. | Target 1.c—Student can use correct conventions in writing when citing evidence from the text. | Target 1.d—Student can clearly communicate ideas in writing. |
|---|---|---|---|---|
|  |  |  |  |  |
|  |  |  |  |  |
|  |  |  |  |  |
|  |  |  |  |  |
|  |  |  |  |  |
|  |  |  |  |  |

Notes:

_____

_____

_____

*Source: White Pine Middle School.*

Figure 2.3: Language arts teacher data tracker.

*Visit **go.solution-tree.com/rtiatwork** for a reproducible version of this figure.*

Sometimes the most qualified adult was the person with the strongest content knowledge or strongest understanding of pedagogy. Sometimes it was the person with the best relationship with those who needed the intervention. The important point is that teachers made judgments as a partnership, responding in real time to the deficit that they had diagnosed. When a child falls and scrapes a knee, parents don't wait a week for a team meeting to determine that the child needs a bandage. Most minor interventions can be applied effectively and immediately if adults know there is a need and know what the need is.

The data trackers, which had been developed by collaborative teams during planning time, helped co-teachers and regular teachers better clarify what students were supposed to learn (PLC question 1). As co-creators of the data trackers, co-teachers had a deep understanding of the targets because they had been part of the discussion while developing them.

Data trackers were the tools that teachers kept on their clipboards to keep real-time progress on each student in the class in relation to the learning targets that were embedded in the essential standard. Teachers would record a progress score most days for each of their students. Lynn S. Fuchs and Doug Fuchs (1986) tabulate that when teachers had graphic representations of student progress, a 26-percentile-point (or 0.70 effect-size) gain was achieved.

Teachers recognized that the research also supported students tracking their own progress. Marzano (2010) reports an average effect size of 0.92 or a 32 percent gain when students track their progress. Teachers thus developed student data trackers (figure 2.4) that allowed students to track their own progress in the essential standards and specific learning targets.

## Knowing Students Well

The same co-teacher followed the same group of approximately thirty students through each of their core classes. Because the co-teacher was with the same thirty students most of the day, he or she was able to develop a firm grasp on their individual needs. The co-teacher developed relationships with those students and their families, making regular calls and, in some cases, visits home. For those students who needed it, the co-teacher provided consistent behavioral interventions and revisions to help make necessary changes for success. Intentionally, students were placed based on their academic and social needs, or by the root cause of their struggle, with the co-teacher who we believed had the talents best suited for helping those students. Buffum, Mattos, and Weber (2012) explain that cause is different than the symptom. Cause is why a deficit exists. In order to be successful in treating the child, we have to diagnose the cause, not the symptoms. Students were often moved from one co-teacher to another as a revision. Buffum, Mattos, and Weber explain that we must revise our intervention strategies if they are not producing the desired result.

| Essential Standard | | 1 Date/ Score | 2 Date/ Score | 3 Date/ Score | 4 Date/ Score | 5 Date/ Score |
|---|---|---|---|---|---|---|
| 1 | I will cite textual evidence to back up a claim through writing. | | | | | |
| Learning Targets | This is my progress so far in: | | | | | |
| 1.a | Making a logical claim that's connected to the text. | | | | | |
| 1.b | Finding relevant evidence in a text to back up a claim. | | | | | |
| 1.c | Using correct conventions in my writing when citing evidence from the text. | | | | | |
| 1.d | Clearly communicating my ideas in my writing. | | | | | |

| Date | Reflection notes. For example: "I need more practice with my conventions," or "I need some help from Mrs. Petersen or Ms. Bybee to improve in making logical claims." |
|---|---|
| | |
| | |
| | |
| | |
| | |

*Source: White Pine Middle School.*

Figure 2.4: Language arts student data tracker.

*Visit **go.solution-tree.com/rtiatwork** for a reproducible version of this figure.*

The co-teachers used their intimate knowledge of each one of "their" students in the grade-level team meetings to make assignments for additional weeklong Tier 2 interventions provided by the team during schoolwide intervention time (CAT Time) if the in-class Tier 1 intervention hadn't been sufficient. The co-teachers took the lead in the data portion of a team meeting. They were expected to come with lists generated before the meeting, recommending which students needed extra time and support in the specific learning targets that they had been tracking on their data trackers throughout the week.

The co-teachers used the data that they had been collecting to determine what interventions the team should provide, and the team determined who was best qualified to provide the intervention for the particular group of students. In most cases, a language arts teacher would provide the support in a language arts standard. However, other circumstances may have been factored in. For example, while visiting one team meeting, the male eighth-grade science teacher, who also happened to coach baseball, offered to work with a group of six eighth-grade boys who were struggling with a math standard. His team agreed to let him work with these at-risk boys not because he was a math expert but because he had a relationship with them and because of his extensive coaching experience with boys. Over the course of the week, the boys were able to become proficient in the standard.

When a student failed to respond to the interventions that the team provided, the student was referred to the student support team to determine whether the student was in need of more intensive intervention.

## What We Learned

At first, we struggled with targeting the in-class intervention to the specific learning target in which a student was deficient. But going through the process of attempting to intervene every day in every core class helped our staff realize that we had to get much clearer about what we wanted students to learn every day, and we had to become better at assessing specific learning targets. We also learned that we didn't have an adequate way of tracking student progress in real time. The process also helped us get better at formatively assessing student needs quickly.

Another challenge was establishing clarity around the roles of the core teacher and the co-teacher. Although the guiding coalition had worked to develop clarity before starting the first year, many issues had to be clarified later to ensure that goals were being met and to ensure that staff members' talents were used in the best possible way. Table 2.1 represents the basic roles that were developed over time.

**Table 2.1: Core Teaching and Co-Teaching Responsibilities**

| Core Teacher | Co-Teacher |
|---|---|
| Determine essential outcomes in department teams. | Use core-teacher lesson plans to develop vocabulary acquisition strategies and help students who struggle with literacy to access the text. |
| Develop frequent formative assessments and common formative assessments. | Monitor student progress in data trackers. |
| Develop and deliver the core lesson. | Provide support during core instruction. |
| Give summative grades and manage the gradebook. | Work collaboratively with grade-level team to provide CAT Time interventions. Use student data to take the lead in team meetings and determine student needs. |
| Provide in-class intervention and enrichment. | Provide in-class intervention and enrichment.<br><br>Know your students' needs and build a meaningful relationship with students and communicate with their parent(s). |
| Work collaboratively with grade-level team to provide CAT Time interventions. | Provide behavior supports to students. |

Even after articulating roles, it was still necessary to continue to establish clarity through continuous conversation. As with any initiative, we struggled at times with individual adults fulfilling their roles to the greatest degree. Relying heavily on our PLC culture, teachers regularly discussed what was working better in one classroom as compared to another, following the practice of kindness but honesty. Job-embedded and continuous professional development was provided through the collaborative teaming process. In addition, co-teachers and core teachers engaged in peer observations and debriefed about their roles in an effort to get clear about what each role should look like in practice. Powerful relationships of trust were developed.

Because the state assessment cut scores and the assessments themselves have changed constantly since 2007, the best way to see student learning gains at WPMS is by looking at cohorts of students over time, as compared to their peers across the state of Nevada (table 2.2, page 52).

The school was ranked highly in the state accountability system due to the individual growth among students.

Although student-achievement gains in comparison to their peers across the state are impressive, other results may be less recognizable to the casual observer. For example, teachers knew a student's learning progress in relation to the standard better than they ever had before. Teachers were able to track each student and know the student's specific level of learning according to the standard at any given time. The principal, or any stakeholder for that matter, could ask, "Where is Jimmy in math?" and an answer could be given immediately. "He is proficient in standard 1. He is not yet proficient in standard 2, because he is struggling in learning target 2a. He has been assigned to CAT Time for the week. Jimmy and I have had a conversation, and his student data tracker is up-to-date. He knows which learning target is giving him trouble. He has committed to me to give his best effort to learn it. His mother has been contacted, and he is staying after school today to work with me during Mandatory Tutoring." A similar conversation could be had with a student. Using the student data tracker, the student could pinpoint his or her learning progress.

One of the great benefits for students was that the model was a blending of the elementary and secondary models. Students enjoyed the benefits of having one go-to teacher with them for the majority of their day, just as in elementary school, yet they were exposed to the content experts of a traditional secondary school. Also, in this way, the system capitalized on the strengths of the faculty's heavy elementary background. The co-teacher was able to use the intimate knowledge he or she gained about each of "his or her kids" to tailor the intervention to meet students' individual needs, instead of teaching to the middle, as so often happens in traditional secondary classrooms.

The bottom line was that the strategy allowed us to do what we intended to do, which was on a daily basis, better answers to the four fundamental PLC questions. By having a clear vision and being willing to rethink traditional structures, the co-teaching teams made it possible to accomplish what seemed like only those who were superhuman could accomplish before.

Table 2.2: Learning Gains at WPMS Compared to Those of Students Statewide (Nevada)

| The Same Students Over Time (Graduating Class of 2016) | ELA | | | Math | | | Science | | |
|---|---|---|---|---|---|---|---|---|---|
| | WPMS | Nevada | Difference | WPMS | Nevada | Difference | WPMS | Nevada | Diff |
| 2008–2009 (fifth grade) | 32 percent | 52 percent | –20 percent | 46 percent | 62 percent | –16 percent | 52 percent | 66 percent | –14 percent |
| 2009–2010 (sixth grade) | 63 percent | 65 percent | –2 percent | 66 percent | 64 percent | +2 percent | No test | No test | NA |
| 2010–2011 (seventh grade) | 53 percent | 56 percent | –3 percent | 71 percent | 72 percent | –1 percent | No test | No test | NA |
| 2011–2012 (eighth grade) | 59 percent | 49 percent | +10 percent | 71 percent | 62 percent | +9 percent | 65 percent | 50 percent | +15 percent |

# References and Resources

Buffum, A., Mattos, M., & Weber, C. (2012). *Simplifying response to intervention: Four essential guiding principles.* Bloomington, IN: Solution Tree Press.

DuFour, R., DuFour, R., Eaker, R., & Many, T. (2010). *Learning by doing: A handbook for professional learning communities at work* (2nd ed.). Bloomington, IN: Solution Tree Press.

DuFour, R., & Eaker, R. (1998). *Professional learning communities at work: Best practices for enhancing student achievement.* Bloomington, IN: Solution Tree Press.

Fuchs, L. S., & Fuchs, D. (1986). Effects of systematic formative evaluation: A meta-analysis. *Exceptional Children, 53*(3), 199–208.

Hattie, J. A. C. (2009). *Visible learning: A synthesis of over 800 meta-analyses relating to achievement.* New York: Routledge.

Marzano, R. J. (2010). *Formative assessment & standards-based grading.* Bloomington, IN: Marzano Research Laboratory.

National Governors Association Center for Best Practices & Council of Chief State School Officers. (2010). *Common Core State Standards for mathematics.* Washington, DC: Authors. Accessed at www.corestandards.org/Math/? on March 10, 2014.

 **Luis F. Cruz, PhD,** upon graduating from high school, found himself working for a Lucky grocery store in Baldwin Park, California, as what was then called a courtesy clerk—the person who bags groceries for customers. Life was good. He figured that over time he would be promoted to checker and maybe one day enter management, allowing him to make a decent living. Fortunately, this plan was suddenly disrupted when a customer in the store who also happened to be the director of bilingual services for the Baldwin Park Unified School District heard Luis speak fluent Spanish while helping a customer. Intrigued by the fact that being an instructional aide paid $10.00 an hour, which far exceeded the $3.35 minimum wage at the time, Luis accepted the invitation to apply for a position, and two weeks later found himself passionately working with first-grade students, who—like him years earlier—were learning English as a second language. It was this experience that would allow Luis to find his lifelong calling of serving low-income students as a public school educator.

Propelled with a new and improved reason to graduate from college, in 1994, Luis entered the teaching profession as a fifth-grade bilingual teacher and later entered administration as an assistant principal and then a principal at the middle school level. In 2006, he accepted what today he refers to as the most challenging and rewarding position of his career thus far, principal of the largest school in the Baldwin Park Unified School District, Baldwin Park High School.

Today, Luis holds a doctorate in institutional leadership and policy studies from the University of California at Riverside and is a sought-after educator and speaker.

You can follow Luis on Twitter @lcruzconsulting.

To book Luis F. Cruz for professional development, contact pd@solution-tree.com.

# The Most Effective Intervention Is Prevention

Luis F. Cruz

**Editors' Note**

Between 70 and 80 percent of students who fail in the first year of high school do not graduate (Wyner, Bridgeland, & Diiulio, 2007). Unfortunately, many high schools allow incoming ninth graders the opportunity to fail before providing extra help. In most cases, this means "too little, too late." Early identification is the key to preventive interventions. Predicting which incoming students are likely to need this support is hardly difficult; at-risk ninth graders usually have a history of struggling in school long before entering high school. As most students enter high school from predictable feeder school(s) within the same district or region, a high school could begin identifying incoming students who may need intensive support during the second semester of the previous school year.

As this chapter demonstrates, Baldwin Park High School does not take a "wait to fail" approach. To this end, the school's Guided Studies program possesses two critical characteristics. First, the staff identify at-risk ninth graders before they have a chance to fail. By working with the middle schools that send students to Baldwin Park High School, students enter high school with daily support beginning the first day of ninth grade. Second, Baldwin Park does not track these students into remedial core classes. To learn at high levels, students must be taught at high levels. The Guided Studies program supports students in meeting rigorous college-prep expectations.

While this chapter focuses on ninth grade, these practices are just as applicable in middle school. A proactive middle school can work with its feeder elementary school(s) to identify incoming students who are likely to need additional support.

Baldwin Park High School is located thirty miles east of Los Angeles and serves approximately 2,400 students in a mostly low-income Latino suburb of Los Angeles County. Over 95 percent of the students qualify for free and reduced lunch, thus allowing the school to be designated Title I. Approximately 25 percent of the students have been identified as English learners, and a significant portion of the students come from immigrant families, predominantly from Latin America. At the time it was built in 1952, district leaders designated Baldwin Park High School as a school focused on athletic prowess, while the other high school across town was identified as one that would focus on academic achievement. These same leaders believed that offering community residents two distinct high schools, each with a different focus, was ideal. Over time, but especially during the early nineties, and true to expectations, Baldwin Park High School developed a reputation for athletic achievement at the expense of academic accomplishment. The onset of federal and state accountability to ensure academic achievement for all students proved to be a challenge for the established culture at Baldwin Park High. While evidence of student learning was occasionally achieved, there was continuous evidence that, for most students, learning seemed impossible. The collective adult sentiment on campus unintentionally created what Kent D. Peterson (2002) identifies as a toxic school culture, one in which students were responsible for their own learning, with the majority of adults embracing little if any of that responsibility. In short, the staff sentiment was that if profound academic achievement for all students was to occur, students and their "irresponsible" parents would need to change. Hence, student achievement for all would only be possible if all parents practiced effective parenting and all students entered our school speaking fluent English and having mastered the basic skills necessary for success in both mathematics and English, to name but a few perceived prerequisites to learning. Anthony Muhammad (2009) captures accurately the negative effect of a toxic culture when he states that "educators' personal belief systems may be the most powerful barriers perpetuating learning gaps in our public school system" (p. 14).

Did the staff at Baldwin Park High School care about their students? Did the staff desire a better life for each of them? Undoubtedly, the answer to these questions was a resounding yes, yet the belief that all of our low-income students, many of whom were Latino and learning English as a second language, could excel academically was one that many of us could not imagine or comprehend. In short, we accepted the status quo and ill-conceived notion that the diverse background of our student population acted as too strong a barrier toward achieving optimal student achievement.

# Beginning the PLC Journey

Beginning in 2006, after several influential faculty and staff members attended their first Professional Learning Communities (PLCs) at Work Institute, a professional learning community mindset began to resonate with the educators at Baldwin Park High School. A collective mission statement that incorporated a focus on all students learning began to take form. After nearly three months of professionally discussing and searching for the words that would capture the "business of our business" at Baldwin Park High School, we created the following mission statement: "To graduate all students with high levels of academic and personal achievement ready for post-secondary excellence through research-based instruction in a collaborative system of support."

More importantly, staff members began to embrace the professional satisfaction that came with not only writing a mission but living it as well. In addition, time was created during the day to allow teachers who taught the same subject the opportunity to collaborate around the four essential questions: What do we want students to know? How will we know students have learned? What do we do when students do not learn? How do we expand the learning of those students who have already learned? (DuFour & Eaker, 1998). Strategic and specific, Measurable, Attainable, Results oriented, and Time bound (SMART) goals to provide a schoolwide focus on results indicative of student learning were also created (O'Neil & Conzemius, 2006). Most importantly, leadership spread beyond the parameters of the administrative offices, and individuals discovered the advantages that come with being part of a team focused on working together to accomplish academic goals set for all students (Kirtman, 2014). Essential to our PLC journey as well, veteran and new teachers alike began to embrace the reality that not all students would learn on a teacher's first attempt and that reteaching to reassess learning needed to be part of our schoolwide practice. Between 2006 and 2009, the staff at Baldwin Park worked diligently to move away from the belief that only those students interested in learning could achieve academic success and toward the belief embodied in our collectively created mission statement: Baldwin Park High School would become a place where all students would learn!

While great strides in producing optimal learning for all students were indeed made, Baldwin Park continued to lack a systematic approach to addressing evidence of schoolwide nonlearning, especially for those students entering the school as ninth graders.

Year after year, the adult sentiment on campus regarding incoming ninth graders played like a scratched record: "If only these students were more responsible and academically ready for the rigors of high school, we could better prepare them for postsecondary excellence." An extensive analysis of both qualitative and quantitative data did in fact reveal that, while many students were demonstrating learning within the four-year time frame high schools are allotted, a significant number of students had demonstrated an inability to master key academic concepts, often since their time in elementary school, and were failing. Moreover, a significant number of ninth-grade students were entering high school without the necessary academic foundation to complete the sixty-credit expectation their first year demanded. As a result, the likelihood of these students graduating on time, if they graduated at all, was greatly diminished.

Concluding that to do nothing about this severe and apparent problem was unacceptable, administrators and teachers agreed to work collaboratively with district and middle school administrators to identify eighth-grade students bound for high school who did not possess the required academic foundation to secure success. The criteria for identifying these students was simple: Any student who had experienced three or four years of consecutive low grades (mostly Ds and Fs) in core academic areas and whom prior teachers felt would benefit from a collective effort to better secure academic success in high school would be targeted. As a result, the identified students would be mandated to enroll in Baldwin Park High School's new Guided Studies class, a one-year, ten-credit course designed to prepare students academically and socially for learning at the high school level by providing immediate academic intervention when necessary. The goal of the Guided Studies course was simple: to ensure that students who enrolled in the course ended their freshman year credit current.

## Confronting the Brutal Facts—as a Team

A careful examination of data confirmed that less than 50 percent of the ninth graders at Baldwin Park High School completed their first year of high school with the sixty credits required to successfully move on to tenth grade. Having come to the realization as a faculty and staff that a 74 percent graduation rate was unacceptable, the focus turned to what could be done to better prepare ninth graders for academic success. Since ninth graders who did not complete all of the required credits their first year were three times more likely not to graduate from high school (Milliken, 2007), it was blatantly clear that addressing this issue early on would be a worthwhile endeavor.

If there was one lesson that the PLC journey had confirmed up to this point, it was that initiating change in systems and practices that a majority of adults would support required a collective approach. The task force assembled to explore how to best address the issue with ninth graders had to create what Michael Fullan (2008) identifies as *purposeful peer interaction*. In other words, the proposed action plan could not be forced on us by the administration or completely handed over to teachers without any direction or administrative support. Hence, the administrator and three teacher leaders who composed this intervention task force would have to work together to explore best practices aimed at directly addressing the "ninth-grade dilemma" at Baldwin Park High School, and in order to solicit overwhelming support for any proposed idea, they would have to include in their action plan a process for supplying those not on the team with a firm understanding of the problem and possible research-based solutions (Marzano, 2003).

The administrator and teacher leaders embraced collective inquiry as a way of further exploring this challenge (DuFour & Eaker, 1998). Realizing that the purpose of data is often to generate additional questions, not necessarily answers (Johnson, 2002), the team decided to probe which essential questions required further inquiry. These questions included:

- What specific skills did ninth graders lack?
- Which ninth-grade courses proved to be the most challenging for ninth graders, and why?
- Was the failure of credit completion for ninth graders an issue of lack of skill or lack of responsibility? Was it a combination of both?
- What advice would educators from the two middle schools that fed into Baldwin Park High School have for the task force?
- How have other schools in the area with similar demographics addressed this issue?
- What did current and former ninth-grade students identify as the biggest issue preventing them from successfully accomplishing all of their credits?

By taking the time to carefully explore collectively the multiple questions that the initial data prompted the task force to ask, we gained a clearer understanding of the issue. As our collective inquiry efforts led to possible solutions, the literature on how schools effectively respond to evidence of nonlearning proved to be a crucial element of support. In their work titled *Pyramid Response to Intervention: RTI, Professional Learning Communities, and How to Respond When Kids Don't Learn*, Buffum, Mattos, and Weber (2009) provide the necessary blueprint the task force needed to formulate a response to the ninth-grade dilemma. For example, the decision as to which incoming ninth graders would be required to enroll in the proposed Guided Studies course would need to be based on "highly specific data," so as to ensure that the correct students were enrolled (Buffum et al., 2009, p. 7). Additionally, the class needed to be structured in such a way that "timely interventions at the first indication that they needed more time and support" would be provided when common formative assessments indicated a need for remediation (Buffum et al., 2009, p. 8). Lastly, our initial idea to mandate this class for the identified incoming ninth graders, an idea that some staff members were originally concerned would ignite a negative reaction from parents and students, is validated by Buffum and colleagues (2009), who write that "this process should be directive rather than invitational, so that students get the extra help they need consistently and without interruption *until they are successful*" (p. 8). In short, by collectively engaging in the literature on how to best respond to students when evidence of nonlearning is present, task force members were able to generate research-based approaches to the issue at hand.

In addition, task force members expanded their outreach to additional influential members of the faculty and staff and invited them to attend local conferences presented by Austin Buffum and Mike Mattos in order to build on the knowledge that would guide the school's effort to successfully address the ninth-grade challenge. While there is no doubt that collectively studying the research related to how schools create a systematic response to nonlearning was essential, equally important was strengthening the communication and knowledge base among additional faculty and staff members in order to spread the relational trust that would be required for successful implementation of the ideas being generated (Bryk & Schneider, 2002).

## Including the Right Stakeholders: A Lesson Learned

As word of a new class for the 2009 school year spread, a group of well-intentioned legitimate representatives from the district's teacher association made an appointment to meet with the principal to discuss questions that had developed as a result of hearing about the potential for a new course on campus: What qualifications would a teacher assigned to teach this new class need? What process would be initiated to select a teacher? What curriculum would this teacher be expected to use? What kind of support would be offered to the selected teacher, since teaching ninth graders with a history of failure would obviously be challenging? As principal, I realized on meeting with the union representatives that failure to include members of the teachers' union in discussions relevant to the thought processes surrounding the creation of the proposed class was a mistake, since uncertainty is often a recipe for uninformed opposition. As a result, I included union leadership in future discussions surrounding the elements of the Guided Studies course.

In their book *District Leadership That Works: Striking the Right Balance,* Robert J. Marzano and Timothy Waters (2009) write that "contrary to the opinion that district leadership has no relationship to student achievement or is an impediment to student achievement, our findings suggest that district leadership has a measurable effect on student achievement" (p. 12). This statement proved to be true for Baldwin Park High School. The more the task force included district leaders in the collective inquiry process, the more informed and supportive they became. When prepared with all of the necessary thinking and planning needed for implementation, district leadership proved to be an ally in the process.

Because members of the task force agreed that the Guided Studies course needed to offer elective credits to ensure families of students enrolled that time spent in the course would not only better prepare their child for the rigors of high school but also provide credits toward graduation, the team would need to present to the district's curriculum council a detailed explanation of the purpose of the course, as well as other important elements of the class. The Guided Studies course was officially explained as follows:

> This course is designed to assist students who have not been successful in school to develop the habits necessary for them to achieve in school, to be on track for graduation, and to set education and/or career goals beyond high school. Emphasis will be placed on recognition of students' strengths, successes, and growth as well as their personal assets. Time will be spent in building the assets students will need for school success, developing effective strategies to deal with personal challenges or past school failure, and setting goals for the future.
>
> Instructional time will be spent on developing students' organizational and study skills, including the maintenance of a three-ring binder. Students will learn strategies for effectively functioning in their academic courses, with special emphasis on core subjects. (Baldwin Park High School Guided Studies Task Force, personal communication)

Considering that a critical component of the collective-inquiry process included visiting nearby La Serna High School to explore the success it had experienced with a similar form of intervention for tenth graders, which they called Oasis, the task force members decided to include the development of organization and study skills, in addition to immediate academic intervention. With the approval of the district curriculum council, the stage was set for initiating the Guided Studies course in the fall of the 2009–2010 school year. Some critical questions still remained: Who would teach it? How would the students be selected? Which classes would be postponed to make room for Guided Studies on the schedules of ninth-grade students selected to be part of this course? How would we communicate to participating students and parents that Guided Studies was an attempt to help secure academic success in high school and not a punishment?

Members of the task force had done a superb job communicating with key members of the faculty and staff, including union leadership. Their detailed data and research as to the need for ninth-grade intervention had generated not only majority acceptance for implementing the Guided Studies course but also support for the need to analyze current programs and practices. Several years earlier, as part of a long-standing practice, Baldwin Park High School had hired a teacher for the purpose of managing a detention room for students who would be issued "in school" detention during the day. The teacher hired for this purpose, Brandi Lopez, was armed with multiple-subject credentials and a passion for working with at-risk student populations. Brandi's tough-love approach to working with students experiencing both emotional and academic challenges had earned her the respect of both adults and students on campus. Fair, strong, and knowledgeable in a multitude of academic disciplines, Brandi was an ideal fit for teaching students in the Guided Studies course. When approached with the invitation to teach and help further develop the Guided Studies class, she enthusiastically welcomed the challenge.

Because preventing the need for more intense intervention in the future of ninth graders was one of the desired outcomes of the Guided Studies course, Brandi, along with counselors from Baldwin Park High School, worked collaboratively with middle school counselors and administrators to identify students who would benefit from this class. Characteristics of ideal Guided Studies students included:

- A history of low academic achievement
- A low grade-point average
- Being identified by counselors as having the potential to do well with additional support
- Low scores on the end-of-the-year state exam

Figure 3.1 is a copy of the Campus Watch Referral Sheet used when attempting to identify students eligible for the Guided Studies course at Baldwin Park High.

**Campus Watch Referral Sheet**

PLEASE RETURN THIS FORM TO: _____

Student's Name and ID: _____

Middle School: _____

Need for Intervention: _____ Low    _____ Medium    _____ High

**Please check ALL areas of concern.**

*Academic Issues:*

\_\_\_\_\_ Poor academic progress (Multiple Fs)

\_\_\_\_\_ Poor attendance and/or truancy (SARB, SART, and so on)

\_\_\_\_\_ Chronic underachiever

\_\_\_\_\_ Released from Special education (Date released if available)

\_\_\_\_\_ 504 Plan, EL, and so on (Attach plan or level if possible)

*Family Issues:*

\_\_\_\_\_ Homeless (Motel/relative)

\_\_\_\_\_ Foster care/group home

\_\_\_\_\_ Single-parent home

\_\_\_\_\_ Domestic violence/abuse

\_\_\_\_\_ Death in family (Recent, date if known)

\_\_\_\_\_ Victim of a violent crime

\_\_\_\_\_ Parent in jail

*Social Issues:*

\_\_\_\_\_ Suspension(s)/expulsion (Reason)

\_\_\_\_\_ Suspected substance abuse

\_\_\_\_\_ Probation (Officer's name if Available)

\_\_\_\_\_ Suspected gang involvement (Affiliation)

\_\_\_\_\_ Suspected graffiti crew Involvement (Affiliation)

\_\_\_\_\_ Chronic Misbehavior/discipline

*Emotional Issues:*

\_\_\_\_\_ Depression (poor self-esteem)

\_\_\_\_\_ Anger management

\_\_\_\_\_ Mental health issues

\_\_\_\_\_ Currently in counseling (Agency if available)

\_\_\_\_\_ Eating disorder

\_\_\_\_\_ Suicide ideation

\_\_\_\_\_ Self-mutilation

**Educational placement if applicable:**

\_\_\_\_\_ RSP        \_\_\_\_\_ LH        \_\_\_\_\_ SH        \_\_\_\_\_ SED

**Alternative program placement if applicable:**

Name of program/reason: _____

*Source: Baldwin Park High School.*

Figure 3.1: Campus watch referral sheet.

Continued on next page →

Medications / Health Issues: _____

_____

Comments: _____

_____

_____

High school use only: _____

_____

_____

Visit **go.solution-tree.com/rtiatwork** *for a reproducible version of this figure.*

Once the students were identified, Brandi made sure to contact families and explain the reason why students had been chosen to take part in the program. In addition, the administration, Brandi, Diana Ruvira (the school parent and community liaison), and the counseling department hosted multiple meetings at both the students' middle school and high school in both English and Spanish, to ensure clarity about the school's intentions. The words of Buffum and colleagues (2009) are important to consider.

> Schools that design and implement a PRTI (Pyramid Response to Intervention) often fail to communicate the system's goals and procedures to students and parents. While we might assume that offering extra help to students would be embraced by them and their parents, they may not, if the school does not also clearly articulate how the program works and what its aims are. Potential pitfalls in communication include students' and parents' perception of the intervention as either punitive or remedial. (p. 142)

Administrators and counselors, with the support of district office leaders, decided that postponing the required one semester of health and one semester of computers education that ninth graders were usually expected to take would allow enough space in the master schedule to produce four sections of Guided Studies. The teachers' union's concern for ensuring that Brandi had the support needed to be successful was addressed when it was decided collaboratively that the Guided Studies course would only admit twenty-five students at one time, far lower than the thirty-six-student maximum in other classes. In addition, Brandi would have two prep periods at the end of the day (one more than other teachers were allotted) in order to communicate with parents and core teachers of students enrolled in Guided Studies and plan her class accordingly. The necessary communication and collective planning had taken place for one hundred incoming ninth graders to be enrolled in Guided

Studies the following year. While there were undoubtedly additional incoming ninth-grade students who might have benefited from the proposed Guided Studies course, members of the task force and district personnel knew that the initial implementation of the course would present unanticipated challenges the first year and that keeping the course at a manageable state was critical. Therefore, the Guided Studies class began with one hundred students—four sections of twenty-five each—a number that would grow in later years in multiple grade levels.

## Guided Studies Intervention Begins

At the start of the 2009 school year, information acquired from middle school counselors allowed high school counselors to make sure the newly assembled classes did not unintentionally create a disruptive combination of students in a specific class period. Therefore, the master schedule first placed Guided Studies students in their designated classes before scheduling each student's remaining periods. In addition, an even number of males and females in each class period was included in the scheduling.

To address both the academic and emotional needs that many students enrolled in Guided Studies required, each student received a copy of the book *The 7 Habits of Highly Effective Teens* by Sean Covey (1998) to help them identify characteristics in themselves that required self-reflection and evaluation. Administrators frequently visited the class as an additional means of support for Brandi. While occasional discipline challenges did take place, the positive demeanor Brandi developed over time allowed her to channel the necessary patience and attitude required to effectively work with the Guided Studies students.

Over time Brandi realized that while students initially reacted to certain expectations with defiance, she could develop personal relationships with these students to help them realize that the purpose of the class was to help them succeed. This approach, combined with high degrees of patience and optimism, as well as a refusal to send defiant students to the discipline office for minor infractions, created a classroom culture whereby the collective will of the adults for students to succeed triumphed over the collective will for students to not want to succeed.

Figure 3.2 (pages 68–71) shows a copy of the syllabus Brandi distributes to students who are enrolled in the Guided Studies course and their parents. Figure 3.3 (pages 71–72) is the form she distributes to parents inviting them to a conference.

**Guided Studies Syllabus, 2013–2014**

Course Description:

This is a yearlong course that is designed to provide students with the skills necessary to be successful in high school. The class will be focused on assisting students in all academic courses in which they are enrolled. There will be strong communication between students, parents, and teachers. The course will foster a connection between the students and their school. Throughout the class, students will discover and develop their individual strengths and set goals for their future.

**Guided Studies Goals:**

- Improve academic skills to ensure success in all classes
- Improve study habits and time-management skills
- Improve behavior and citizenship
- Develop ownership, accountability, and appreciation for your education
- Develop positive self-esteem
- Earn Cs or above in all classes
- Graduate from high school ON TIME!

**Policies:**  These policies will help our class function smoothly.

- Everyone participates!
- Restroom use will be limited (not allowed during instruction) to 5 MINUTES.
- Restroom use is not allowed during the first and last 15 minutes of class.

**Required Materials:** All students are expected and required to enter class prepared for class activities. Students are required to bring the following EVERY DAY:

1. Three-ring binder
2. Subject dividers for five academic classes
3. Zipper pouch to hold writing utensils
4. Lined paper
5. Black- or blue-ink pen
6. Pencil
7. Highlighter
8. Spiral notebook (at least 70–100 pages) for Guided Studies class ONLY
9. Agenda
10. Homework (assignments to work on in class)

(FIRST Notebook Check will be held on Friday, August 16.)

**Grading:** Students will earn credit for assignments and work in the following areas:

- Participation and Classroom Behavior
- Attendance and Tardies
- Organization (WEEKLY notebook checks)
- Weekly Progress Report
- Daily Warm-Ups
- Tests/Quizzes

**Grading Scale:**

| | |
|---|---|
| 100–89.5 percent | A |
| 89.4–79.5 percent | B |
| 79.4–69.5 percent | C |
| 69.4–59.5 percent | D |
| Below 59.4 percent | F |

**\*Late Work:** Any late work can be turned in for partial credit at teacher's discretion.

**Absences:**

Attendance is a significant part of a students' overall grade. It is imperative that students are in class EVERY DAY. It is the students' responsibility to get all missed work from the teacher.

**Tardies:** Students are required to be on time to every class. This means you are in your seat and ready to work when the bell rings. Excessive tardies will result in a loss of attendance points and detention according to the schoolwide-discipline plan.

**Required Paperwork:** The grade in this class is primarily based on completion of work for other classes. Each week students must turn in a Weekly Progress Report. This form will be given to students each Friday and must be turned in by Monday. It is the students' responsibility to have their parent/legal guardian sign it and to turn it in by Monday. This form provides excellent information to the students, parents, and Guided Studies teacher regarding the students' progress in each class.

**RULES:**

- Treat everyone with respect (no put-downs, profanity, or interruptions).
- Follow directions and cooperate.
- Do not argue with the teacher or other students.
- Be responsible and work hard.

*Source: Baldwin Park High School.*

Figure 3.2: Guided Studies syllabus.

Continued on next page →

- Electronic devices CANNOT BE OUT OR TURNED ON DURING CLASS.
- No gum/eating/drinking in class (water is allowed).
- Follow school rules.

**CONSEQUENCES** (FAILURE TO FOLLOW THE RULES MAY RESULT IN ONE OR MORE OF THE FOLLOWING):

1. Warning
2. Student-teacher conference
3. Loss of participation points
4. Phone call home or parent conference
5. Detention
6. Referral
7. Parent, student, counselor, and/or administrator

**Guided Studies Routines:**

| | |
|---|---|
| Every Day: | Daily 5—complete sentences detailing the answer to the reflection question asked at the beginning of each class period **MAJOR PART OF YOUR GRADE!!** |
| Once a Week: | Notebook Check (Must contain all notes and materials from your other classes) |
| Every Thursday: | SSR (MAKE SURE TO HAVE A READING BOOK!) |
| Every Friday: | Weekly Progress Report (due on Monday) |
| Tuesday Through Thursday: | WORK DAYS!! Bring work from other classes!!! |

**Guided Studies Exit Requirements at First Semester:**

- 2.5 GPA—You must have a C or better in English, math, science, and Guided Studies on first-semester report
- No more than five off-campus suspension days
- No more than eight tardies and no SART contract
- No poor attitude/behavior/citizenship comments on first-semester report

**Office Hours/Assistance:**

I am available to provide extra help during my conference period 11:30–12:30. Please feel free to come and see me if you have any questions or concerns.

I look forward to working with you and for you! Let's have a great year!!!!

By signing this document, I am agreeing to follow all of Brandi's policies and rules.

Student Name: _____

Student Signature: _____

I acknowledge that I have read the information for Brandi's class. By signing this document, I am accepting the policies and rules set by Brandi.

Parent Signature: _____

*Visit **go.solution-tree.com/rtiatwork** for a reproducible version of this figure.*

**Guided Studies**

Student Name: _____

Parent Involvement

This class is an excellent tool to help struggling students in high school. Parents play a major role in student achievement. Please ask your son or daughter each night to see his or her homework or any completed assignments. These questions, in addition to signing the Weekly Progress Reports, will give you an excellent view into your son or daughter's progress at school. Please feel free to call or email me at any time for any reason. In order to generate strong communication between students, teachers, and parents/guardians, we will be holding a mandatory conference on the following dates. Please check the date that you would like to attend.

☐   Tuesday, Sept. 8 (6–7:30 p.m.)

☐   Thursday, Sept. 10 (6–7:30 p.m.)

☐   Saturday, Sept. 12 (10–11:30 a.m.)

I look forward to meeting you!

Sincerely,
Brandi
Guided Studies Teacher

*Source: Baldwin Park High School.*

Figure 3.3: Invitation to a parent-student conference.

*Visit **go.solution-tree.com/rtiatwork** for a reproducible version of this figure.*

The development of a positive approach toward working with Guided Studies students, combined with the fact that students were engaged throughout the class period, meant that very few interruptions on account of discipline interfered with the goals of the course. Over time, it was discovered that the academic success of students enrolled in Guided Studies was directly linked to the students' attention, engagement, and behavior while in class (Buffum et al., 2009).

## The Need for Real-Time Data

Using technological support called Illuminate that the school district had purchased, the district kept a strict daily record of students' academic performance in core classes their freshman year. This resource allowed teachers to post grades and comments in real time with rich detail regarding which assignments, if any, were missing, as well as what assessments students were expected to be prepared for in each of their classes. Teachers were expected to update student profiles at the end of each week. While most teachers complied, several had to be reminded and held accountable by administration. With access to each of her students' profiles, Brandi was easily able to provide immediate academic intervention once an academic deficit was identified. For example, on discovering that a particular student was failing algebra 1 due to his or her inability to solve quadratic equations, intervention in this specific area would be provided daily during the Guided Studies class. If during intervention it was discovered the student lacked a foundation in arithmetic, time during Guided Studies would also address this specific deficit. Careful monitoring of the student's progress or lack thereof by Brandi and the assigned counselor would generate additional inquiry and often conversations between the teacher, parents, and the student to search for additional support aimed at providing the student with the necessary resources to generate learning.

Since Baldwin Park High School generated and mailed home a student progress report every six weeks in an attempt to keep parents abreast of their child's academic status, Brandi, the counselor, and the administrator overseeing the Guided Studies course used this same six-week grading period as a means of monitoring the class and making necessary adjustments to produce the desired goal of credit completion in all academic areas by the end of freshman year. Hence, by using the six-week progress report (a typical report card with grades for each course students were currently enrolled in) as a sort of formative assessment to inform specific changes needed in the Guided Studies program, adjustments to the class could be made, and any support Brandi herself needed could also be offered. In short, if the goal of the Guided Studies course was to have all ninth-grade students enrolled in the class earn the required sixty credits necessary to be deemed credit current at the end of their ninth-grade year, then the gauge used to determine success at the end of the semester would be the number of students who had earned thirty credits midway through the year.

## Making Necessary Changes Along the Way

Even though each of the four Guided Studies courses enrolled only twenty-five students per class, having only one teacher per twenty-five students still proved challenging. After numerous meetings collaborating on how to best support Guided Studies students with a "human" resource that would allow for specific individualized-academic intervention for each student, a return to the observation made at La Serna High School during the school's collective inquiry phase proved insightful. It was observed that La Serna High School's Oasis program used fellow students as academic tutors to support the school's intervention efforts. Why could Baldwin Park High School not do the same? After much discussion, the school implemented a new idea. Rather than have eleventh- and twelfth-grade students who had demonstrated academic excellence via their participation in honors and Advanced Placement courses earlier in their academic career gain elective credits in classes teaching skills such as "clerical assistant," it was decided that their academic accomplishments would be put to better use as academic tutors assisting students in Guided Studies. As many as five to six academic tutors were assigned to each section of Guided Studies ensuring individual support for students requiring assistance. The district's curriculum council approved the following course description for academic tutors.

> This course meets graduation requirements for elective credits. This course is for mature junior and senior students to assist teachers in tutoring students in grades 9, 10, 11 or 12. Students will lead tutorial sessions and also serve as role models for younger students. This course is ideal for students who might want to become teachers or who wish to gain valuable leadership skills.

Evidence of a team and peer approach toward ensuring the success of Guided Studies students spread, and on more than one occasion, academic tutors were observed assisting Guided Studies students outside of the class.

## If at First You Don't Succeed, Reflect, Revamp, and Try Again!

At the end of the 2009–2010 school year, none of the students enrolled in Baldwin Park High School's new Guided Studies class completed his or her first year of high school with the entire sixty credits needed to successfully end their ninth-grade year. No one was more disappointed than Brandi. With tears in her eyes, she met with the principal at the end of the year and concluded that the Guided Studies course, in her opinion, had been a failure. But a closer examination of the data told a different story. While it was true that none of the students had completed all sixty credits, the data revealed that:

- 3 percent of the students had earned 55 credits
- 10 percent of the students had earned 50 credits
- 10 percent of the students had earned 45 credits
- 13 percent of the students had earned 40 credits
- 12 percent of the students had earned 35 credits

- 9 percent of the students had earned 30 credits

- 7 percent of the students had earned 25 credits

- 10 percent of the students had earned 20 credits

- 8 percent of the students had earned 15 credits

- 9 percent of the students had earned 10 credits

- 9 percent of the students had earned 5 credits

While the school's initial goal of ensuring students enrolled in Guided Studies would end their first year with sixty credits, over 58 percent of the students had completed thirty credits, half of the credits desired. Keeping in mind that students with the characteristics that made Guided Studies students eligible for the class in the first place usually ended their first year with ten credits at most, the collective effort at establishing a Guided Studies course had indeed proved worthwhile.

No one was more determined to improve results for Guided Studies students the following year than Brandi. That summer, she engaged in professional reading to better understand how to best motivate and assist students labeled at risk. While administration and other teacher leaders further explored the definition of quality instruction aimed at producing an overflow of student learning at Baldwin Park High School in general, Brandi continued to strengthen her skill set as the Guided Studies teacher in an effort to close the achievement gap between regular ninth graders and those enrolled in her class (Thernstrom & Thernstrom, 2003). Administration also worked with counselors to ensure that this time an ample number of academic tutors would be available for all of the following school year. The school's parent liaison also vowed to work more closely with parents of students enrolled in the Guided Studies class by providing classes that would teach parents how to support and hold their children accountable to academic expectations set by the school and parents jointly. The adults on campus made a determined effort to significantly enhance the number of designated ninth graders in Guided Studies who would end the year with more credits than the previous year.

## At Last, Solid Evidence of Student Learning!

By the semester break in the 2010–2011 school year, 39 percent of the students enrolled in Guided Studies had successfully passed all of their classes, thus earning thirty credits. By year's end, 18 percent of students completed their first year with sixty credits. Equally impressive was the fact that 83 percent of the students enrolled in Guided Studies during the 2010–2011 school year successfully completed more than half of the credits required of their ninth-grade year, a feat that would be repeated and improved on over the next several years. By the end of the 2012–2013 school year, Baldwin Park High's graduation rate had increased by 18 percent to an impressive 92 percent, far exceeding the state of California's graduation rate of 80 percent. The 2013 senior graduation from Baldwin Park included 42 percent of the original students enrolled in the Guided Studies course, students who—counselors report—in the past would not have graduated on time. While having close to half of all Guided Studies students graduate on time is certainly reason to celebrate, a focus on "continuous improvement" (DuFour & Eaker, 1998) will certainly increase the percentage of Guided Studies students who graduate on time in the near future.

While quantitative data have revealed that the effort put forth to create the Guided Studies course proved to be a worthwhile investment, qualitative data in the form of student voices captured in letters written to Brandi by former Guided Studies students also reveals a powerful impact. One student wrote, "I feel blessed to have had such a useful class. While at the beginning I just wanted to get out, I slowly realized how much I needed this. This class is such a release." Another student wrote, "Since being in Guided Studies, I have not had a sip of alcohol, have not touched any drugs, I have stopped hanging out with negative friends, and I no longer wear oversized clothing. More importantly, I do my work and am determined to graduate." These and many other student testimonials revealed the important contribution the Guided Studies course had made to both academic achievement and life enhancement.

Currently, the Guided Studies course has been expanded to tenth and eleventh grades, and student testimonials have concluded that for many students the Guided Studies course has undoubtedly supported their goal of graduating on time. Brandi continues to teach the course and is still seeking new and improved ways of reaching a 100 percent success rate with each ninth-grade class that she inherits.

# References and Resources

Bryk, A., & Schneider, B. (2002). *Trust in schools: A core resource for improvement.* New York: Sage Foundation.

Buckingham, M., & Clifton, D. O. (2001). *Now, discover your strengths.* New York: Free Press.

Buffum, A., Mattos, M., & Weber, C. (2009). *Pyramid response to intervention: RTI, professional learning communities, and how to respond when kids don't learn.* Bloomington, IN: Solution Tree Press.

Covey, S. (1998). *The 7 habits of highly effective teens.* New York: Free Press.

DuFour, R., & Eaker, R. (1998). *Professional learning communities at work: Best practices for enhancing student achievement.* Bloomington, IN: Solution Tree Press.

Fullan, M. (2008). *The six secrets of change: What the best organizations do to help their organizations survive and thrive.* San Francisco: Jossey-Bass.

Johnson, R. (2002). *Using data to close the achievement gap: How to measure equity in our schools.* Thousand Oaks, CA: Corwin Press.

Kirtman, L. (2014). *Leadership and teams: The missing piece of the educational reform puzzle.* Boston: Pearson.

Marzano, R. (2003). *What works in schools: Translating research into action.* Alexandria, VA: Association for Supervision and Curriculum Development.

Marzano, R., & Waters, T. (2009). *District leadership that works: Striking the right balance.* Bloomington, IN: Solution Tree Press.

Milliken, B. (2007). *The last dropout: Stop the epidemic.* Carlsbad, CA: Hay House.

Muhammad, A. (2009). *Transforming school culture: How to overcome staff division.* Bloomington, IN: Solution Tree Press.

O'Neil, J., & Conzemius, A. (2006). *The power of SMART goals: Using goals to improve student learning.* Bloomington, IN: Solution Tree Press.

Peterson, K. D. (2002). Is your school culture toxic or positive? *Education World, 6.*

Thernstrom, A., & Thernstrom, S. (2003). *No excuses: Closing the racial gap in learning.* New York: Simon & Schuster.

Wyner, J. S., Bridgeland, J. J., & Diiulio, J. J., Jr. (2007). *Achievement trap: How America is failing millions of high-achieving students from lower-income families.* Leesburg, VA: Jack Kent Cooke Foundation.

 **Paul Goldberg** is assistant superintendent for district improvement in Schaumburg School District 54 and the former principal of both Robert Frost Junior High and John Muir Literacy Academy, both located in Illinois. He is a former elementary school teacher and is a Solution Tree response to intervention (RTI) and professional learning communities at work (PLC at Work) associate. In 2005, less than 75 percent of Robert Frost's students were proficient on state assessments, and in 2007, the school was not making adequate yearly progress. By 2011, Paul's fourth year as principal of the school, 98 percent of Robert Frost's students were proficient in reading and math on the state assessment, and it was one of two public secondary schools in Illinois to be recognized as a National Blue Ribbon School. Through Paul's leadership of effective system implementation, the school became a three-time winner of the Academic Excellence Award given by the Illinois State Board of Education and is one of about eighty secondary schools in America featured on www.allthingsplc.info. Paul has been selected as the North Cook County Principal of the Year and was nominated for Illinois Principal of the Year in 2014.

You can follow Paul on Twitter @paulgoldberg00.

To book Paul Goldberg for professional development, contact pd@solution-tree .com.

# Three Doses of Intervention and Acceleration

Paul Goldberg

**Editors' Note**

If you are reading each chapter of this anthology in order, we hope that some recurring themes are starting to emerge. One of the most important is that successful interventions don't begin with interventions. They start with getting clear on what you want students to learn and then creating and administering targeted common assessments to identify students who need additional help. This point can be demonstrated by looking once again at the four critical questions that guide the professional learning community (PLC) process (DuFour, DuFour, Eaker, & Many, 2006).

1. What do we want our students to learn?

2. How will we know they are learning it?

3. How should we respond when they are not learning?

4. How should we respond once they have already learned?

Providing students with interventions and extension are addressed in questions 3 and 4. But think about it—a school cannot effectively answer the latter questions if it has not first adequately answered questions 1 and 2. This point is so important that we want it to be consistently reinforced from chapter to chapter, yet we also want to provide different examples of how these outcomes were achieved.

We like Robert Frost Junior High School's story, because it is a great example of tiered interventions. In response to intervention (RTI) research, a system of interventions is represented in the shape of a pyramid, with Tier 1 representing grade-level core instruction, Tier 2 supplemental interventions, and Tier 3 intensive student support (figure 4.1, page 80).

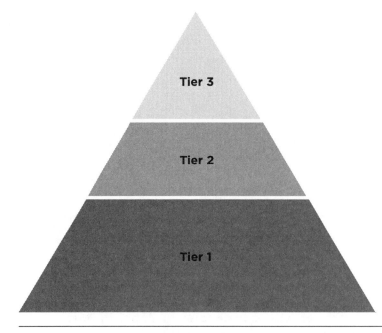

Figure 4.1: The RTI pyramid of intervention.

> Robert Frost Junior High School's "three doses" represent student support at every tier. Equally important, its master schedule makes it possible for a student to potentially receive all three tiers, if needed. For example, a particular student might need a short reteach in science, supplemental help in math, and intensive help in language arts. This can be achieved if the student's science teacher provides common formative assessment intervention and acceleration time during Tier 1, the student's math teacher works with the student during tenth period, and the student is assigned to an extension language arts class for intensive help. The goal of every school should be to build a master schedule where students can receive Tiers 1, 2, and 3 . . . not Tier 1, 2, or 3.

Robert Frost Junior High School is a suburban seventh- and eighth-grade school of about six hundred students. In 2006, the school decided it would embark on the journey to increase student learning by becoming a professional learning community. At the time, there weren't structures at the school for collaboration, intervention, or acceleration to support student learning. After assessments were delivered, it was typical for 25–50 percent of the student population to produce nonproficient results. The need to help students beyond initial instruction was clear. Our assessment data were telling us that students needed extra time and support. We needed to find time to help students who were struggling or who didn't learn after initial teaching.

We determined that no one intervention or acceleration model alone is multifaceted enough to achieve what our students needed, so we would need to add layers until it was. When we initially recognized our students needed extra time and support, we evaluated our curriculum to make sure our focus was on a guaranteed and viable curriculum. During Tier 1 initial instruction, common formative assessments were created to monitor student progress so we could intervene and extend for every student.

Recognizing that more support was needed for all students beyond initial instruction, we removed three minutes from each period and added a tenth period without lengthening the school day. Instead of having nine classes of about forty minutes, we now had nine classes of about thirty-seven minutes and one additional thirty-minute class. This extra, half-hour-long tenth period allowed us to flexibly intervene and extend for all students.

We eventually realized we needed still another dose of support for our students. Some needed an extra class of literacy and math to advance their skills to grade level. Extension classes were therefore created in literacy and math, and taught by teachers with a strong expertise in each area.

Throughout this chapter, we will explicitly identify the structures and specific details that were implemented across our three doses of intervention and acceleration.

- Tier 1: common formative assessment intervention and acceleration
- Tier 2: tenth period
- Tier 3: extension classes

Each layer of support brought us closer to achieving our mission of ensuring success for all students.

## Tier 1 Supports: Common Formative Assessment Intervention and Acceleration

Our staff began their journey to intervene for students with no idea how to find the time. We knew students needed extra time and support and daily initial instruction to not fall further behind, and we knew that multiple doses of intervention and acceleration were required to support all students. During our staff development time, our school leadership team, made up of our administration, teacher leaders, support staff, and a parent, presented the research supporting intervention in schools. Our teachers were presented with evidence of best practice as we leaned heavily on the work of DuFour, DuFour, Eaker, Marzano, Buffum, Mattos, and Weber. After our teachers were given time during staff development to read key excerpts from these authors' research, our school leadership-team members led conversations in small groups with the staff. This built our collective capacity and enabled us to rely on facts to make decisions in the best interests of students. DuFour and Marzano (2011) provide an outline to help us focus our efforts.

> Effective plans of intervention will ensure that students receive additional time and support for learning in ways that do not remove those students from new direct instruction. Furthermore, if the current level of time and support a student is receiving is not resulting in his or her learning, the school plan will include additional tiers that provide the student with even more time and additional support. (p. 182)

This first dose of intervention and acceleration didn't require an extra class or a change to the master schedule, since these interventions occurred in Tier 1 classes in lieu of initial instruction. We knew that if we focused on the most critical skills all students needed to know in each course, assessed student learning of those skills using common formative assessments, and built in an extra day after each test to intervene and extend for all students, we had the makings of an initial intervention and acceleration model. But how did we find the time? In most of our content areas, the teachers were doing common formative assessments every three to four weeks. Given that the school year is roughly forty weeks long, resulting in about ten common formative assessments in each course per year, we knew we needed approximately ten days for intervention and acceleration after each assessment. We referred to the time after a common formative assessment as common formative assessment intervention and acceleration.

Our teacher teams in each subject and course found the time for this intervention by paring away nonessential skills and assignments that we were providing students. The teachers teaching each course as a content-area collaborative team went through their respective curricula and determined what all students truly needed to know and be able to do. We first looked at the value of the projects and assignments our students were being required to complete. Some were fun assignments, and some were even favorite units, but they were not part of our curriculum. Others took considerably more instructional time than was necessary for the students to learn the standard. If the students could demonstrate mastery on a particular standard in two weeks, why did we spend four weeks teaching it? Once we evaluated our projects and the time we taught a unit, relative to the data we had about student proficiency on those standards, we used Doug Reeves's (2011) process for determining power standards so we could identify what we would expect all students to know and be able to do.

There are three criteria that can be applied to develop power standards: endurance, leverage, and necessity for the next level of instruction. The property of endurance implies that the standard has lasting value. The principle of leverage is related to the application of a standard to multiple academic disciplines. The third criterion for a standard is the degree to which it is necessary for the next level of learning. (p. 110)

When we first went through this process, our teacher teams used most of a professional development day to map out the year by identifying approximately eight-to ten-power standards per trimester. Every team, including the core subjects (math, language arts, science, and social studies), electives, and physical education teachers, completed this process for the whole year but made changes and adaptations throughout the year. Teams made changes prior to each trimester as learning data indicated whether a particular standard required more or less instructional time. Figure 4.2 shows a completed sample trimester planning guide.

This document is to be completed by each department prior to each trimester. It supports curriculum alignment in the reading and math extension classes. Identify the standard each student must demonstrate mastery on by the end of the trimester. Document how long the standard will be taught.

| Trimester 1 | Trimester 2 | Trimester 3 |
|---|---|---|
| Write and evaluate variable expressions. | Solve linear systems by graphing, substitution, and elimination. | Simplify radical expressions. |
| Simplify numerical expressions using the Order of Operations. | Identify and apply special solutions to systems of linear equations. | Perform operations with polynomials. |
| Translate words into mathematical symbols. | Simplify expressions using the properties of exponents. | Factor polynomials. |
| Solve multistep equations. | Use the discriminant to determine the number of solutions to a quadratic equation. | Solve rational equations. |
| Determine the slope of a line from a graph. | Factor polynomials. | Use the Pythagorean Theorem, Distance, and Midpoint formulas. |
| Write, solve, and graph linear inequalities with one variable. | Perform operations with polynomials. | Perform operations with radicals. |

*Source: Robert Frost Junior High School.*

Figure 4.2: Sample trimester planning guide.

*Visit* **go.solution-tree.com/rtiatwork** *for a reproducible version of this figure.*

We needed to come into close alignment about what all students needed to know and be able to do and when those standards would be taught in each course so that teams could work together to write assessments, share best practices, and intervene for students. In this case, being tightly aligned meant that all members of the team agreed to teach the same standards and to assess the students on the same day. While teachers had autonomy in how they taught our power standards, the only way to effectively have a common assessment cycle was for teachers to spend very similar lengths of time teaching each one. After power standards were established, teams utilized long-term planning documents and a school calendar to map out their time lines for each standard. Figure 4.3 shows a sample trimester calendar.

Once we made time by being purposeful in identifying our standards, common formative assessments were created to monitor student progress and to intervene and extend for every student at the conclusion of each common formative assessment cycle. The teams began with the planning guide and calendar, so the power standards were laid out for the course. Our common formative assessment cycle occurred in the following ten steps within each department and course.

| 2013–2014 Trimester Calendar | | | | |
|---|---|---|---|---|
| Monday | Tuesday | Wednesday | Thursday | Friday |
| 8/19/2013<br>Institute Day—No Class | 8/20/2013<br>Institute Day—No Class | 8/21/2013<br>First day for 1–6 | 8/22/2013 | 8/23/2013 |
| 8/26/2013 | 8/27/2013<br>First day for kindergarten | 8/28/2013<br>Write CA 1 | 8/29/2013 | 8/30/2013 |
| 9/2/2013<br>Labor Day—no class | 9/3/2013 | 9/4/2013 | 9/5/2013 | 9/6/2013<br>Administer CA 1 |
| 9/9/2013 | 9/10/2013<br>Reflect on CA 1 | 9/11/2013 | 9/12/2013 | 9/13/2013 |
| 9/16/2013 | 9/17/2013 | 9/18/2013 | 9/19/2013 | 9/20/2013 |
| 9/23/2013 | 9/24/2013 | 9/25/2013<br>½ day inservice | 9/26/2013<br>Write CA 2 | 9/27/2013 |
| 9/30/2013<br>Reflect on CA 2 | 10/1/2013 | 10/2/2013 | 10/3/2013 | 10/4/2013 |
| 10/7/2013<br>Administer CA 2 | 10/8/2013 | 10/9/2013 | 10/10/2013<br>½ day parent conference | 10/11/2013<br>Parent conferences—no class |
| 10/14/2013<br>Columbus Day—no class | 10/15/2013 | 10/16/2013 | 10/17/2013 | 10/18/2013<br>Write CA 3 |
| 10/21/2013 | 10/22/2013 | 10/23/2013 | 10/24/2013 | 10/25/2013 |
| 10/28/2013 | 10/29/2013<br>Administer CA 3 | 10/30/2013 | 10/31/2013 | 11/1/2013<br>Reflect on CA 3 |
| 11/4/2013<br>Write CA 4 | 11/5/2013 | 11/6/2013 | 11/7/2013 | 11/8/2013<br>End of trimester |

*Source: Robert Frost Junior High School.*

Figure 4.3: Sample trimester calendar for 2013–2014.

Continued on next page →

| Dates to Include on Calendar | |
|---|---|
| Throughout Trimester | At Least Every Three Weeks:<br><br>Identify date to write CA prior to instruction.<br><br>Identify date to administer CA.<br><br>Identify date to reflect on CSA using CA Synopsis.<br><br>If applicable, identify dates when pre-assessments will occur. |
| End of Trimester: | |

1. A team of teachers teaching the same course identifies the power standard and what all students need to know and be able to do in the next unit.

2. The team identifies a time line for teaching the standard and a date to write the assessment.

3. The team writes a common formative assessment prior to teaching the unit to assess student progress and inform future instruction. The teachers determine what proficiency looks like on the test.

4. The unit is taught for a length of time agreed on by the team, and the assessment is given to all students in that course on the same day.

5. The team of teachers analyzes the results of the assessment to learn which students need extra time and support and which need acceleration.

6. Students are placed by the team of teachers in the proper group for intervention or acceleration instruction.

7. The team discusses effective instructional strategies for each group.

8. The team intervenes and extends for each group of students.

9. The team assesses student progress.

10. The cycle begins anew with the next set of agreed-on power standards.

After delivering common formative assessments, regrouping and reshuffling across teachers occurred, and all new instruction stopped in order to give students timely intervention and acceleration. We found that some students needed small-group support targeting deficit areas from the assessment. Others demonstrated proficiency and warranted acceleration. Based on the results of the assessment, we often found that some teachers advanced learning for our highest students and others demonstrated a knack for intervening for students who struggled. At this point, our teams collaborated on what strategies would be most effective and who would best teach each group. After each common formative assessment, approximately every three to four weeks in all content areas, teacher teams analyzed their results and answered the following three questions.

1. Based on the results of the assessment, which students need more time and support with each standard?

2. Based on the results of the assessment, which students require extension?

3. Based on the results of the assessment, who would be the most appropriate person to teach each group of students needing intervention and extension?

This work was done by each of our teams after every common formative assessment. The teachers then used assessment data to determine who would work with students needing intervention and who would extend for the proficient students.

Table 4.1 (page 88) shows how a math team could carry out this ten-step cycle via a common assessment focusing on congruence and similarity in an eighth-grade geometry course. The team predetermines that the unit will take four weeks, identifies a date to write the assessment and a score that indicates proficiency, begins teaching the standard, and builds in informal assessments along the way. The common formative assessment is then administered and analyzed. Students are regrouped, and the team uses best practices and data to formulate an intervention and extension plan. The intervention and extension process occurs, there are checks for understanding, and this common assessment cycle concludes.

This assessment tested five skills aligned with the standard.

1. Describe angle relationships of parallel lines intersected by a transversal.

2. Describe angle relationships of the interior and exterior angles of triangles.

3. Demonstrate rotations, reflections, and translations (line segments, lines, parallel lines, angles).

4. Verify that 2-D figures are congruent using transformations.

5. Demonstrate the similarity of 2-D figures using transformations.

The team spent a little over a week teaching transformations and a little over two weeks teaching angles, and allowed time for individual informal assessments to occur prior to the team-determined common formative assessment.

**Table 4.1: Sample Ten-Step Common Assessment Cycle for Geometry**

| | |
|---|---|
| 1. Identify what students will need to know and be able to do. | Understand congruence and similarity using physical models, transparencies, or geometry software. |
| 2. Identify the time line for teaching the standard and a date for assessment. | Four weeks—including time for individual classroom informal assessment.<br><br>Date: October 14 |
| 3. Write the test—determine proficiency. | The team will write the test on September 17. The students will need to get 80 percent correct on each skill to be proficient. |
| 4. Teach, then deliver the common formative assessment. | The team will assess students on October 14. |
| 5. Analyze assessment results. | Team will analyze results on October 15 to determine the plan for intervention and extension. |
| 6. Group students for intervention or extension. | Three teachers teach sixty-six eighth-grade geometry students during first period. Ten were nonproficient and work with one teacher, and fifty-six were proficient and work with the other teachers. |
| 7. Discuss effective instructional strategies for each group. | Strategies that were found to be effective based on the results of the common formative assessment are identified to support the struggling students. The team determines extension activities beyond the expected standard. |
| 8. Intervene and extend. | Intervention and extension occur on October 17 in Tier 1. |
| 9. Assess progress. | Informal assessment will occur on the deficit standards during intervention on October 17. |
| 10. Begin the cycle again. | |

The team analyzed the results by classroom, student, and standard, and the results drove intervention and extension decisions. Teacher 1 in table 4.2 did particularly well with the students who struggled on these skills earlier in the unit, so the team chose her to teach the intervention group. The shaded cells in each class indicate students whose informal assessments indicated that they struggled early in the unit and at the time were nonproficient. As you can see, Teacher 1 moved five previously nonproficient students to a proficient level above 80 percent—three of them to 100 percent.

**Table 4.2: Percentage of Correct Answers After Geometry Skills Intervention and Extension**

|  | Teacher 1 | Teacher 2 | Teacher 3 |
|---|---|---|---|
|  | Describe angle relationships of parallel lines intersected by a transversal. | Describe angle relationships of parallel lines intersected by a transversal. | Describe angle relationships of parallel lines intersected by a transversal. |
| 1 | 90 | 60 | 80 |
| 2 | 90 | 80 | 60 |
| 3 | 80 | 90 | 90 |
| 4 | 80 | 60 | 100 |
| 5 | 80 | 90 | 100 |
| 6 | 80 | 100 | 60 |
| 7 | 90 | 100 | 80 |
| 8 | 100 | 90 | 90 |
| 9 | 100 | 60 | 60 |
| 10 | 100 | 80 | 100 |
| 11 | 90 | 80 | 100 |
| 12 | 80 | 60 | 100 |
| 13 | 60 | 80 | 80 |
| 14 | 90 | 80 | 80 |
| 15 | 80 | 100 | 90 |
| 16 | 80 | 100 | 90 |
| 17 | 80 | 90 | 100 |
| 18 | 90 | 60 | 80 |
| 19 | 100 | 80 | 60 |
| 20 | 100 | 100 | 80 |
| 21 | 100 | 80 | 90 |
| 22 | 90 | 80 | 90 |
|  |  |  |  |
|  | Percentage Correct on Skill | | |

The team completed the data collection for all five skills but noted that this skill—describing angle relationships—was the main deficit area for some students; on the other four skills, all students were proficient and got at least 80 percent correct. To support the ten nonproficient students during the common formative assessment intervention and acceleration time, the teacher who intervened provided the students with additional labeled angle measures than the expected standard required. She then began pulling away this scaffolded support until just one angle measure remained, which was similar to what was asked on the test. Once intervention occurred and the scaffolds were no longer needed, the teacher provided an on-the-spot assessment to determine whether the students were proficient.

In the extension groups, two teachers worked with twenty-eight students each to advance this skill beyond what was expected during initial instruction. An algebraic component was added for these students to move the skill beyond the standard to a more rigorous level. The students were asked to solve for the variable in an algebraic expression using their knowledge of angle relationships. These proficient students advanced their learning beyond the course standard during this time.

During common assessment intervention and acceleration, our first dose, teacher teams across all content areas were able to intervene and extend for their students based on the results of assessments. To support nonproficient students in language arts, for example, a teacher might use multiple pieces of poetry to model how to identify elements of figurative language and then have the students write their own poem in order to assess their progress and provide feedback. In math, a teacher might work with a small group of students using manipulatives to model how to solve an algebraic word problem. The teacher would then allow the students to demonstrate this skill first with the manipulatives and then ideally without any scaffolded support. In science, a teacher could demonstrate how to use the scientific method to draw conclusions based on a set of data. The teacher might begin by modeling this process with a small group and then allow the students to demonstrate mastery with their own lab or data. In social studies, a teacher could teach the students how to analyze the differences between world political systems through role play and eventually allow the students to apply the skill through a written analysis.

Teachers like our art, media, band, and chorus teacher who were singletons within the building adapted differently, since there weren't multiple teachers to regroup students between. After each assessment, one might see the following:

- Art—In art class, the teacher might have proficient students adding detail to a piece of pottery while he or she works with a small group of nonproficient students on the pottery wheel. The teacher would likely model the skill the students struggled with during their performance assessment by teaching it with a different strategy and would then have each student practice the skill again and coach him or her with specific feedback.

- Media—In media class, proficient students could be asked to use a specific form of propaganda to design a commercial within certain advanced criteria. A small group of students who were nonproficient would typically be retaught the learning objective and then would be asked to either take a different assessment on the deficit skill(s) or demonstrate mastery through a performance assessment.

- Band—During band, proficient students often continued working with like instrument groups to prepare for a final piece. Our band director would often pull a group of students with similar performance challenges or appropriate instrument groups and work on the side with them to overcome a particular challenge. One would often see him model the proper use of the instrument and then give immediate corrective feedback to a student. Perhaps most importantly, these students transitioned back to the full band for the ultimate reassessment: How would they perform with the whole group?

Other situations certainly arose that required problem solving. What did we do when two teachers were teaching a course during a period and fifty students were proficient and only three were nonproficient? Did one teacher teach fifty students? Is that appropriate for those students? Given that the period was forty minutes long, we would have one teacher take twenty-five proficient students for teacher-directed extension while the other took twenty-two students for an independent extension activity and the three students for intervention. About twenty minutes into the period, the proficient students would switch rooms and teachers. We ensured that the classes were taught in close proximity to one another—often in adjacent rooms—that transition expectations were taught and practiced, and that the transition was closely monitored to ensure that minimal instructional time was lost. This allowed the students to all receive a balance of teacher-directed extension (twenty minutes) and an independent extension activity (twenty minutes). The teacher working with the three nonproficient students continued intervening.

What did we do when the assessment required a lengthy turnaround time to grade—for example, an essay in language arts? In this case, the team set a date to have the assessment graded, perhaps a week after the test. They analyzed the results at that team's agreed-on time and built-in an intervention and acceleration day a couple of days later. While the teachers graded the essays, the next unit began. It then paused for a day of intervention and extension on the prior skill and then immediately continued.

Our biggest challenge was supporting students who struggled even after a period of intervention using this model. We did what most schools do. We relied on individual teachers to find time, perhaps during lunch, after school, or even between classes. Of course, reliance on individuals instead of systems is the antithesis of RTI. More importantly, though, our teachers recognized that this couldn't be a solution for us, and that our students needed another layer of support.

Dose one worked wonders for our students, and student learning immediately began increasing, but more was needed. Our leadership team and department chairpersons asked, "What else can we do to ensure student success?"

## Tier 2 Supports: Tenth Period

Because some students did not learn all the standards taught in Tier 1 even after our common formative assessment intervention and acceleration, our school leadership team and department chairpersons recognized that more support was needed. They also saw that our proficient students needed additional extension to continue making growth, so we added a tenth period to our schedule. Our teacher leaders speculated that this would be the answer for many students, because it met the criteria Buffum, Mattos, and Weber (2009) suggest. Tenth period was:

- Urgent
- Directive
- Timely
- Targeted
- Administered by trained professionals
- Systematic (Buffum et al., 2009, p. 61)

It was urgent in that students received support when it was needed, directive because it was mandatory, and timely because it was immediate and extra. The intervention provided was matched to student need, which made it targeted. Intervention and extension were provided by content area, special education, or English learner teachers. Lastly, it was systematic because it wasn't teacher or team dependent and was structured in a way that every intervention happened on purpose. Further detail about how it was orchestrated is the focus of this section.

Students who were struggling worked with a teacher in small groups in this period to receive targeted support. Students who were successful participated in extension and enrichment activities, since they previously demonstrated proficiency on the standard. In part, this was different from what occurred during our first dose, because students were often taught in a preteaching or proactive manner. Through informal data collection, our teachers could identify students they speculated would struggle with or exceed the standard on the next common formative assessment. This dose enabled our teachers to reach those students earlier and more often by pulling out these students during tenth period. The extra period also gave our teachers time after a test to support students who didn't learn all of what they needed during our common formative assessment intervention and acceleration time. Some students needed more support, which is precisely why we layered this support for them.

To create tenth period, classes went from roughly forty minutes a day to roughly thirty-seven minutes a day. Figure 4.4 shows before-and-after bell schedules that include three-minute passing periods.

| Period | Before | After |
|--------|--------|-------|
| 1 | 7:40–8:20 | 7:40–8:18 |
| 2 | 8:23–9:03 | 8:21–8:57 |
| 3 | 9:06–9:46 | 9:00–9:38 |
| 4 | 9:49–10:31 | 9:41–10:18 |
| 5 | 10:34–11:14 | 10:21–10:59 |
| 6 | 11:17–11:59 | 11:02–11:40 |
| 7 | 12:02–12:43 | 11:43–12:21 |
| 8 | 12:46–1:28 | 12:24–1:02 |
| 9 | 1:31–2:15 | 1:05–1:40 |
| 10 | | 1:43–2:15 |

*Source: Robert Frost Junior High School.*

Figure 4.4: Before-and-after bell schedules with three-minute passing periods.

We used this schedule on Tuesdays and Thursdays. Teachers identified students needing intervention or extension during tenth period by using formal and informal assessments, in most cases after dose one—the common formative assessment intervention and acceleration. Homework completion, student behavior, and project completion were never considered valid criteria to request a student during this block. For any student who was choosing not to complete homework, we had a built-in homework and project completion intervention during lunch and a secondary support that occurred after school. A systematic process to intervene for students who were struggling behaviorally was also in place. In our model, tenth period was not the time for a behavioral consequence or overdue homework completion unless a student was participating in a study hall. It was the time to help students learn our standards.

The tenth-period block truly required all hands on deck. We needed to account for six hundred students while providing as many as possible with small-group intervention and moving proficient students into extension or enrichment classes. As shown in table 4.4, all students were assigned a base location that they would report to during tenth period, unless they were asked to go to another course or teacher.

**Table 4.4: Base Locations for Tenth-Grade Block**

| Base Locations | Number of Students Assigned |
|---|---|
| Cafeteria—Study Hall (Students assigned by need and supported by teachers and peer tutors—often for work completion) | 150 |
| Library—Study Hall (Students assigned by need and supported by teachers and peer tutors—often for work completion) | 100 |
| Science Lab (Students assigned who participated in enrichment science program) | 50 |
| Chorus (Chorus students assigned) | 50 |
| Media (Media students assigned) | 25 |
| Band (Band students assigned) | 50 |
| Foreign Language (Foreign language students assigned) | 50 |
| Gym (Physical education) | 100 |
| Art (Art students assigned) | 25 |

These base locations were a way to assign every student to an area each trimester before any students moved to teacher-requested content areas. Some students were assigned to electives for extension or enrichment, and others were provided study hall time when staff felt that opportunity would be beneficial.

Table 4.5 contains a sample of where students might move to for tenth period. Note that many students would not go to their base location, regardless of its type, and would immediately report to an intervention or extension by teacher request.

**Table 4.5: Numbers of Students Per Content Area During Tenth Period**

| Teacher Content Area | Approximate Number of Students per Group | What Was Occurring? | Number of Teachers Assigned |
|---|---|---|---|
| Language Arts Intervention | 20 | Small-group targeted instruction | 2: language arts, 1: special education, 1: reading specialist |
| Language Arts Extension | 40 | Extension instruction | 2: language arts |
| Math Intervention | 20 | Small-group targeted instruction | 2: math, 1: EL |
| Math Extension | 40 | Extension activity or task | 2: math |
| Social Studies Intervention | 20 | Small-group targeted instruction | 2: social studies |
| Social Studies Extension | 20 | Extension activity or task | 1: social studies |
| Science Intervention | 30 | Small-group hands-on activity | 3: science |
| Science Extension | 20 | Lab extension | 1: science |
| Physical Education | 80 | Aerobic activity | 3: physical education |
| Guided Study Hall in Cafeteria | 100 | Tutoring by staff and students | 1: social studies teacher, 1: social worker, 2: teaching assistants |
| Guided Study Hall in Library | 50 | Tutoring by staff and students | 1: library teacher, 1: teaching assistant |
| Band | 50 | Band practice | 1: band |
| Foreign Language | 30 | Extension activity | 1: foreign language |
| Art | 20 | Extension project | 1: art |
| Media | 20 | Extension project | 1: media |
| Chorus | 40 | Chorus practice | 1: chorus |

Every staff member was involved in tenth period, including administration, guidance staff, support staff, special education, and English learner teachers. As principal, I worked with our department chairs to make sure that enough teachers were available for each content area on a given day, so there were appropriate teacher-to-student ratios. As you can see from the table, we placed teachers in areas where they had expertise. Some flexibly worked in varying content areas. For example, special education teachers worked in language arts, math, science, or social studies, depending on the needs of the students. Other versatile staff members, like the librarian, flexibly supported content areas they had expertise in, or supported a study hall.

In most junior highs and high schools, students get a schedule for the semester that rarely changes. We needed to flexibly move all of our students multiple times a week to the class they needed during our tenth-period block. We did our best to keep it structured and simple by relying on our base locations. The day prior to the tenth-period block any teacher could make a request to see a specific student for extension or intervention.

This list of requested students was electronically submitted to a member of our guidance staff, who acted as point person and decided where each student would go based on a rotating prioritization schedule. It took our point person roughly thirty minutes to organize the tenth-period block. While this was an extra responsibility for her, she had always served as the coordinator of our RTI and special education services. Given how many more students were having their needs met proactively through our doses of support; she had considerably more time in her day than she did before, when we were using reactive processes. One day, language arts might have first priority; the next day, it might be science. We attempted to ensure that all content areas had an opportunity to see the students they needed within as short a time frame as possible. This was necessary because those students who struggled across multiple content areas would be requested by more than one staff member on a given day. Figure 4.5 shows a sample prioritization schedule that systemized where our guidance staff assigned students. The first course listed had first priority on that day and the last course had lowest priority.

| Day 1 | Language Arts, Math, Science, Social Studies, Specials, PE |
| --- | --- |
| Day 2 | Math, Science, Social Studies, Specials, PE, Language Arts |
| Day 3 | Science, Social Studies, Specials, PE, Language Arts, Math |
| Day 4 | Social Studies, Specials, PE, Language Arts, Math, Science |
| Day 5 | Specials, PE, Language Arts, Math, Science, Social Studies |
| Day 6 | PE, Language Arts, Math, Science, Social Studies, Specials |

*Source: Robert Frost Junior High School.*

Figure 4.5: Sample prioritization schedule.

The schedule shown in the table could cycle continuously throughout the year, or based on your school goals, it could fluctuate. At various points, our goals indicated that we needed to make progress in the areas of reading and math, so we often needed to make language arts and math the top priority on additional days. Let your schedule mirror your priorities.

Once the point person assigned all of our students, she printed passes that informed every student where to go for tenth period. A pass would include a student's name, the room assignment for tenth period, and the name of the teacher who requested the student. Student helpers distributed those passes during ninth period, and a master list was distributed to all staff to take attendance. Students knew where to go, because they either went where their pass dictated or they stayed in their base location. Attendance was just as mandatory as every other period of the day. Students were required to attend the course they were assigned.

After students attended the tenth-period block for an appropriate number of sessions, the collaborative teams reassessed the struggling students to determine if they had mastered the power standard in which they previously demonstrated a lack of proficiency. As with all other common formative assessments, the collaborative teams used the data to identify individual student progress but also to discuss strategies that were effective. Teachers used the student learning results to celebrate proficiency, adjust their methods, and when necessary add an extra dose for a student who continued to struggle.

This dose-two block was timely, targeted, systematic, and organized. It was helpful to many students, but we weren't yet "ensuring student success" for all. An extra dose was needed.

## Tier 3 Supports: Extension Classes

Despite multiple layers of intervention and acceleration, we found that we were not helping *all* students be successful. Some needed daily interventions in literacy or mathematics, so we decided to make changes to the schedules of those students. In a typical nine-period student schedule, there were two elective periods. It was apparent to our staff that more literacy or math support was needed for our students, so we scheduled struggling students into this extension course in lieu of one of their electives. A student needing this level of support would now take reading or math extensions and would take one elective instead of two. Students in reading or math extensions needed targeted instruction to be on track for high school and college curriculum. After all, as Timothy D. Kanold (2012) writes, "Access to a college preparatory mathematics curriculum has typically been restricted to a small group of students. The idea of tracking students into lower-level mathematics courses is a typical and ineffective school response to failed student performance" (p. 113). The same is also true of language arts. Students were placed in this course with the goal that they would be on track for high school college-track courses.

In determining the instructional model that would best support student learning, we focused on curricular alignment for these courses. Nicholas Jay Myers (2012) explains:

> When designing balanced literacy intervention lessons, teachers should focus on addressing the same skills, concepts, and vocabulary that are simultaneously being delivered during initial instruction. In other words, teachers provide students with in-depth exposure to the same content delivered during initial instruction, but in a differentiated, small-group context. Furthermore, teachers should select a different teaching strategy for small-group interventions than was used during initial instruction. (p. 78)

These expectations were true of our interventions across content areas, specials, and physical education, even though we only had extension classes in language arts and math. Intervention in specials and physical education were curriculum aligned, differentiated with a new strategy, and delivered in small groups.

Each year, we adapted and organized our model, and it was evident that we needed to be systematic to maintain structure for our students and staff. As we know, "A successful system of interventions will require not only a collective effort, but also a coordinated one" (DuFour, DuFour, & Eaker, 2008, p. 257). We ensured there was coordination across each dose of intervention, in flexibly scheduling students, and in collaboration between teachers. Our extension teachers and Tier 1 teachers were in regular communication. The Tier 1 teachers planned at least a trimester ahead, and when changes were needed to the scope and sequence, we communicated those changes to the extension teachers in advance of each unit. This structure and the communications that occurred often through email and our intranet resulted in the curricular coordination our students needed so they could be pretaught and retaught our power standards. Additionally, the Tier 1 teachers provided our intervention teachers with a copy of each student's common formative assessment as soon as it was graded, so they could use that information to guide intervention and support. Whenever possible, often during staff development, additional time was provided to our extension and Tier 1 teachers for collaboration. Without this coordination, we would have had a combination of chaos and curriculum "dis-aligned" instruction, which we know does not work. Richard L. Allington (2009) acknowledges the all-too-familiar problem that occurs when dis-alignment happens in a school: "The vastly dominant instructional model [is] one that [creates] curricular and strategy conflicts for struggling readers" (p. 91).

We worked hard to avoid these conflicts during this third dose of instruction and ensure curricular coherence by maintaining a logical connection between the strategies used during initial instruction and those that were used during extension classes. When students struggled to use or retain a skill or strategy, we found that by teaching the standard multiple times with different approaches, our students experienced exponentially greater gains. For example, let's assume our language arts classes were learning to determine how incidents in a story propel the action, reveal aspects of a character, or provoke a decision. In Tier 1, the teachers would define *propel the action* the same way it would be defined in the extension class. However, in Tier 1, the skill might be modeled through whole-group instruction via an on-grade-level text. In Tier 3, it might be taught through an instructional-level text, with a graphic organizer or different scaffolded support in a small group. Throughout the week, the goal would be to remove the supports provided to the student and increase his or her ability to independently complete the task. Alignment in our school occurred when common language was agreed to by all members of the team and used during every dose of support, when the time lines for teaching the standards were the same and when appropriate differentiated strategies were used. This alignment occurred throughout Tiers 1, 2, and 3.

Our primary structure for determining who received this course was our districtwide internal assessment—Northwest Evaluation Association's Measures of Academic Progress. We typically looked at multiple data points, but if a student was performing below the 40th percentile based on national norms, he or she was usually assigned to this course. This test was given three times a year, and student enrollment in this intervention was always reevaluated after these assessments. As principal, I typically acted as gatekeeper for entry into this course, but teachers and parents were always welcome to provide input, and other reliable data (for example, common formative assessments) were always considered.

These extension classes were taught by teachers highly qualified in language arts and math. At various times, these were new teachers with strong literacy or math backgrounds, literacy or math specialists, or former math or language arts teachers. Regardless, these courses were typically taught many times throughout the day. To achieve targeted support and cohesion, we did the following:

- Our Tier 1 math and language arts courses were planned long term, a trimester at a time, to enable the extension class teachers to plan in a corresponding manner. This allowed each teacher of an extension class to both preteach and reteach the standard that was taught in Tier 1.

- The teachers of an extension class provided scaffolded support and consistently developed the independent application skills of the students. As this newly acquired skill was transferred and used in the core classroom, student confidence was boosted.

- Teachers of an extension class began most days by modeling for about ten minutes how to use the skill and strategy for the day. Then, typically, two small groups of students each day received guided reading or math instruction. This small-group instruction, which occurred for approximately thirty of the forty minutes, was a tight expectation to ensure student progress was monitored and explicit corrective coaching was provided to individual students. Small-group instruction enabled the teachers to provide "high-quality, intensive instruction that is appropriate for every member of the group" (Fountas & Pinnell, 2001, p. 217). It was during this guided instruction that prerequisite skills—decoding, math facts, writing a basic paragraph, and so on—were taught at the student's instructional level.

In the case of students performing consistently well below grade level, we attempted to find structured ways to meet their needs. After all, what secondary school doesn't have students struggling with basic skills—decoding in literacy; adding, subtracting, multiplying, and dividing in math; or constructing a basic paragraph in writing? We approached these students in a multifaceted way, recognizing that their needs were vast and curricular alignment was key. Students receiving near-maximum intervention may have received the following academic support.

- Initial instruction: During initial instruction they would be exposed to the grade-level standard during shared or whole-group instruction. They would also receive regular small-group guided instruction at their instructional level, where decoding could be taught, numeracy skills embedded, or independent writing supported.

- Tenth period: Students would typically see prerequisite skill development occur through an embedded structure. As they learned the grade-level standard, the teacher would often use a "name and notice" model. The teacher might say in a math class, "Notice how I'm determining the sum of these two double-digit numbers. Now you try it." While this wouldn't be the focus of most secondary grade-level standards for the entire period, it does allow for numeracy development to occur without the gap widening further on the grade-level skill.

- Extension class: Daily guided reading would result in on-level word work, comprehension support, and guided writing support.

- Resource: During an EL or special education resource, our teachers worked to achieve not only the grade-level standard but the student's individualized education program (IEP) or English goals. It was common to see practice of prerequisite skills and the grade-level standard occurring simultaneously during this block. During this time, our students learned basic skills like decoding and math facts.

In the rare instance where an academic struggle was not rectified or at least improved at an accelerated rate after these doses of support, we began a formal problem-solving process involving the team, the psychologist, the student, and the parent. The team first analyzed the student's data, identified a hypothesis for the root cause of the problem, and identified solutions to support the student and his or her challenge. For instance, one student was failing common formative assessments due to what the team speculated was his not knowing his basic facts in math. The team determined a systematic way of utilizing manipulatives and common language across all doses of support to intervene for the student. The data indicated that by the end of the year, he was proficient in his math facts and had moved from the 5th to the 25th percentile based on national norms.

Only one student in four years went through the problem-solving process into a case study and was determined eligible for special education. That student's needs were determined to be behavioral and not academic. Despite not identifying one new student in four years with a learning disability, over 90 percent of our students with IEPs were proficient on state assessments in both math and reading. This can be attributed to (1) giving all students the support they need, (2) ensuring every student participates in initial instruction, (3) teaching students with their nondisabled peers to the maximum extent possible, and (4) holding all students to high expectations.

Our goal was continuous improvement—continuously improving our guaranteed and viable curriculum so all students could be successful, continuously improving our intervention and extension structures so they mirrored our priorities, and continuously improving our professional expertise. As Richard L. Allington (2012) writes, "Schools must enhance classroom instruction so that the number of struggling readers is minimized and then put into place an organizational strategy that ensures that the children who need intensive, expert instruction receive it" (p. 175). In a short time, three doses of intervention and extension were in place, and learning levels reached all-time highs.

This didn't happen without challenges. When we started on this journey, we had no collaborative planning time for teachers to discuss and identify our standards and to share best practices. The idea of new classes or additional classes beyond Tier 1 instruction that might be necessary to help students learn at high levels was in its infant stages. We were excellent at qualifying students for special education, pulling them from core instruction, remediating, and hoping for the best. We certainly did not know how to change our master schedule to overcome our challenges. Making this task more challenging, we did not have contractual language within our school board and association agreements describing how a schedule could be changed.

Year by year, we worked through each challenge. Figure 4.6 shows a schedule for a seventh-grade team before grade-level content-area teachers were provided collaborative planning time.

|  | 1 | 2 | 3 | 4 | 5 | 6 | 7 | 8 | 9 |
|---|---|---|---|---|---|---|---|---|---|
| LA | T | T | T | T | L | * | S | T | T |
| LA | T | T | T | S | T | L | * | T | T |
| LA | T | T | T | L | S | T | * | T | T |
| LA | T | T | T | * | L | S | T | T | T |
| Math | T | T | T | * | T | L | T | T | S |
| Math | * | T | T | T | L | T | T | S | T |
| Math | T | T | T | T | * | L | T | T | S |
| Science | * | T | T | S | T | T | T | L | T |
| Science | T | T | S | T | T | T | L | T | * |
| Social Studies | S | T | T | L | T | * | T | T | T |
| Social Studies | T | S | T | T | T | T | L | * | T |

T: Teaching period—most periods are roughly 40 minutes. Language arts classes are two 40-minute periods (80 minutes). Math classes are one and a half 40-minute periods (60 minutes).

CP: Collaborative planning (N/A)

S: Supervision

L: Lunch

*Empty periods were individual preparation times.

*Source: Robert Frost Junior High School.*

Figure 4.6: Seventh-grade core subject sample schedule based on a nine-period day.

Figure 4.7 demonstrates how we added both collaborative planning time and a tenth period. Notice how all seventh-grade teachers in each content area have a collaborative planning time.

| | 1 | 2 | 3 | 4 | 5 | 6 | 7 | 8 | 9 | 10 |
|---|---|---|---|---|---|---|---|---|---|---|
| LA | T | T | T | T | * | * | CP | T | T | A |
| LA | T | T | T | T | * | * | CP | T | T | A |
| LA | T | T | T | T | * | * | CP | T | T | A |
| LA | T | T | T | T | * | * | CP | T | T | A |
| Math | T | T | T | * | * | T | T | T | CP | A |
| Math | * | T | T | T | * | T | T | T | CP | A |
| Math | T | T | T | * | * | T | T | T | CP | A |
| Science | * | T | * | T | T | T | T | CP | T | A |
| Science | T | T | * | T | T | T | T | CP | * | A |
| Social Studies | * | CP | T | * | T | T | T | T | T | A |
| Social Studies | T | CP | T | * | T | T | T | * | T | A |

T: Teaching period—most periods are roughly 40 minutes. Language arts classes are two 40-minute periods (80 minutes). Math classes are one and a half 40-minute periods (60 minutes).

CP: Collaborative planning

A: Tenth-period acceleration

*Empty periods are lunch or individual planning time.

*Source: Robert Frost Junior High School.*

Figure 4.7: Seventh-grade core subject sample schedule based on nine-period day with tenth-period acceleration.

Collaborative time was now built into the school day. As Timothy D. Kanold (2012) points out, "Collaborative teams are required to orchestrate strong interventions and supports for each student in a course or grade level. In a professional learning community, you cannot allow teachers to provide response to intervention in isolation from one another" (p. 114). Our teams' collaboration not only supported instruction but also built a culture of helping all students succeed. This was the result of our department chairpersons and school leadership team coming together to prioritize collaborative planning over other important variables, like hallway supervision and interdisciplinary planning time. Our teachers found this time to be much more helpful and focused on improving student learning.

At the time we started this endeavor, we had no contractual language to substantiate a change like the one we knew we needed for our students. So we found solutions. Our administration and leadership team took the responsibility of researching the interventions we were lacking. We visited schools within our district and schools in other parts of the state to "borrow" elements of what was working for them. Our administrative team, including our assistant superintendent for human resources, met frequently with our building and district-level association leadership. We asked and answered each other's questions about past practice, the contract language as it relates to instructional and planning time, and the impact on various constituent groups—working toward a solution that met the needs of our students. Once we achieved a solution, we brought the details to our staff. This whole staff conversation was led by me and our school association leadership team. We answered the staff's questions honestly and found solutions to challenges, including collaborative planning time and students who needed support across multiple content areas. Together we did the work that our students needed.

We faced several additional challenges that we eventually overcame during implementation of our three doses of intervention and acceleration. Some staff were concerned that their course would lose instructional time, and we faced concerns from students who may have chosen an elective over an extra reading or math class. We were working with early adolescents, and many struggled in reading or math for quite some time. Given those academic struggles and the engaging nature of our elective courses, we needed to ensure that our extra math and reading courses were just as engaging and our justification for joining those classes was very purposeful.

Our solution was multifaceted. We met one-on-one with teachers who had questions and addressed their concerns. Teachers expressed concerns that losing two-to-three minutes per period to our tenth-period intervention and acceleration block would be detrimental to learning, so we worked as a staff to improve our transitions and to maximize instructional time. This was successful largely because of our efforts to train students to use time more effectively. We practiced transitioning efficiently, coming prepared, and getting started right away. Teachers used timers to keep track of time saved and lost during each period. The students were rewarded for saving time with tickets to use during the lunch hour for food items they enjoyed, and before we knew it, we had saved more than a couple of minutes during each period just by maximizing our instructional time.

To address other staff concerns, we continued to demonstrate our commitment to the arts, foreign language, and physical education. We recognized that our students needed a balanced curricular experience and typically made sure that every student maintained at least one elective, along with physical education, to preserve balance in the student's day. I often met one-on-one with students who qualified for this intervention course and showed them their academic progress in relation to their peers and where we needed them to be to exit the course. Because we did not want this course to feel like a punishment, we made sure that the teachers who taught it were highly engaging and adept at building relationships with our adolescent students. Parent concerns were few and far between. We regularly communicated with them on their child's progress and where they needed to be to get to college-track courses in high school and always met with parents who had concerns. I personally provided each parent with a letter about the course, the research, and data that supported its purpose, and met with parents. The teachers provided monthly progress reports, in addition to meeting with parents after report cards and during conferences. In my four years as principal, only four parents requested that their child drop this course. Over one hundred students a year successfully took the course, and our data indicated that over 90 percent saw gains in the range of two years for every one year in the program.

As we added doses of intervention, isolating variables to determine the sole effect of any intervention became more challenging. To monitor student, group, and school progress, we used the following method.

- Throughout our implementation process, we used nationally normed tests, state assessments, common formative assessments, and formal progress monitoring assessments. Formal progress monitoring like AIMSweb was usually used when students were receiving Tier 3 supports.

- At multiple points in the year, we analyzed these results to determine the following:

  - Are individuals in each level of intervention improving at an accelerated rate?

  - Is the collective group in each intervention progressing at an accelerated rate?

  - Is the school accelerating learning at every level—Tier 1, Tier 2, and Tier 3—and are students exceeding standards?

This process of analyzing our progress was undertaken not only by the school administrators but also by teachers. The school leadership team and department chairpersons were given these data during monthly meetings with the principal, where they were analyzed from a macro level. Equally important, those teaching these courses were provided with data about not only the performance of their students but also that of all other similar classes. After all, without comparative data, how does one really know if one's instructional practice is the most effective? We found over time, however, that after implementing each intervention, the answer to that question was yes. Our students and tiers of support were working. In fact, performance improved exponentially.

Student results skyrocketed throughout the course of our three doses of intervention and acceleration implementation. Student growth reached all-time highs and was near the 99th percentile nationwide. By 2011, every subgroup of students was performing above 90 percent proficient. Table 4.9 shows the progress of two of those groups.

**Table 4.9: Percentage of Students Meeting and Exceeding Illinois State Standards on State Test**

| Group | Content Area | Pre-Intervention / Extension 2007 | Post-Intervention / Extension 2011 |
|---|---|---|---|
| Special Education | Reading | 67 | 91 |
| Special Education | Math | 70 | 95 |
| Low Income | Reading | 79 | 92 |
| Low Income | Math | 79 | 96 |

Progress wasn't simply limited to subgroups. All students were making progress. In 2004, prior to professional learning communities and intervention implementation, just over 70 percent of students were proficient on state reading and math exams. By 2011, about 98 percent were proficient. This amounts to over 150 additional proficient students.

Our mission is "ensuring student success." While our work is never done, through a collective commitment to our students, we were much closer to achieving this goal than ever before. No one intervention or acceleration model alone was multifaceted enough to achieve what our students needed, so we added layers of support until it did. Did we fix everything or get every student where we wanted him or her to be? No. What we did do was put results before intentions, learning before teaching, and students before self. Three doses later, we made the time needed to ensure student success.

# References and Resources

Allington, R. L. (2009). *What really matters in response to intervention: Research-based designs.* Boston: Pearson.

Allington, R. L. (2012). *What really matters for struggling readers: Designing research-based programs* (3rd ed.). Boston: Pearson.

Buffum, A., Mattos, M., & Weber, C. (2009). *Pyramid response to intervention: RTI, professional learning communities, and how to respond when kids don't learn.* Bloomington, IN: Solution Tree Press.

Buffum, A., Mattos, M., & Weber, C. (2012). *Simplifying response to intervention: Four essential guiding principles.* Bloomington, IN: Solution Tree Press.

DuFour, R., DuFour, R., & Eaker, R. (2008). *Revisiting professional learning communities at work: New insights for improving schools.* Bloomington, IN: Solution Tree Press.

DuFour, R., DuFour, R., Eaker, R., & Many, T. (2006). *Learning by doing: A handbook for professional learning communities at work.* Bloomington, IN: Solution Tree Press.

DuFour, R., & Marzano, R. (2011). *Leaders of learning: How district, school, and classroom leaders improve student achievement.* Bloomington, IN: Solution Tree Press.

Fountas, I. C., & Pinnell, G. S. (2001). *Guiding readers and writers, grades 3–6: Teaching comprehension, genre, and content literacy.* Portsmouth, NH: Heinemann.

Kanold, T. D. (Ed.). (2012). *Common Core mathematics in a PLC at work, leader's guide.* Bloomington, IN: Solution Tree Press.

Myers, N. J. (2012). *Getting district results: A case study in implementing PLCs at work.* Bloomington, IN: Solution Tree Press.

Reeves, D. B. (2004). *Making standards work: How to implement standards-based assessments in the classroom, school, and district* (3d ed.). Englewood, CO: Advanced Learning Press.

**Bob Sonju** is the executive director of learning and development for Washington County School District and an adjunct professor of education at Dixie State University in Utah. He is the former principal of the nationally recognized Fossil Ridge Intermediate School and has served as a high school administrator and special education teacher.

With a passionate focus on student learning, specific interventions, and sustaining an effective school culture, Bob and the staff at Fossil Ridge developed a professional learning community that produces extraordinary results. Fossil Ridge was selected as a 2013 National Breakthrough School by the National Association of Secondary School Principals (NASSP), and its work as a school has been featured in *Principal Leadership* magazine and on www.allthingsplc.info. The Fossil Ridge staff regularly assist other school teams on their PLC journey by hosting frequent visits to this high-performing school.

Bob was named 2011 Principal of the Year for Middle-Level Schools by the Utah Association of Secondary School Principals and was one of three finalists for National Principal of the Year by the NASSP. His work has been published in *Principal Leadership* magazine and *Impact Journal*, a publication of the Utah Association of Secondary School Principals.

To book Bob Sonju for professional development, contact pd@solution-tree.com.

# A Promise to Learn at High Levels

Bob Sonju

This chapter is an excellent example of exactly how to implement a secondary supplemental intervention program. Fossil Ridge Intermediate School was able to create a master schedule that provided students flexible time and additional support every week. Here are a few critical elements of this school's model.

- The "REACH" intervention period supports every subject and course—not just English language arts (ELA) and mathematics. This is important for two reasons. First, a school should want students to succeed in every class, not just the subjects that are weighted most on state assessments. (This is especially important to successful implementation of the Common Core State Standards, as they require students to demonstrate higher-level thinking across disciplines.) Second, every teacher will feel the effects of shaving minutes off each class to create an intervention period. If this time is then used to support students only in core classes, this means the teachers in the nonpriority subjects have lost this time. But if every subject and all teachers benefit from this intervention time, then the time is not lost but simply banked and used for students who need help in their classes.

- REACH sessions are not merely glorified study halls. Students are identified "by student and by standard," so targeted reteaching takes place.

- REACH does not come at the expense of advanced students. Sessions are offered to support all classes, including students in honors and accelerated coursework.

Without question, REACH does not represent a cure-all for every student who needs help—undoubtedly, some students will need additional intensive support. But we have never seen a secondary school create a successful system of interventions without supplemental intervention time built into the master schedule. Fossil Ridge Intermediate School is an exceptional example of how this time can be used effectively.

---

Winston Churchill (n.d.) once wrote:

To every man there comes . . . that special moment when he is figuratively tapped on the shoulder and offered the chance to do something unique to him and fitted to his talent. What a tragedy if that moment finds him unprepared or unqualified for the work which would be his finest hour.

As Churchill himself knew, there are indelible moments that profoundly define who we are and what we truly believe. One of these moments happened for Fossil Ridge in the spring of 2007. A single mother working two jobs and trying to raise her son, Dylan, had requested a meeting with his teachers, his counselor, and our school's administration. From all outward indications, this was going to be like many of the meetings that take place in schools each day all around the country. But for some unforeseen reason, it turned out to be a meeting that served as the stimulus for profoundly changing our school.

Overcome by emotion, Dylan's mom sat in an office full of professional educators describing the challenges she was having with her son. He was not listening to her, not doing what he was supposed to, and falling woefully short of even a minimal level of proficiency in all his classes. Through tears, she pleaded with the educators in that room, "Please . . . please help my son." Keep in mind, our community's perception of Fossil Ridge Intermediate School was that ours, like many schools across our nation, was a good school. But this particular plea from a panicked mother brought a personal dimension to learning that had never been truly considered. Suddenly, Dylan was more than a statistic; he was more than a "nonproficient" student on the end of level assessments; he became more than a number. Dylan was failing, and so we were failing. We began to realize that we could no longer blame him (or any of the "Dylans" in our school) for choosing not to do the essential work that we had assigned and expected.

Research assured us what Dylan's most likely fate would be if he didn't learn the critical skills needed to be successful and prepared. Like Dylan's mom, we too felt helpless. We couldn't promise Dylan's mom that he would learn. We realized that in our current system and with our current thinking we could not promise high levels of learning for every student. After the meeting, I was immediately approached by one of Dylan's teachers. She frustratingly avowed, "We have to change. I never, ever want to feel that helpless again." At that moment, we knew deep down that we had to become better.

## A Critical Look

Far too often, school leaders attempt to improve student learning by immediately adding structural changes to their systems, yet fail to address the culture of a school. These structural changes often come in the form of policies, procedures, or the newest program. Our work began immediately with a focus not on implementing immediate structural change, but on the culture of our school.

> Culture is like the auto-pilot or mindset of a school. It is a combination of all the attitudes, beliefs, and values that guide the behavior of those in the school. If you attempt to implement reforms, but fail to engage the culture of a school, nothing will change. (National Association of Secondary School Principals [NASSP], 2009, p. 5)

Like many educational institutions, ours had its share of dedicated professionals who worked very hard each day. We also had a few people on our staff who simply didn't believe that all students could learn at high levels. Within departments, it was common to see teachers working extremely hard . . . individually, and subsequently producing results that varied wildly. As a result, we were not united in our beliefs or coordinated in our efforts and subsequently produced results that were less than extraordinary. If we were to move toward extraordinary, we needed to do more than just add structural changes, until we had developed a culture that was prepared, focused, and committed to ensuring that all students learned at high levels. And this needed to happen soon. Dylan and many others just like him depended on it.

The decision was made to begin the crucial conversations with our leadership team. We had to come to consensus on, and articulate answers to, some critical questions regarding the culture of our school before we could make the necessary structural changes that we desperately needed. Questions such as "What is our fundamental purpose?" and "Do our current behaviors and practices align with this purpose?" needed to be answered. This approach is reinforced by Richard DuFour, Rebecca DuFour, Robert Eaker, and Thomas Many (2010), who write in *Learning by Doing: A Handbook for Professional Learning Communities at Work (Second edition)* that "a principal benefits by working through the issues with a small group of key staff members . . . before engaging the entire faculty" (p. 21). With a population of nearly nine hundred sixth- and seventh-grade students (over half of whom were considered at risk), we had to create a culture that was committed to learning and a coordinated system of structures and processes that would ensure that every Fossil Ridge student learned.

Our cultural work began with the development of a clearly defined purpose, followed by a vision for our school and, finally, a series of collective commitments. Through the committed work of our faculty, we came to consensus on our fundamental purpose: to make sure that each of our students learned at high levels. Our next step was simple—to describe our vision of an exemplary school. Through this vision work, we were able to articulate the kind of instruction, assessment, intervention, leadership, and culture we would need in order to effectively accomplish our newly agreed-on purpose.

Our next step became very clear: to agree on the commitments we were willing to make that would align our beliefs, behaviors, and practices with this vision and purpose. These collective commitments would serve as a driving force behind our day-to-day work. One of our agreed-on collective commitments was to provide immediate, specific, and effective intervention for students who don't meet a given standard.

This had to become more than just words on paper. If we were going to ensure that every student learned the critical skills for each course and grade level, it became imperative that we take a critical look at our current system of interventions, to determine if our practices and systems aligned with this newly developed collective commitment. As we did, we were dismayed by what we discovered.

Our interventions were meager at best. One of the more popular ones was common in schools around our country: "Come in before or after school." In other words, we made assistance available only if a number of factors aligned perfectly: (1) the student was not one of the 80 percent who rode the bus to and from our school; (2) the student could convince a parent to bring him or her to school early or leave work and pick the student up late; and (3) the student had the courage to walk through the gauntlet of intimidating closed doors toward the academic halls, and then hope that the teacher was there and not making copies, answering email, and engaging in the myriad activities busy teachers do before school. If these events aligned perfectly, the student could then receive extra assistance. Needless to say, only the non–bus-riding, courageous, lucky students, who most commonly wanted to raise their score from a 97 percent to a 99 percent, were the students we saw before or after school. We were not seeing the students we most desperately needed to see.

We also evaluated our study halls—classes with fancy names such as Educational Enrichment, Math Enhancement, and so on. Essentially, these were classrooms of students who had been placed there for a variety of reasons, with a charge to the teacher assigned to the class to simply catch all of them up! We discovered that our intervention approach was almost completely ineffective and in no way aligned with our freshly agreed-on purpose.

Our inadvertent message was clear: If you were fortunate enough to grasp the concepts that were taught the first time, great. But if you didn't, our response was random and haphazard at best. Embarrassingly, we realized that we were unsystematically tossing interventions (such as study hall, slowing the curriculum down, and "come in before or after school") at students hoping one of them would work. More often than not, it didn't. It was a bitter pill to swallow.

Taking a critical look at ourselves and identifying and exposing our weaknesses and inadequacies is difficult work, but it is absolutely critical if we are to ensure high levels of learning for every student and improve as schools. We discovered that in no way did our current intervention practices align with our purpose, our vision, and the commitments we had made. It became evident that we needed to think differently about our school. We needed to function not as a collection of individuals, but as highly performing teams drawing on the expertise and skills of everybody in the building. These teams decided the critical concepts and skills they wanted the students to learn within each course and grade level. Once teams came to agreement on these, they developed common assessments to determine which students understood the critical concept or skill and which did not. Through this focused work, teams began identifying students who lacked proficiency in the concepts or skills that the team had determined were critical for every student to learn. Following this, the next step became clear: teams (and our school) had to create a systematic way to respond to those students who didn't demonstrate proficiency in those concepts and skills. As a result, the PLC process became more than just words and began to be deeply embedded in our daily practices and culture.

It's important to note that all teams did not move at the same pace. Some understood the process and moved very quickly, while a few, for a variety of reasons, took longer. The key is that the expectation was there, and that all teams were moving toward accomplishing our purpose.

## Thinking Differently: An Overview

It was becoming evident to us that although schools looked differently than they did many years ago, what happened in schools had not dramatically changed. We came to the realization that if we were going to make a significant, substantive change, we had to think differently about the beliefs, practices, and structures in our school.

> Having been provided with the knowledge and skills to effectively respond when students don't learn, only one question remains: Are you willing to do the hard work necessary to make these outcomes a reality? (Buffum, Mattos, & Weber 2009, p. 169)

As our work to develop a system of interventions that would provide both teachers and students extra time for learning began, we made the commitment that our decisions about intervention and learning should satisfy a number of criteria:

- Interventions had to occur immediately and would not be optional.

- Time had to be flexible, with learning as a constant.

- Students needed to be grouped according to the concept or skill they needed to learn and not simply because they were failing a class.

- The extra learning time that all students would receive would not be perceived as punitive.

- We needed a schoolwide systematic approach that included all members of our staff.

With these factors in mind, we immediately began our work. Utilizing the work in *Pyramid Response to Intervention: RTI, Professional Learning Communities, and How to Respond When Kids Don't Learn* (Buffum et al., 2009), we thoughtfully developed a pyramid of interventions that ensured immediate, specific, and directive support for every student in each of the academic areas. Instead of waiting until the reporting period to identify struggling students, our intervention team—consisting of the principal, the assistant principal, counselors, and the attendance secretary—met every two weeks and reviewed lists of students who had fallen below proficiency in core areas. These lists were generated through the simple process of running a "flag" list of those students who had fallen below a minimal level of proficiency in a core class (determined by the faculty to be 70 percent).

It is important to note that this was a general list of students who had fallen below proficiency and did not name the specific skills or needs of the student. This initial information was communicated to the student's teacher (most often through email) with a request for specific input regarding the student's performance, needs, and recommended intervention placement. This communication became important because our teachers were seeing anywhere from 120 to 240 students per day and a student could easily get lost in the sheer number of students that teachers were managing. Based on this information and feedback, the leadership team next identified the specific student and the cause of the lack of proficiency and immediately assigned a specific intervention. Was the process perfect? Absolutely not. But it was a critical first step to providing a focused, schoolwide effort to identify individual students who traditionally had fallen through the cracks.

Next to our students, time became our most valuable resource. The phrase *time is of the essence* took on a much deeper meaning for us. Through work and commitment, we were quickly becoming an educational institution that was completely and passionately focused on student learning—but we still had one barrier: we had to find a systematic way to divide students based on their specific need in a skill or a concept.

# The Process: Schoolwide Intervention by Concept

For far too long, we have looked at students as data points from end-of-level summative assessments. In order to be truly effective at intervening with students, we had to get very specific on the names of the students and the skill in which they were deficient. Our students had to be more than just data points. As a 2004 NASSP report put it, "Student 'anonymity' has been the most consistent criticism of America's school. It must end, whatever it takes" (p. xi).

Again, inspired by the work of Austin Buffum and colleagues (2009) in the landmark *Pyramid Response to Intervention*, we had a much clearer sense of what we needed to do. Specifically, interventions needed to be immediate, specific, and systematic—drilling down to the student and the skill. After much work, the current Fossil Ridge REACH (Reinforce, Extend, Achieve, Challenge, and Help for all) system became the school's answer to meeting the specific needs of all students.

Using the model of Pioneer Middle School in Tustin, California, we developed a Tier 2 intervention that would allow teachers and students critical extra time for learning. Early in the process, this intervention time occurred Tuesday through Thursday between second and third periods. As we continued to revisit and evolve, the intervention time moved to between fifth and sixth periods. Currently, as shown in figure 5.1, the Fossil Ridge REACH system occurs each day of the week.

| First Lunch | | Second Lunch | |
| --- | --- | --- | --- |
| Period | Time | Period | Time |
| Announcements | 7:45–7:48 (3) | Announcements | 7:45–7:48 (3) |
| First | 7:48–8:37 (49) | First | 7:48–8:37 (49) |
| Second | 8:40–9:29 (49) | Second | 8:40–9:29 (49) |
| Third | 9:32–10:21 (49) | Third | 9:32–10:21 (49) |
| First Lunch | 10:21–10:49 (28) | Fourth | 10:24–11:13 (49) |
| Fourth | 10:49–11:38 (49) | Second Lunch | 11:13–11:41 (28) |
| Fifth | 11:41–12:30 (49) | Fifth | 11:41–12:30 (49) |
| REACH | 12:34–1:08 (34) | REACH | 12:34–1:08 (34) |
| Sixth | 1:11–2:00 (49) | Sixth | 1:11–2:00 (49) |

*Source: Fossil Ridge Intermediate School.*

Figure 5.1: Schedule showing REACH system periods.

As we began, we saw that it was essential that teams identified the guaranteed skills that every student would need to know, that the teams developed and used a common pacing guide, and that they developed common formative assessments to effectively diagnose a student's progress and deficiencies in these guaranteed skills. Using the data from these common formative assessments, teams collaborate and identify which students need immediate assistance in a critical concept or skill.

Time for teams to collaborate became so critical that we had to be innovative in finding it. Common prep times were created, and substitute teachers were hired sporadically throughout the year; creative assembly supervision also created time for teams to focus on this work. During this collaborative time, teams also used the data to decide who was best suited to reteach the concept. These conversations were essential if we were going to use the very best practitioners to ensure that our students learned at high levels. During these collaboration meetings, teams also identified the specific skills or concepts (based on the results of the common formative assessments) that they would intervene with during that two-week period of time. These intervention offerings were sent to an administrative assistant in the main office and compiled into a master schoolwide intervention offering for the upcoming two weeks. These offerings changed every two weeks and aligned with a team's pacing guide. Students who did not demonstrate proficiency during REACH time were assigned to a more intense intervention.

Grouping the students according to concept or standard need became our next challenge. Student planners (handbooks that include a daily calendar of the school year) were identified as the most effective tool to make this happen. Our students are required to carry their planners with them at all times, and each teacher is given an ink stamp indicating, "Intervention required." The teacher places a stamp in the student's planner on the day the student is required to attend the concept intervention. Students are assigned to the teacher identified by the team as most effective in teaching that particular concept, based on the results of the common formative assessments and the professional discussions that take place with the team. All students with a stamp in any of the deficient concept areas are directed to this closed session that focuses on their specific concept need.

For example, after a two-week unit of instruction focusing on adding and subtracting integers, a math team would use a collectively developed assessment to determine proficiency. The team asks five questions ranging in complexity in each area (adding integers and subtracting integers) for a total of ten questions on the common assessment. The team has also made the collective decision that a student would need to score at least a four out of five in order to be proficient. Once the team has administered the common formative assessment, members come together in collaboration to review the assessment. Student names are quickly sorted as proficient and nonproficient in each of the assessed areas. A discussion then takes place about who is the best candidate to reteach adding integers and who is best to reteach subtracting integers (ideally, they are the teachers who demonstrated the best results on the assessment). The names are given to each of these teachers so they know whom to expect in the intervention class. The offerings for each REACH time are also posted on the school's website, and hard copies are placed around the school so students know what offerings will be available during that two-week period. At the conclusion of a closed intervention session, the teacher gives a short reassessment that focuses on the concept that was retaught. If proficient, a student's new score replaces the existing score in the gradebook. If the student does not demonstrate proficiency following two attempts, the student is referred to a more intense, targeted intervention. This is often a Tier 3 intervention that focuses specifically on the student's need. This process continues until the student demonstrates a sufficient level of proficiency in the concept or skill.

The learning momentum in our school was palpable, but we quickly discovered that with it came a new set of challenges. What were we going to do with the students who didn't receive a stamp? And what about students with multiple stamps on the same day?

Each team was expected to provide two closed sessions (based on concept or skill need) and one open session staffed by a member of the curricular team. Open sessions are also supervised by library staff, aides, and counselors—in some cases, any adult who is in the building—and often include free reading, supervised homework, extra assistance, musical practice, and so on. We decided that students who do not receive a stamp are allowed to choose where they will receive assistance in any of our open sessions—an educational offering that occurs during our schoolwide intervention time. In this way, all students receive valuable extra learning time each day. The only difference between a student who is stamped for concept intervention and one who is not is simple: choice. If the student has received a stamp, we direct that student where to go during the extra learning time. Some innovative curricular teams are even beginning to use peer tutoring during these sessions as a means for additional support. The actual process becomes simple: A bell sounds indicating that students need to prepare for REACH time by having their student planners in their hands. An announcement is then made giving last-minute reminders about the purpose of REACH time. Students are dismissed to move to their REACH time class. This Tier 2, schoolwide intervention includes every adult in the building. From secretaries to custodians, and from teacher aides to college interns, every adult takes part. Custodians and secretaries stand by exit doors (to make sure a student doesn't decide to go outside for intervention); teachers stand in the halls by their classroom doors and check student planners for stamps (ensuring they are in the correct area); and students hurriedly move to their assigned intervention class. It really is an amazingly coordinated sight to see. If an open session is at capacity (as determined by the teacher), the student is directed to another one. It takes approximately four minutes to move approximately 850 students to their sessions. Attendance is taken in each session by simply requiring each student to sign a roll that is delivered to the main office at the conclusion of the period.

It's important to note that each of the schoolwide intervention days looks very different depending on which students have been stamped for a particular concept. For example, a student might be stamped for a math intervention on Tuesday, receive no stamp on Wednesday, and have a stamp for a specific concept in language arts on Thursday. In the classroom, most teachers stamp the student planners while students work independently on an assignment such as their daily bell work. Furthermore, the intervention schedule changes every two weeks as new concepts and skills are introduced and assessed. To keep the offerings in order, each department chair submits to a designated main-office administrative assistant what the team's offerings are going to be for the upcoming two weeks. Figure 5.2 shows a partial example.

To guarantee that all of our students learn at high levels, we used the greatest capital we had in our school: flexible time and the collective skills and talents of every person in the building. At first, this was a messy process, as we worked through a variety of challenges. For example, in our initial attempt, we had intervention classes that were completely overloaded and students who were confused as to where to go. One student decided his intervention should take place outside of the school at the local convenience store! We learned a great deal early on in the process. Detailed training takes place at the beginning of the year regarding the REACH purpose and process. This has decreased the confusion for students. And teams now understand that their stamps can control the number of students in an intervention class. Student learning was increasing, but a challenge remained—what to do with students who had multiple stamps each day.

## Schoolwide Intervention Challenges

As Michael Fullan (2001) notes, "transformation would not be possible without accompanying messiness" (p. 31). For instance, we discovered that a number of our students were receiving multiple stamps each day, meaning that more than one teacher had requested the student for intervention. This new challenge was discussed at length in a faculty meeting, and it was proposed to designate one of the schoolwide intervention days as a priority for each of the core subject areas.

| Teacher | Room | Grade | Mon | Tues | Wed | Thurs | Fri |
|---------|------|-------|-----|------|-----|-------|-----|
| Felder | 600 | 6 | Open: Story elements | Open: Story elements | Open: Story elements | Open: Story elements | Open: Story elements |
| Heaton | 602 | 6 | Closed: Paragraph hooks | Closed: Paragraph hooks | Closed: Paragraph hooks | Closed: Paragraph hooks | Closed: Paragraph hooks |
| Jae | 604 | 6 | Closed: Conclusions | Closed: Conclusions | Closed: Conclusions | Closed: Conclusions | Closed: Conclusions |
| Thomas | 607 | 7 | Closed: HF assess | Closed: HF assess | Closed: HF assess | Closed: HF assess | Closed: HF assess |
| Lynn | 608 | 7 | Closed: Paragraph | Closed: Paragraph | Closed: Paragraph | Closed: Paragraph | Closed: Paragraph |
| Gillett | 609 | 7 | Open: LA assist | Open: LA assist | Open: LA assist | Open: LA assist | Open: LA assist |
| Morby | 610 | 6/7 | Open: Homework | Open: Homework | Open: Homework | Open: Homework | Open: Homework |

*Source: Fossil Ridge Intermediate School.*

Figure 5.2: Sample one-week intervention schedule.

Tuesday was the math priority, Wednesday was the language arts priority, and Thursday was dedicated to science. If a student had more than one stamp, he or she would go to a class based on the priority for that day. Teachers in these areas were guaranteed to see students needing intervention at least once per week. Currently, this schedule has now evolved to include priorities in all discipline areas.

- Monday: Social studies and career technical education
- Tuesday: Math
- Wednesday: Science
- Thursday: Language arts
- Friday: PE and fine arts

The belief that all students will learn is prevalent in the daily culture and structures of Fossil Ridge. Because the whole school is taking part, REACH is not viewed as punitive. There is nothing more inspiring than to see one of our students excitedly moving to an extra learning time opportunity and proudly stating, "I'm getting help with part of the scientific process that I didn't understand!"

## Barriers

Our journey hasn't been without barriers. There were those on the staff who immediately saw the vision and committed to the process, while some could be considered "fence sitters," reserving judgment or complete commitment until they could get a sense of how and if the process would work. And then there were those few who were openly resistant to the idea that all students could learn at high levels. As a school with a high number of socioeconomic and other demographic challenges, justifications for why our students couldn't learn were abundant: our students were too poor, they did not have enough support at home, they lacked the necessary prerequisite skills—the list went on and on. Creating additional learning time within the schedule also met with extreme opposition for a variety of reasons. It's important to note that during this process, we often referred back to our collective commitments as a touchstone. These commitments have helped to guide our work and focus on what we committed to do. And once all voices were heard and the will of the group became evident, we reached consensus and fervently pressed forward.

During a faculty meeting, one of our language arts teachers stated that she had been stamping students for intervention, but they had been going to math intervention, because the math teachers were strongly encouraging them. The math teachers sheepishly admitted that they had, in fact, been pressuring the students to attend their intervention, because some had missed critical math concepts. Frustrated, the language arts teacher heatedly explained that her team needed the students for intervention. There was a lively debate about which team would get the opportunity to intervene with our students. As I watched, it became clear to me: we were moving in the right direction!

The year following implementation of REACH, we discovered that we faced another barrier. A teacher who appeared to be extremely frustrated told me that her team had been stamping students for intervention, yet the students were not showing up. I questioned one of the students who had been stamped. As I reviewed this student's planner, it was evident that there was no stamp! Curious, I went back to the team and shared this. As we delved further into our latest challenge, we made an amazing discovery. A handful of students figured out that if they reported to one of our secretaries that they had lost their planner, they could purchase another. Utilizing two planners allowed these highly creative students to manipulate the system. I was reminded of a universal truth when working with students: they are smart! This challenge was quickly remedied by querying the list of extra handbooks that had been sold (and making our financial secretary aware of the latest maneuverings of a few of our students).

## Becoming Better

Exemplary businesses, organizations, and schools have an inherent desire to get better at what they do. They have a certain unrest with the status quo. It's this desire that propels organizations to change; to become better. As Atul Gawande (2007) writes, "Better is possible. It does not take genius. It takes diligence. It takes moral clarity. It takes ingenuity. And above all, it takes a willingness to try" (p. 246).

After five years of refining and modifying our schoolwide intervention system, teams have started to find that this extra learning time could be used in a variety of ways. Teams are designating students not only for concept intervention but also for extensions. Students who have already met proficiency in a concept are afforded extension opportunities during REACH time by curricular teams on the team's non-priority day. Extensions generally focus on the guaranteed skills or concepts but at a deeper, more complex level of learning. For example, while sixth-grade students are learning the identified critical elements of our solar system, students who have already demonstrated proficiency in the critical concepts are building a solar system, to scale, in the hallway outside of the science classrooms. The REACH open sessions continue to evolve and even include the opportunity to learn a new language.

The REACH intervention is certainly not perfect. Many adjustments have been made over the course of five years, but one thing has not changed: the commitment and work of the dedicated educators at Fossil Ridge Intermediate School. Changes in personnel and leadership have not diminished the effective culture of our school.

Even during the most challenging times, returning to our old, ineffective practices was never considered. As an educational professional, this is what I am most proud of.

## A Promise

Perceptions of our school have definitely changed. With a change in purpose and a clear focus on learning for all, we have moved from being a good school to being a *nationally recognized school*, one where learning is not optional. In spite of our high-risk population, Fossil Ridge students continue to produce significantly higher scores than state averages in all academic measures. As figure 5.3 shows, gains in achievement in all core areas have increased by an incredible 15–32 percent since 2008. Best of all, the lessons that were learned and the changes that are attributed to these gains are free, and they work!

## Reflecting: Lessons Learned

Through the process, we learned a number of powerful lessons, each of which has increased our effectiveness in meeting the individual and varied needs of our students. First, addressing the culture of our school was an initial, critical part of the process. Next, we had to come to consensus on our purpose and vision for an exemplary school and make collective commitments that would focus our efforts and drive our work. Once we articulated these things, we made a critical examination of our current practices and decided if they aligned with our commitments. Additionally, we learned that interventions must be immediate, directive, systematic, and most of all effective, getting down to the specific student and skill.

One of the most powerful lessons we learned was that persistence, creativity, and frequent communication with staff and teams are the antidotes for combating barriers. And the final lesson learned is simple: stay committed to doing what is best for *all* students. In the forum we call school, we often resort to what's easiest or causes the least amount of discomfort for the adults in the building. But if we are to change, we desperately need courageous, transformational educators who have the ability to create a vision, ignore the accompanying noise that comes with change, tackle the difficult issues, and change schools, learning, and most importantly student lives.

During the quiet months of the summer, I like to sit and reflect on the positive changes that have occurred at Fossil Ridge. During these times, I often drift back to that defining meeting with the distraught single mother who was the impetus for change. As difficult as that meeting was for those involved, it profoundly changed us. At Fossil Ridge, we can now make the promise that all of our students *will* learn at high levels.

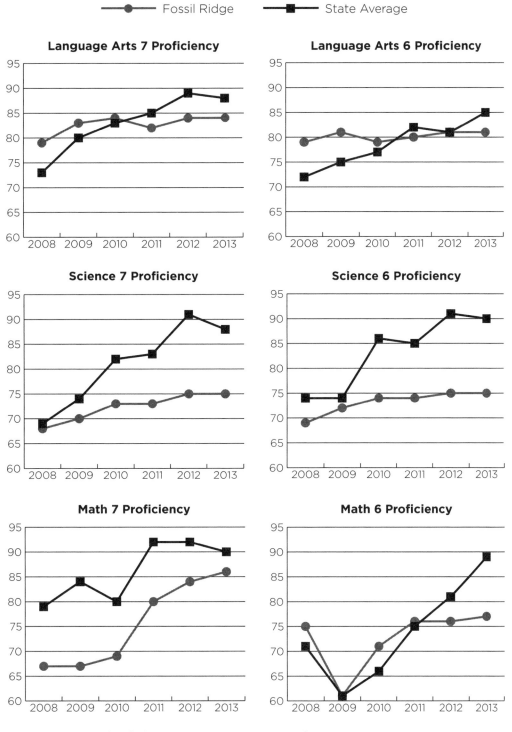

*Source: Utah State Office of Education (USOE) Cognos/Data Display.*

Figure 5.3: Fossil Ridge Intermediate School proficiency data.

# References

Buffum, A., Mattos, M., & Weber, C. (2009). *Pyramid response to intervention: RTI, professional learning communities, and how to respond when kids don't learn.* Bloomington, IN: Solution Tree Press.

Churchill, Winston (n.d.). *Quotations.* Accessed at https://sites.google.com/site /byuheroesofhistory/winstonchurchill on July 19, 2014.

DuFour, R., DuFour, R., Eaker, R., & Many, T. (2010). *Learning by doing: A handbook for professional learning communities at work* (2nd ed.). Bloomington, IN: Solution Tree Press.

Fullan, M. (2001). *Leading in a culture of change: Personal action guide and workbook.* San Francisco: Jossey-Bass.

Gawande, A. (2007). *Better: A surgeon's notes on performance.* New York: Metropolitan.

National Association of Secondary School Principals. (2004). *Breaking ranks II: Strategies for leading high school reform.* Reston, VA: Author.

National Association of Secondary School Principals. (2009). *Breaking ranks: A field guide for leading change.* Reston, VA: Author.

Pausch, R. (2008). *The last lecture.* New York: Hyperion.

 **Joe Doyle** has been working in education for two decades. He began teaching English to at-risk students. His later years in the classroom included teaching honors English and speech, and he was actively involved supporting students through coaching tennis and student philanthropy. After earning a master's degree from Butler University in school administration, he began working as an assistant principal at Bloomington High School South. In the fall of 2014, he stopped coaching the tennis team to have more time coaching his four children. During his time as an administrator, he has been involved with curriculum programming for students, which includes the development and implementation of what is known as Plus Time at Bloomington High School South.

To book Joe Doyle for professional development, contact pd@solution-tree.com.

# Creating Plus Time and the Culture to Use It

Joe Doyle

**Editors' Note**

Monitoring student attendance during a flexible block of intervention time can be challenging. Many secondary schools have solved this problem by assigning all students to a specific intervention session for three to four weeks. That way, the school can more effectively take student attendance. The weakness of this approach is that many students will learn a given session's targeted outcome before the end of the session. These students can't get help they might need in another course until the end of the session. For a supplemental intervention period, it is therefore best if teachers and students can change interventions weekly. Bloomington High School South solved this problem through the use of technology. By utilizing their school's student-management data system, staff revise offerings every week, account for every one of their almost two thousand students, and do not have to ask staff members to complete laborious paperwork to identify and track students who need additional help.

We also like South's tiered support for students who lack the motivation or study skills necessary to succeed. We are often asked, "What do we do with students who just won't try?" Academic behaviors such as motivation, volition, and organization are not genetic. Students struggling in these areas must be taught these skills, not just punished or failed for not already possessing them. South's PACE program offers tiered support to first ensure that students have learned these academic behaviors, then holds students accountable for applying them. By offering this help, South can offer interventions that address both skill and will.

Bloomington High School South is a vibrant school in the heart of Hoosier land—Bloomington, Indiana. Being just minutes away from the campus of Indiana University means that South enjoys the benefit of having many students who plan to attend postsecondary school. Our student population consists of nearly 1,800 students of many cultures and ethnicities, another result of being a college town. However, because many of the businesses that once called Bloomington home have left due to outsourcing and efforts to cut costs, a significant portion of families—over 20 percent are on free and reduced lunch—struggle to make ends meet.

With a focus on open enrollment, an Advanced Placement (AP) program, technical honors courses, a career center, and a variety of fine arts options, South tries to provide the best opportunities for every student. In these attempts, the school consistently garners recognition both locally and nationally through various scholarships, teacher recognitions, academic and athletic teams, and award-winning choirs, musicians, and artists.

## The Purpose and Process for Making Time

Our focus, like that of many schools, has been on continuous improvement, which is why we began the practices of a professional learning community (PLC). The PLC model offered a framework to keep our efforts focused on providing students the skills and opportunities to do what they hope to do after high school. What we had not yet done was create a means to provide academic supports in a timely, direct, and systematic way to every student in the school, in addition to the instruction that all students were receiving. Our school staff agreed that if we could add time to our school day, we could create a system to support students who were failing classes, and we could also provide extension opportunities to students who were performing well.

When we began the conversation about needing additional time to support students, the school day for our district was the state minimum 6.5 hours. Our school system was promoting a referendum to request additional tax dollars to add an hour to the school day. The school system led a very rigorous campaign through forums, mailings, and literally going door to door. The grassroots effort worked, and the community approved our referendum, which was one of only a few in the state to be approved.

Once the referendum was passed, each school in our district began discussing the specifics of how the time would be used. The common expectation shared by the school board, teachers, and parents was that it must be used for instruction. Another aspect of the additional time agreement was that Wednesday mornings would start an hour late for students in order to provide uninterrupted time for teams of teachers to collaborate on curriculum mapping, create assessments, and compare the data from formative assessments. Figure 6.1 shows the new schedule.

|  | **M, Tu, Th, F** | **Wednesday** |
| --- | --- | --- |
| Period 1 | 7:40–8:50 | 8:30–9:40 |
| Pass | 8:50–8:55 | 9:40–9:45 |
| Period 2 | 8:55–10:00 | 9:45–10:50 |
| Pass | 10:00–10:05 | 10:50–10:55 |
| SRT (Monday) Flex Time (T TH F) | 10:05–10:50 | |
| Pass | 10:50–10:55 | |
| Period 3 | 10:55–12:35 | 11:03–12:35 |
| Pass | 12:35–12:40 | 12:35–12:40 |
| Period 4 | 12:40–1:45 | 12:40–1:45 |
| Pass | 1:45–1:50 | 1:45–1:50 |
| Period 5 | 1:50–2:55 | 1:50–2:55 |

*Source: Bloomington High School South.*

Figure 6.1: Daily schedule for Bloomington High School South.

Discussions about implementing our new time began within our administrative council. This group is a collection of department chairpersons from each of our nine departments, our technology coordinator, and our administrators. This group meets twice a month to share information about school topics. We first assessed one existing program for students: our student advisory period, or Student Resource Time (SRT). Because SRT met once a week for fifty minutes, we cloned that time schedule and used it for enrichment and remediation on three days of the week. We believed, after looking at what other schools were implementing, that devoting the entire fifty minutes to our additional time was warranted because students would need it to be able to complete assessments that they were taking in class. Looking at other secondary schools that successfully accomplished targeted reteaching and extension opportunities confirmed our belief that a period of less than fifty minutes would limit what we could do.

Our staff agreed that the main objective we should accomplish with our new time was to reduce failures. One reason the program was supported by teachers so readily is that we also agreed reducing failures meant we must collaborate with more focus than we ever had before. Since the alternative was for each teacher to create, manage, and sustain an individual program to reduce the number of individual struggling students, the choice was easy.

## Creating Plus Time

Knowing that culture devours structure faster than a thirty-second time-out (sorry, this is Indiana, a basketball reference was needed!), our department chairs agreed that as a first step to giving the new time some identity in the community, it was important to name it. Panther Plus Time was suggested by a department chair, and it seemed to work. The name was shared with the entire staff, it was agreed to by the school, and so the process began.

We split our planning process into two parts.

1. Determining what we wanted to accomplish with the time

2. Determining how the program would work

We agreed as a school that the following three goals would drive our planning for this additional time.

1. Increase opportunities to provide timely, systematic, and direct support to all students.

2. Increase opportunities to provide students unique academic experiences during the school day.

3. Increase students' awareness of how they are performing in a particular course.

Our process for determining what we would offer during Plus Time was similar to the process we use to discuss any significant issue. Our administrative council begins by sharing information and having discussions with our department chairs. Our department chairs take information back and forth between their department members and the council. Our entire faculty meets monthly to discuss and review topics—and this topic was all we discussed for three months. We shared information with the entire faculty and then discussed it when we came together as a group. Through the process of meeting in administrative council and then vetting our work in faculty meetings, we came up with the "what" of Plus Time, as follows:

- Create terminology that would enable students to easily understand the program (see page xx). For example, every event that we offered was referred to as a lab.

- Document the labs students attended during each session.

- Ensure that all students and teachers were engaged in a lab.

- Provide a continuum of support for students ranging from remediation in basic skills to AP courses.

- Agree that enrichment would be offered to students who were demonstrating mastery.

- Allow students to choose their labs if they were meeting specific criteria and not requested by teachers (this proved to be a huge benefit for us during implementation).

- Agree that only academic supports would take place during this time.

- Guarantee that every department would receive a priority day on which its requests to see students would trump those of other departments.

- Agree that teachers would not spend time with intentional nonlearners.

With regard to nonlearners, our prior work had led us to realize that despite our best efforts, some students would refuse to engage. If a student was failing a course, had two missing assignments, and had not completed the missing work within one week, he or she was deemed as not giving his or her full effort and was provided supports through our counselors and principals. We agreed as a faculty that if teachers were going to reteach assignments and focus on students who were struggling, then students needed to give us their full effort. The focus for nonlearners was learning skills like note-taking, basic organization, and a system for organizing their work. This group of students was also given encouragement from their counselors about their ability to complete the work. Many of these students were resigned to believing that even with effort they couldn't complete their work, so convincing them otherwise was both important and difficult.

The specifics of how the program would work was left to a much smaller group, because it involved the technical aspects of creating a web-based program that would track what teachers and students were doing. Every idea that we agreed to when creating what we wanted the program to do would influence how the program would be constructed. Concepts for this section included:

- A visual layout that would allow teachers to register students needing assistance quickly

- A menu that would be very intuitive for students and teachers with limited options

- The mechanism that would provide teachers the ability to have a priority day without allowing other departments to trump their choices

- Reporting ability that would show all stakeholders where students had attended

- The ability to take attendance

These basic components led to a skeleton sketch of the program, which we shared with the entire teaching staff about a month into our discussions. With constant discussion and a framework of what we wanted the program to do, the evolution of our intervention program slowly took shape. By midsummer, we had tested the web-based program and began sharing the common language with parents. We also created videos showing how students would use the program. To view the student video on tutoring, search YouTube for Panther Plus Fall 2013 (or go to www.youtube.com/watch?v=Z7oQs_ogH5c). Visit **go.solution-tree.com/rtiatwork** to find reproducible versions of some of the support materials we send out to parents and teachers explaining Plus Time, such as the parent letter and the information sheet given to staff to help focus our purpose and create a common language; with some minor modifications, this information sheet was sent to all parents as well. (Visit **go.solution-tree.com/rtiatwork** to download these and other resources.)

## The Research

We had seen through our work over the previous ten years that if students were significantly credit deficient at the end of their sophomore year (which to us meant that a student had earned fifteen credits of a possible thirty), then they were at great risk to not complete high school. Our school was operating on a trimester system, which means that students have three twelve-week terms. During each term, students take five courses, and over the course of a year can earn fifteen credits, so the students we were targeting were basically failing five classes a year. We tried to be proactive, by providing mandatory after-school tutoring for all freshmen and sophomores as soon as they had missing work and a failing grade in a course. We had already created additional time for our target audience by adding an additional term of instruction to some of our freshman and sophomore courses. While this did reduce our number of failures, it was basically an adjustment in the way we had provided instruction to all students, and it did not address how to provide instruction for students who were struggling.

We believed, as a faculty, that in order to meet our goal of reducing failures, we would have to work in teams to collaborate around student learning. We had been to PLC workshops and specifically spent some time studying *Pyramid Response to Intervention: Paths to Degree Completion From High School Through College* (Buffum, Mattos, & Weber, 2009). The concept of response to intervention (RTI) is well documented, and we were convinced that we could improve learning for students if we dedicated our new time to providing additional instruction to students who needed it based on their performance on common assessments. We also had to come to some agreements about what wasn't working in regard to motivating students. Specifically, we knew that failure was not a motivator for our most struggling students. For students who had struggled in school for years, our task was to motivate them to see that they could actually learn, not assume that they would fear failing— they didn't, and we had the failure rates in core classes (nearly 20 percent at times) to prove it. A major influence on our efforts was Marina Krakovsky's "Effort Effect" in the *Stanford Review*, which provided a very tangible summary of Carol Dweck's growth mindset idea, which is that students with a fixed mindset believe that their intelligence is fixed and don't learn from their mistakes. Students with a growth mindset get excited about challenges and look at failure as an opportunity to learn. The important point is that "Dweck has shown that people can learn to adopt the latter belief and make drastic strides in performance" (Krakovsky, 2007).

Paul Tough's (2012) *How Children Succeed: Grit, Curiosity, and the Hidden Power of Character* provides great evidence that motivation may be more important than cognitive ability. Motivation, and more specifically providing for autonomy, mastery, and purpose, is a concept we discussed after hearing Daniel Pink (2009) share his research on motivation. Our efforts also coincide with the number-one learning strategy that John Hattie (2009) documents in *Visible Learning: A Synthesis of Over 800 Meta-Analyses Relating to Achievement*, student self-reporting. Simply put, as teachers, we need to ensure that students are making accurate judgments about their ability levels, because students often only perform to whatever expectations they already have of their own ability. We see on a daily basis that requiring students to be responsible for knowing how they are doing and letting them make their own choices for what labs they attend during Plus Time, along with taking those choices away when they are not performing, is far more motivating than a failing grade.

Because our teachers had seen that directing students to supports in a timely manner was helping them reach their goals in our classrooms, prior to implementing this additional time, we implemented several practices that helped our program gain traction. Here are some of the key elements that we implemented.

- Grading had been a discussion point, and common grading practices were being used by teachers teaching the same courses. For example, the English department used common rubrics for grading essays. We looked at "The Case Against Zero" by Douglas Reeves (2004) as a starting point for our discussions about the importance of intentional, consistent grading practices. Cohorts of staff members also had training in Robert Marzano's work on scales.

- In the spring of 2008, extensive committee work in our "What Do We Do When Students Don't Learn" group (which we deemed WD40) came up with some important distinctions among students who struggle that were well known to the staff. One of these distinctions involved different types of support for students who can't, don't, or won't do the work. By the time these students get to high school, struggling is more of a way of life than a surprise to them. We have found that this group's needs are far different than those of students who have not grown accustomed to failing. We adopted Mike Mattos' term *intentional nonlearner* as a way to categorize this very complex set of students. While we never use this term when talking to students themselves, its use does evoke urgency when we try to plan supports for them.

- One of the key components of WD40, which was merged into our eventual Plus Time program, was a mandatory after-school tutoring program for students with missing work. We named the program PACE (Panther Achieving Credit and Enrichment), as it encouraged students to pick up the pace when they were struggling. While the acronym has faded, the practices of the program are essential to our school culture.

See figure 6.2 for a thorough collection of our pyramid of interventions by tier.

## Obstacles

One major obstacle that we met was that the approval for the additional time was granted in the spring of 2010, and the school year ended before all of the details could be shared with our students, parents, and even teachers. In an ideal situation, we would have been able to share these details the year prior to the program. In addition, the technology component was not finished, so teachers did not have the summer to experiment with the logistics of the program. They had to take a leap of faith that everything would be ready when they returned from summer. This created some anxiety for us, but we had so much enthusiasm about implementing Plus Time with our staff that the thought of 1,800 students attending a flexible schedule of labs three times a week did not send us into paralysis. In fact, the anxiety created a practice that we found very valuable: when school started in the fall, we took the first three weeks to review the program in a variety of ways.

We showed all of our students the video again, we had a principal review it in grade-level meetings, and a counselor and principal demonstrated how to use the program in a live demonstration at convocations for each grade level. After students

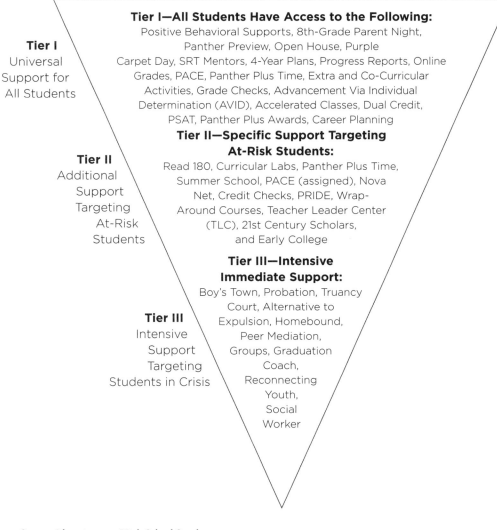

*Source: Bloomiongton High School South.*

Figure 6.2: Bloomington South pyramid of interventions.

had heard about the program three additional times, we asked all SRT teachers to review it with their students again in a small-group setting before we sent anyone to a lab. SRT teachers also helped students register the first week. These deliberate measures were done because we felt that, although we had been very diligent in our planning, Plus Time needed to work the first time. We felt that every student needed to know how to register and where he or she was going, and we did not want any students in the hall when the first bell rang. Spoiler alert . . . it worked!

# Determining Weekly Offerings

Because this work is grounded in PLC practices, our weekly teacher collaboration time is an essential component of Plus Time. When teachers meet, they use data to determine which students need to attend which labs, and they agree which labs each teacher will run for the week. It is critical that team members view every student in their course (for example, ninth-grade English) as someone they are collectively responsible for supporting during Plus Time. Teachers also determine how many students set a maximum number of students for each lab. In general, areas that have higher levels of direct instruction needed to meet mastery have smaller numbers of students attending.

Four basic types of labs are offered for most core courses.

1.  Students who failed a lesson on a common formative assessment are directed to a reteaching lab for that lesson.

2.  Students needing to master essential skills are sent to a retest lab until their unit assessment result is sufficient. Teachers are now promoting every unit test as an opportunity for reteaching, correcting mistakes, and student learning!

3.  Students needing general assistance with coursework can select or be sent to a homework help lab.

4.  Students who are not missing work and not failing can attend enrichment.

Aside from these basic labs offered by each department, there is also the PACE program, which began as an after-school homework completion idea. When we expanded the day, it was a natural fit for Plus Time. The goal of PACE is to have students become responsible for their own learning, and to accomplish this goal, we use counselors and administrators rather than the classroom teacher. This part of Plus Time is for students who are not engaging in our efforts to support them. We have the group split into three tiers, with each one having a different goal.

- PACE I is for students missing work and failing one course. Since it can be complicated to determine if a student like this is a failed learner (meaning he or she is trying and not grasping the concepts) or intentionally not participating, we allow teachers to pull students out of this lab into the class they are failing. Teachers determine the maximum number of students for each lab by department. For an intentional nonlearner, instruction often isn't the issue; therefore, we are trying to motivate these students to put forth effort on material they have the skills to master. The goal for this group is to be out of PACE within one week. The loss of choosing where to go is a motivator for most of these students.

This tier is supervised by one administrator whose focus is to remind students to complete missing work. Many of these students would gladly take a zero on assignments with the hope of doing make-up work or earning extra credit before the term ends. By setting a standard that work will be done on time, we help develop time-management skills. Many, but not all, students would rather turn the work in on time than attend PACE I.

- PACE II is assigned when students do not complete their work in PACE I. It is a three-week assignment. Our focus is helping students understand why they are not turning in work and what they can do to pass classes. We review organization strategies and help them plan how to complete their work. The focus is not on tutoring students needing content help; rather, it is to help them with the intangible skills of how to study and stay organized. This tier is supervised by our counseling department and our technology coordinator.

- PACE III is assigned if students still do not participate in their learning. Basically, this section is for students who refuse to work. It is an indefinite placement. This tier is monitored by one of our special education teachers who has extensive training in behavior management.

## The Identification Process

Determining which students will be required to attend a particular lab occurs every Wednesday during team-collaboration time, when course-alike teachers meet on a delayed student start for an hour. During this time, teacher teams determine which students need which supports for the following week. This results in three scenarios for determining where students go.

1. Students missing no assignments and passing all their courses with Cs or greater have the ability to select what lab they attend if no teacher selected them for a lab.

2. Teachers select by student and by skill what they will provide during labs. The nature of the intervention needs to be very specific, because if labs are set up for broad topics like freshmen English or algebra, then the tendency will be for teachers to just see their own students and help them complete work. We want students to receive direct instruction in homogenous groups based on their need for support in a specific skill.

3. Students who are deemed intentional nonlearners are assigned to labs run by people other than classroom teachers in PACE.

Plus Time is three days a week, but once a week each department has a priority day. So if a student is struggling with an English skill, the teacher will register the student at least one day the following week for English, during the English priority day, with the option of scheduling up to three days.

Once each team determines student placement, each teacher is responsible for logging these student assignments into our web-based Plus Time program. The screen allows teachers to see every student on their roster organized by class period, and they click the Assign tab to send students to the activity they need to attend for their department. They are assigning only students who meet the criteria their teacher team determined to see that week. We later added the ability for every teacher to assign students to any activity, not just their department's labs, so that SRT teachers, teachers of record in special education, and guidance counselors could also assign students to labs when needed. This is done through Assign +. Figure 6.3 shows an example of the teacher screen.

## Bloomington South || Panther Plus Time

**Teacher Menu:** | Assign | Assign + | Switch | Locate | Notify | Attendance | Slip | Rosters | Change Password | Logut |

12-2 Help Lab (Open) - TOSTI, KYLA - Thursday ▾

Select Activity

Fetching students from p1

Fetching students from p2

Fetching students from p3

You do not have any students during p4

Fetching students from p5

† — Teacher Assigned

| | Thu Oct 24 13 | |
|---|---|---|
| **Student** | **Current Assignment** | **Assign** |
| ADORNO-CANCEL, JOSE | ECA † | ☐ |
| AI, HUAN | Not Assigned | ☐ |
| BALABAN, HOPE | Girls PE 1 (Synchron † | ☐ |
| BRAUN, ALEXANDER | Reading lab † | ☐ |
| BREWSTER, BARBARA, J | Not Assigned | ☐ |
| CHAN, CHUN | Nomenclature practic † | -- |
| CORNWELL, ETHAN | Weights and Conditio † | ☐ |
| EADS, JARED | Not Assigned | ☐ |
| JACOBS, JOSHUA | ECA † | ☐ |
| JESSMER, DUSTIN, L | Not Assigned | ☐ |
| MASSENGALE, KYLE | Not Assigned | ☐ |
| MITCHELL, CHASE | PACE II † | -- |

*Source: Bloomington High School South.*

Figure 6.3: Teacher screen for Plus Time program assignments.

This teacher has selected an activity for Thursday, October 24, and can see which of her students are already assigned and which ones haven't been assigned yet. The deadline is midnight Sunday for labs happening in the upcoming week. A symbol shows teachers which labs were assigned by teachers. Note that in the Assign column, two of the students do not have a box next to their names. This is because Thursday is a priority day for science, and the students have already been selected by a science teacher. The second student is in PACE II, which is our second tier for failed learners, and we do not allow students to be pulled out of that lab.

Students who are current on all their work and have not been selected by a teacher for a targeted lab can select an activity they want to attend each day by logging into the Plus Time database through a web-based student portal. Students click on the day they are trying to schedule, and every lab offering for that day is listed. Some labs are open, which allows students to register themselves, and others are closed, which means only teachers can assign students to them. Labs are deemed closed for two reasons: (1) if direct instruction is needed because students failed a skill, closing the lab allows the teachers to have complete control of the class population; and (2) occasionally, so only students taking that course can attend. We offer several art labs, for example, that allow students from previous terms to work on their portfolios, and "closing" the lab signals to them that they can't attend that particular day.

The layout for the student labs shown in figure 6.4 also shows a feature unique to the student page—the announcement section highlighted in gray. Announcements for presentations are placed in this section as a way to notify students about upcoming enrichment activities.

### Bloomington South || Panther Plus Time

**Sign Up**

| Date | Current Assignment | Select |
| --- | --- | --- |
| Thu, May 2 13 | IU Brass Quintet Concert - P230 | Assigned |
| Fri, May 3 13 | Independent Silent Reading - AUD | ▾ |
| Tue, May 7 13 | We the People Help - A111 | Assigned |
| Thu, May 9 13 | Independent Silent Reading - AUD | ▾ |
| Fri, May 10 13 | Independent Silent Reading - AUD | ▾ |

submit

LOGOUT

- The **deadline** for signing up for Panther Plus Time for next week is Sunday night.
- If you sign up for next week before the deadline you will be **allowed to make** changes up until the night before Panther Plus Time.
- **If you do not sign up** for next week and are assigned to the Auditorium you will not be able to make adjustments next week.

Announcements
- **Student Council Election**
  - Ballot is online. Click here to vote.
- **PHYSICAL EDUCATION**
  - If you are signed up for a Physical Education lab, **please bring clothes** (t-shirt, shorts, tennis shoes) to change out into, a towel, and a lock. If it is a swim lab, please bring a swimsuit, towel, and a lock to class.
- **Computer lab** available during Panther Plus Time:
  - General Purpose Computer Lab for completing assignments/projcets with Mr. Cartwright in Lab A129.

Figure 6.4: Student portal of Plus Time database.

If teachers do not assign a student to a lab and the student doesn't select one, the student attends Silent Reading Lab in the auditorium, supervised by an athletic director, study hall aide, or principal. Generally, we have about 150 students of our 1,800 in this room. It is incredibly quiet, and students are productive during their visits to the Silent Reading Lab.

## The Monitoring Process

The response a student receives depends on what lab that student is attending and whether he or she demonstrated knowledge of the desired skill. If a student was in a lab for students deemed intentional nonlearners but eventually completed his or her homework and brought up his grade, then we would consider that intervention as having worked. When teachers are working with students in content-specific labs, the intervention is deemed to have worked when the students demonstrate mastery. Generally, students should have to attend only a specific-content lab once during the week for assistance on the deficient skill, which is assessed by a specific task—completing a homework assignment, retaking a quiz, writing a paper, or completing an end-of-unit assessment.

As we assess the entire program, we seek student and teacher feedback and also look at more broad-based data, like attrition into AP and dual-credit classes, failure rates, diploma types, attendance, graduation rates, and so on. If students are demonstrating mastery on essential skills, all of these points should improve . . . and they have. In our third year of the program, we were at record levels for AP and dual-credit participation, graduation rates, and scores on state-mandated graduation exams.

## The Revision Process

If students don't respond to a support, they progress to the next higher level of support or attend the same level but receive new strategies. For example, a student would be placed in a closed lab for English 9 if he or she didn't improve after the first week of being in an open lab. A continuum of supports is provided to students based on how they are performing. We also have the resources (that is, teachers) aligned in such a way as to place students who need the most help in smaller classes.

## The Extension Process

Students who are demonstrating mastery are given the most choice in this system. They can choose to review or practice work in a homework-help lab. However, they can also choose to attend any other open section. We generally have several options during Plus Time for students to revisit courses they have taken before. For example, students could attend an art class if they have taken the course before. We have several students who maintain their connection with art through Plus Time if they cannot work an art class into their current trimester. In addition, there are frequently presentations at which students can extend learning or be exposed to entirely new topics. These include everything from guest speakers on specific topics to a guidance department presentation on financial aid for college. We also run labs for academic electives so that students who are demonstrating success in class can participate in yearbook, newspaper, creative writing, and similar activities. AP teachers run study groups and discussion labs as well. We've found that giving students extra time has encouraged collaboration and the formation of study groups like those they will experience in college.

## Tune-Ups and Adjustments

We began this adventure very deliberately and with great expectations. Because we were lucky enough to talk to RTI expert Mike Mattos prior to fully choosing what our program would look like, we felt that we were ready for what would happen next. While we knew what we wanted the computer aspect of Plus Time to do, there was no tangible model for our web program since it didn't exist anywhere else. With a great deal of trial and error, communication with our teachers, and a desire to get feedback from students during the early stages, we were able to create a program that has changed the culture of our school.

Because of the collective passion of our teachers to implement this idea, we are happy to report that there were no problems delaying the start of the program. We have, however, made several adaptations along the way to the registration process. For example, we implemented an easier process to allow changes of student labs. The original idea was that all the scheduling would be entered prior to the Monday of the upcoming week. Per the plan, we believed managing a week at a time was all the students and teachers could handle. However, students started missing work and make-up tests much faster than expected, so the request was made to allow for teachers to assign students to change labs for situations like that. It basically made the program more real time and even more fluid. We were initially concerned that allowing changes would create unnecessary extra work for the teachers, but it has proved to be beneficial.

We also now allow students to select out of the default reading lab if they did not select a lab prior to the cutoff date. This allows for a student to get real-time, proactive support; although this wasn't an initial intent of the program, we have been able to support it. If a student was assigned silent reading (which means they had no missing work, grades of C or better, and no teachers requesting to see them) and had a homework assignment or project during the week that had just been assigned, that student has the option to go see a teacher and get help before the work is actually turned in for the first time. It allows for a more fluid response from students about their own needs.

The core of the program and the intent are still very much the same as when we started. Our challenges at year three were fairly minimal, and the main theme has remained making sure that we are doing everything we can to engage our struggling students.

## Results

Perhaps the most useful result that we can share is that our teachers report they cannot imagine teaching without Plus Time. It has become an essential component of our PLC work, and because our results are so transparent, it has improved our work on assessment and mapping. A brief video speaking to this is available (Kennedy, 2012) on YouTube (www.youtube.com/watch?v=j_rEmG39ca8).

More specifically, we have seen the number of failed learners nearly disappear. Looking at a course like ninth-grade English, for example, we note the following.

- First and foremost, the actual number of students failing is very small—20 out of 430 freshmen might be failing as opposed to more than 60 students in the past.

- Every student who is failing has been given support throughout the trimester, and we can document what we have tried.

- We may ask students to look at the interventions we have tried and seek their input as to why they are not learning.

- We may ask teachers to look at their mapping and assessment and guarantee that every option to support a struggling student was used.

- There are no surprises. When students start struggling, calls are made to parents, and counselors and principals can see which students they are. More conversations are happening schoolwide to support all students.

While we aren't getting all of our assignments returned, the amount of missing work has diminished immensely.

We had hoped that this program and the idea of trying to target students immediately when they struggle would translate into improved metrics over time. For the graduating class of 2012, our common comparable statistics look promising compared to what they were just a few years ago.

- The graduation rate has risen three years in a row and is up to 95 percent compared to 80 percent in 2007. The state average is 88 percent.

- The percentage of graduates taking the SAT is up to 80 percent from 65 percent in 2006.

- Average SAT scores have remained in the 1080 range even with that increase.

- More than half of the graduating class took an AP exam, up from just 17 percent in 2006.

- The percentage of students earning a score of 3 or better has doubled since 2006.

After starting our third year of Panther Plus Time, perhaps the strongest data we have consist of the repeated sentiment among teachers that "we can't imagine teaching any other way." Teachers are seeing more engagement from students, reflected in more work being turned in, and a greater number of students are performing better. In addition, this process has given even more energy to our teachers' already impressive collective efforts in answering and revisiting the four guiding questions of a PLC. Our mapping, assessments, enrichment, and extension practices have improved over the course of the first three years of the program. More than ever, our culture reflects our belief that it is our obligation to ensure that all students are learning, and we are doing everything that we can to support them. The investment our teachers have made to guarantee that the time added to the school day was used to improve student learning is impressive; student buy-in has been equally impressive. It has been a rewarding experience to witness the creation of Plus Time and the culture it has nourished.

# References and Resources

Buffum, A., Mattos, M., & Weber, C. (2009). *Pyramid response to intervention: RTI, professional learning communities, and how to respond when kids don't learn.* Bloomington, IN: Solution Tree Press.

DuFour, R., DuFour, R., Eaker, R., & Karnhanek, G. (2004). *Whatever it takes: How professional learning communities respond when kids don't learn.* Bloomington, IN: Solution Tree Press.

DuFour, R., DuFour, R., Eaker, R., & Many, T. (2006). *Learning by doing: A handbook for professional learning communities at work.* Bloomington, IN: Solution Tree Press.

*Growth mindset diagram.* (n.d.). Accessed at http://alumni.stanford.edu/content/magazine/artfiles/dweck_2007_2.pdf on March 5, 2014.

Hattie, J. A. C. (2009). *Visible learning: A synthesis of over 800 meta-analyses relating to achievement.* New York: Routledge.

Kennedy, D. (2012, February 1). *Panther plus BHSS* [Video file]. Accessed at www.youtube.com/watch?v=j_rEmG39ca8 on March 10, 2014.

Krakovsky, M. (2007). *The effort effect.* Accessed at http://alumni.stanford.edu/get/page/magazine/article/?article_id=32124 on March 5, 2014.

Pink, D. H. (2009). *Drive: The surprising truth about what motivates us.* New York: Riverhead Books.

Reeves, D. B. (2004). The case against zero. *Phil Delta Kappan, 86*(4), 324–325. Accessed at www.leadandlearn.com/sites/default/files/articles/caseagainstzero.pdf on March 5, 2014.

Scherer, M. (2001). *How and why standards can improve student achievement: A conversation with Robert Marzano.* Accessed at www.ascd.org/publications/educational-leadership/sept01/vol59/num01/How-and-Why-Standards-Can-Improve-Student-Achievement@-A-Conversation-with-Robert-J.-Marzano.aspx.

Tough, P. (2012). *How children succeed: Grit, curiosity, and the hidden power of character.* Boston: Houghton Mifflin Harcourt.

 **Steve Pearce** was the principal at Jane Addams Junior High School in Schaumburg, Illinois, from 2008 to 2013. During this time, Jane Addams went from being the lowest performing of the five junior high schools in Schaumburg District 54 to one of the highest performing as measured by state assessment and Northwest Evaluation Association's Measures of Academic Progress. Steve is currently the assistant superintendent of human resources for Batavia Public School District 101 in Batavia, Illinois.

You can follow Steve on Twitter @StevePearce4.

To book Steve Pearce for professional development, contact pd@solution-tree.com.

# The FLEX Schedule

Steve Pearce

**Editors' Note** Every secondary school already has multiple school schedules, such as a regular daily schedule, a minimum-day schedule, an assembly schedule, and a testing (finals) schedule. If you asked the school why it needs multiple schedules, the staff would say because there are different needs on certain days, and no one schedule can cover all the different scenarios. Providing intervention time is no different—no intervention schedule can meet all the needs of every teacher and student. This point is demonstrated perfectly by the story of Jane Addams Junior High School.

Jane Addams started by creating Flex 1.0, designed to provide two short, timely reteaching times during the school day to targeted subjects. This proved to be highly successful at meeting the desired outcomes, but it did not meet the learning needs of every student. As additional student needs were identified, schedules were created to meet these needs. Notice, too, that Jane Addams first determined student needs, then created a schedule to meet them. They did not first look for the perfect intervention schedule, then fit student needs into it.

Jane Addams Junior High School, in Schaumburg School District 54, may seem from the outside like any other school in the western suburbs of Chicago. But if you drill deeper into what is happening there, it's evident that it is not. During the 2007–2008 school year, Jane Addams was the lowest performing of the five junior high schools in District 54 in every area of testing as measured by the Illinois Standard Achievement Test (ISAT). Name the subject and grade level, and Jane Addams was at the bottom. In 2008–2009, with a deeper understanding of the professional learning community (PLC) process, coupled with the implementation of some simple student support systems, Jane Addams became the highest-achieving junior high in the school district in reading and the second highest-achieving junior high in math. This trend of high achievement as measured by the ISAT has continued. The staff, students, and community are very proud of these accomplishments from a school that has a student body that is 47 percent white, 22 percent Hispanic, 16 percent Asian, 10 percent African American, 5 percent multiracial, and 19 percent students coming from low-income families, with 16 percent of the student population having individualized education programs (IEPs).

## The FLEX Drivers

The staff at Jane Addams could have been satisfied with these results, as they are certainly good. But this wasn't good enough; they wanted their students to achieve at great levels. Our district had begun tracking individual fall-to-spring student growth as measured by the Northwest Evaluation Association (NWEA) Measures of Academic Progress (MAP), and we quickly realized that in terms of individual student growth we had some work to do. Our students were performing well overall in terms of the expected state standards, but not all of our students were learning at the levels that we knew they could achieve.

As principal, I heard comments like the following over the course of the school year:

- "It would be great to have access to students who need the help the most with no other distractions around."

- "If I could get thirty minutes alone with students who need support, my team could do some great stuff."

- "It would be great to work extra with our high-achieving students to push them beyond the standards."

- "We are working very hard to provide intervention during our class periods, but it is very challenging to get the work done while dealing with all of the other students."

- "Our current mode of intervention is okay, but there has to be a better way to help our kids who need my help."

These types of comments were reinforced during one of our annual staff activities. Every year during the month of February, I would ask our staff the same three questions in order to give our entire staff a voice in our efforts to guide school improvement.

1. What three things are going well at our school this year?

2. What are the two challenges at our school this year?

3. What is one thought or question you have?

This was done in February for multiple reasons. First, any new program or system had reached full implementation by then. Second, we were in the midst of our staffing plan for the following school year, and this process aided in proper staff utilization. Finally, and probably most importantly, the month of February always seemed to bring out the raw and honest truth from our staff, which is what I was after. We called this activity 3–2–1, and all staff were required to answer the questions during a staff development meeting. Their ticket out of the staff development session was a completed form. Some teachers took a few minutes to complete the activity; others took thirty minutes or more.

These three simple questions provided phenomenal feedback for me as principal. Once I read through all of the feedback, I compiled and shared it with our staff. For example, the feedback I shared with the staff after our 3–2–1 process in February 2010 contained many expressions of satisfaction and approval. Morale was high, communication with the staff seemed excellent, and people felt the school was focused on the right things. Among the concerns, however, were the following:

- Time for reteaching

- Hallway supervision, more visible staff, consistency of expectations and consequences

- Things we can do as a staff to ensure that 100 percent of our students are successful and empowered

- A better way to track all of our interventions. Database? Share folder?

- Nail down the "intervention progression" and have appropriate goals and consequences to increase motivation for our students who are chronically struggling academically

- A study hall or support time for sixty-minute math students

- An all-school reteaching day or period: fluid, real-time intervention

- More time for co-teachers to plan together

- Continued Positive Behavioral Intervention and Supports, reteaching, check in and check out, and so on

- More purposeful use of team time; time for guidance staff and teachers to collaborate with each other and get updates

I considered this type of transparent sharing combined with planned action to be a type of reciprocal accountability I shared with the staff. Richard DuFour and Michael Fullan (2013) define *reciprocal accountability* as "the obligation to provide others with the resources and assistance they need to meet expectations" (p. 52). This sharing would then shape our plans as we moved forward for the remainder of the year and beyond. I was able to build credibility and trust with my staff by listening to their needs and then collaboratively planning with our school leadership team in order to provide student schedules and student support systems that met the staff-identified needs of our school. A beneficial part of this process was to revisit the results of 3–2–1 in August at the beginning of the school year and show the staff all of the new systems and changes for the coming school year that were collaboratively created, all based on their feedback. To me, this exemplifies this concept of reciprocal accountability to a staff. They saw that their input was not only valued, but acted on.

## The PLC Foundation

Our staff was well versed in the professional learning communities at work (PLC at Work) process, as we had spent time learning about it together during a series of staff development sessions in the fall of 2008. We truly embraced the belief that to make a change together, we must learn together. For instance, we fully embraced Robert J. Marzano's (2003) research, which states that "a guaranteed and viable curriculum is the school-level factor with the most impact on student achievement" (p. 15), as this answers PLC question 1, What do we want all of our students to learn? This research and pursuit of question 1 led our teams to develop agreed-on standards for every course that all students were expected to attain. Our staff also understood the research related to common formative assessments and how these are vital to not only improving our instruction, but to properly supporting students. We embraced formative assessments due to our awareness of research from Dylan Wiliam (2007), which states, "When implemented well, formative assessment can effectively double the speed of student learning" (p. 36), as this answers PLC question 2, How do we know if our students are learning the agreed-on standards?

It was no surprise that we not only saw student growth from fall to spring but double student growth as we worked together to put this research into action. Additionally, we knew from the work of Richard DuFour, Rebecca DuFour, and Robert Eaker (2008) that common assessments are essential to systemic interventions. With this understanding, we worked to answer PLC questions 3 and 4, What do we do if they aren't learning the agreed-on standards, and what do we do if they have already learned the agreed-on standards? We answered these questions by following the research of Austin Buffum, Mike Mattos, and Chris Weber (2009), who recommend that "developing intervention systems that are urgent, directive, timely, targeted, administered by professionals, and systematic" (p. 61) is a key to school improvement. The development and implementation of our FLEX schedules were built on the foundation provided by the four PLC at Work questions.

## The Beginning of FLEX

During the 2009–2010 school year, the 3–2–1 process provided us with the feedback to create more time during the school day to support students. Because of the collaborative process we used to create the FLEX schedule, we encountered few obstacles to putting it together. First, the staff requested a schedule with extra time (twenty-five to thirty minutes) included in it to support students, and the majority of our staff supported this concept. Second, the staff had a voice in the creation of the schedule, which created a sense of ownership that never waned throughout the process. Finally, our teachers' association was purposefully involved. To this day, I am grateful to the association's building representatives with whom I worked to determine how the new schedule would affect students without violating any provisions of our collective-bargaining agreement. I would highly recommend that every administration work proactively with its association in developing a schedule like this, as we all need to be aligned in order to make this happen. The primary concern of our association was whether or not this FLEX schedule was adding time to the instructional day. Our veteran association building rep and I sat down several times as we developed the schedule and did the math on the number of minutes.

Previous to instituting our FLEX schedule, each teacher had a total of 240 minutes of "face time" with our students (six classes of forty minutes each). With the FLEX schedule, the average face time was increased by seventeen minutes per teacher. However, because they saw the value that it would bring, this slight increase in face time was acceptable to the teachers' association. Once our staff gave us direction on creating this schedule, our school leadership team (made up of elected noncertified staff and certified staff along with myself and the assistant principal) went to work. Our traditional schedule had a total of nine periods, with the first and last periods forty-five minutes long to leave time for announcements, and the seven periods in between forty minutes in length. Everyone agreed that we could find thirty minutes during the school day to support students. We decided that was an appropriate amount of time. We had experience with twenty-minute study halls, and the informal feedback from teachers was that it was not enough time to give students what they needed.

Other obstacles involved deciding where the extra time would appear in the schedule and what subject areas would have access to it. Should FLEX be at the same time every day, or should the time be flexible based on when different departments had their collaborative team time? Would all academic areas have access to FLEX, or would this be available only to our core areas? We wrestled with these questions as a school and struggled to get consensus. In the end, we decided that we truly wouldn't know how this would work best until we tried it with our students.

## Learn by Doing: FLEX in Action

Confucius once said, "I hear and I forget. I see and I remember. I do and I understand." We made the decision to follow these words and learn by doing. We began our pilot by asking if any curricular areas would volunteer to participate. Our science and social studies departments volunteered, and in May 2010, we actually ran our FLEX schedule twice with surprising success. We then spent some time processing how it went. We decided that thirty minutes was the right amount of time and that we would schedule it after specific content-area collaborative meetings during the day. Additionally, we felt it was useful enough that we would do it two times per week in the fall, every Tuesday and Thursday. As you can see from figures 7.1 and 7.2, we were able to gain the time for our FLEX period by shortening all periods and by being brief with our announcements, only sharing the essentials at the start of first period. Our staff were comfortable with this arrangement, and that helped soothe any concerns from teachers regarding lost core instructional time.

| Announcements | 7:38–7:45 |
|---|---|
| Period 1 | 7:45–8:25 |
| Period 2 | 8:28–9:08 |
| Period 3 | 9:11–9:51 |
| Period 4 | 9:54–10:34 |
| Period 5 | 10:37–11:17 |
| Period 6 | 11:20–12:00 |
| Period 7 | 12:03–12:43 |
| Period 8 | 12:46–1:26 |
| Period 9 | 1:29–2:10 |
| Announcements | 2:10–2:15 |

*Source: Jane Addams Junior High School.*

Figure 7.1: Jane Addams regular schedule.

| Announcements | Shortened |
|---|---|
| Period 1 | 7:38–8:17 |
| FLEX | 8:20–8:50 |
| Period 2 | 8:53–9:30 |
| Period 3 | 9:33–10:10 |
| Period 4 | 10:13–10:51 |
| Period 5 | 10:54–11:32 |
| Period 6 | 11:35–12:13 |
| Period 7 | 12:16–12:54 |
| Period 8 | 12:57–1:34 |
| Period 9 | 1:37–2:15 |
| Announcements | Shortened |

*Source: Jane Addams Junior High School.*

Figure 7.2: Jane Addams FLEX schedule.

Our staff was excited about the possibilities of implementing this new schedule on a regular basis. Michael Fullan's (2010) research on change states that we have to "give people new experiences in relatively nonthreatening circumstances, and build on it, especially through interactions with trusted peers" (p. 25). This supports all of the work we did in piloting the FLEX schedule in the spring of 2010 and taking the time to collect feedback and process with staff in order to make the schedule effective. Since there were no major flaws, we had our blueprint to begin running FLEX on a regular basis during the following school year.

## FLEX 1.0

FLEX began as a thirty-minute period carved out of our schedule to give core staff the flexibility and opportunity to meet with the students who required intervention. FLEX time was really no different from time taken out from each class for an all-school pep assembly or when a guest speaker came to meet with the whole building. We decided on two times per week because we had also decided to begin implementation with only four core curricular areas. On rotation, this would allow for each of our language arts, math, science, and social studies teachers to have an extra thirty minutes with targeted students once every two weeks. Our school leadership team did make the decision to leave the elective courses out of the mix for FLEX until we could establish the program. The understanding was that we would add the electives when we could implement them effectively. Each FLEX day had one designated curricular area, meaning that only that specific area would have access to students for that FLEX session. Table 7.1 shows the rotation of content areas.

**Table 7.1: Rotation of Content Areas**

|              | Week 1         | Week 2         |
| ------------ | -------------- | -------------- |
| **Tuesday**  | Science        | Math           |
| **Thursday** | Social Studies | Language Arts  |

FLEX interventions are targeted at the skills that the teaching staff have determined collaboratively. In the PLC world, we know that the best people to determine the essential skills that need to be retaught, supported, or complemented are those who have the best handle on those skills—the teachers who are teaching them! Our teachers worked together to group students by skill deficit and shared the responsibility for providing the intervention. Additionally, it's vital to note that none of the intervention was done in isolation; the teachers were always building on the core that was taught during the regular class period. For instance, our social studies department would schedule their common formative assessments a day or two before their FLEX day. Social studies students who didn't hit the benchmark in their proficiency scales would then be required to go to FLEX to get additional time, support, and targeted instruction in order to learn the expected essential learnings. It's also important to note that as FLEX developed, our teaching teams didn't just use this thirty minutes for our struggling learners. At different times during the year, a subject area would use the FLEX period as an opportunity to extend learning. For example, our science department would have an extended thirty-minute FLEX enrichment lab for students who demonstrated mastery on the common formative assessment that was given to all students. This gave those students an opportunity to go beyond the normal standards and learn a concept at a deeper level with an engaging hands-on activity. In both of these examples, the students who are being directed to FLEX, along with the activities and lessons to be completed during FLEX, would be collaboratively processed by the social studies and science teaching teams in their collaborative meeting. There were many options. One FLEX period could be used for students needing support and intervention, and the following FLEX session could be used for students needing extension. Conversely, one FLEX period could be used for students needing support and students needing extension, with different teachers in the same content area providing the support to students as needed.

## Creating Reading Time for Nonparticipants

What about the students and teachers who don't participate in FLEX on a given day? This question is the one that I was most troubled with as principal—not because our plan was bad, but because of my concern for how the parental community would perceive it. We made a decision as a staff to have all students who were not directed to a FLEX period read during that time. Not only did students read, but our staff agreed that they, too, would read as role models during this time. Richard Allington (2001) states, "If I were required to select a single aspect of the instructional environment to change, my first choice would be creating a schedule that supported dramatically increased quantities of reading during the school day" (p. 24). In our FLEX schedule, we had created two thirty-minute blocks of time when students could independently read every week. Additionally, all of our students have independent reading expectations from their language arts teachers, and this gave them an hour a week to enter their weekly reading logs. Just as we reminded students about attending a FLEX session, we would remind them to bring reading material to the appropriate class on the morning of FLEX. Additionally, our language arts and library staff did a great job of putting together book bins full of materials for teachers who needed them. A visitor who walked through our gym during a FLEX period would witness both students and teachers seated in the gym reading. As it turned out, our community was very accepting of this entire reading practice, as they were able to realize the benefits of the entire FLEX period very quickly.

### Communicating About Flex

On the day before a specific subject area's FLEX day, each teacher would be in touch with his or her FLEX students and let them know verbally that they would be attending FLEX the following day. Our teachers worked hard to communicate with students in a sensitive and supportive manner. The message was not "You are bad at solving two-step equations, so you must attend this session as a punishment." Instead, the message was "Guess what? You have the great opportunity to attend FLEX tomorrow. We want you there because we will help you, and we care about you." As a result, FLEX was rarely seen as a negative by the students. Conversely, many teachers had students asking to go to FLEX because they saw the benefit of the process.

Our communication regarding FLEX didn't stop with the students. We realized during the pilot that all of the staff needed to know where students were during the FLEX sessions. Therefore, the other communication expectation was for the members of a department to communicate with their fellow staff on who was expected to attend. On the afternoon before a FLEX day, the department would send out an email with a spreadsheet (table 7.2, page 156) listing which students would be going to which classroom for FLEX. This was later changed to an email with a link to our shared folder on our network.

**Table 7.2: Spreadsheet of Student Assignments for a FLEX Session**

| Student Name | FLEX Teacher | Room |
|---|---|---|
| Student 1 | Burke | 208 |
| Student 2 | Burke | 208 |
| Student 3 | Burke | 208 |
| Student 4 | Burger | 212 |
| Student 5 | Burger | 212 |
| Student 6 | Reinkingh | 214 |
| Student 7 | Reinkingh | 214 |

This system allowed staff to remind (or directly send) students to their FLEX classroom when the FLEX bell rang if the student "forgot." These two communication modes led to incredibly well-attended FLEX sessions! If you were a visitor in our school during a FLEX passing period, you would hear the FLEX bell ring, and you would see anywhere from 75 to 300+ students moving quietly and with purpose to the classrooms they were assigned to. This happens because both the students and the staff know exactly where each student is supposed to be. It is a rarity when a student does not show up at his or her FLEX classroom. If this did happen, the FLEX teacher would make a call to the classroom in which the missing student had been prior to FLEX. If the student was still not found, then the FLEX teacher would notify the main office, and the administrators would work to track the student down.

### Understanding FLEX Success

The real uniqueness of FLEX is twofold. First, FLEX was created so that teachers would not be responsible for students in their classroom who did not need the targeted intervention. Before FLEX time begins, teachers' classrooms are empty because all FLEX periods are backed up to department meeting periods. For example, if the language arts team was off first period for their team planning time, then their FLEX period immediately followed first period. In the same way, if the social studies team was off second period for their team planning time, then their FLEX period immediately followed second period. This limited transitions (we didn't have to move any students out of rooms to make them empty) and allowed the teachers a full forty-minute collaborative period before FLEX to prepare, as needed. It also facilitated giving the teacher a quiet room with only the targeted students present to assist and support during FLEX.

The second unique attribute of FLEX is that it relies heavily on teacher-team autonomy and decision making. The principal is not telling the staff who gets the intervention. It's not up to an unconnected RTI team to determine via meetings and forms. Teachers and department teams had the volition to decide based on their content area's essential standards and formative assessment who would need access to this extra time. The staff of Jane Addams embraced the practice of "doing teaching not as an isolated individual but as part of a high-performing team" (Fullan & Hargreaves, 2012, p. 22). Thus, on any given day, FLEX could be used to support:

- The struggling student who had not mastered a learning target, essential skill, or standard

- The student who had barely shown mastery of a learning target, essential skill, or standard

- The high-achieving student who had demonstrated mastery

Michelle Burke, an eighth-grade science teacher at Jane Addams, summarizes FLEX best when she said, "The beauty of FLEX is that it is just that, flexible. We can use that time to help kids who are struggling, kids who need more time to work on projects, or kids who are looking to learn even more" (M. Burke, personal communication, April 14, 2011).

## FLEX 2.0

As it turned out, FLEX was a success from the onset. The schedule worked, students went to the correct places with relatively no problems, teachers supported students, and our community understood and supported the process. After several weeks of FLEX schedule implementation, we took the advice of Chip and Dan Heath (2010) and "recognized and celebrated the first steps" (p. 250) at a staff meeting, noting the progress we had made with our new schedule. I congratulated our staff on being a group of successful risk takers on behalf of our students and their learning. With this success, a little buzz was beginning among the teaching staff. Comments like "This FLEX schedule is really helping my students" and "I can't believe how smooth this FLEX schedule is running" were heard after every Tuesday and Thursday. Before long, there were small lines of elective teachers outside my office, all with the same thought: "How can we get in on this FLEX action?" Additionally, our core staff were frequently hearing another question from their colleagues: "How can I get more FLEX time?" As I frequently told our school leadership team (SLT), these types of questions from a teaching staff are good problems for a principal to have. Having staff members verbalizing a strong desire to put in extra time with students brought me joy. From these questions, the development of FLEX 2.0 began.

The solution to this first "good problem" was quite simple. Our SLT collaboratively determined that while the four core areas (math, science, social studies, and language arts) had first priority on their FLEX day, if a teacher of another content area wanted a student who wasn't on the priority list, then that student was fair game. In other words, all noncore teachers had to do was scan the published FLEX list, and if the student they wanted to work with was available, they could run FLEX 2.0 with that student. Our Flex 1.0 periods happened after periods 1, 2, 3, and 8. In scanning our noncore teachers' schedules, we found that every single teacher was off one of those periods. This then gave them the opportunity to work with students at least once during FLEX every two weeks, just like a core teacher, provided the student had not been requested by a prioritized core teacher. Problem one was solved! Like regular FLEX teachers, noncore FLEX teachers sent out the email link with the students they were meeting with for FLEX 2.0. The deadline to communicate FLEX 2.0 lists was the same as that for the core teachers—the afternoon before the FLEX day, after the core email link had been sent out.

The second priority for FLEX 2.0 was to create an opportunity to meet with students more than one time every two weeks. The reality was that some teachers not only wanted, but their students needed, more time with them than the one FLEX period every two weeks.

## FLEX 2.0 Option 1

Our SLT was able to make FLEX 2.0 option 1 happen by first compiling a list of teachers who had their off periods during FLEX periods. On a typical FLEX day, all of these teachers were receiving an additional thirty minutes of planning time, since they had no FLEX time responsibilities. Given this, all those teachers agreed to cover another teacher's class when asked to in order to allow their coworker the opportunity to spend more time with and give more support to students who needed it.

For example, Tom Pfeifer, a seventh-grade science teacher at Addams, spent thirty minutes of science FLEX time on Thursday with twenty-four struggling science students. At the conclusion of the thirty-minute session, fourteen of the twenty-four students demonstrated proficiency on the skill being retaught and reassessed. Because one of the science department's Strategic and specific, Measurable, Attainable, Results oriented, and Time bound (SMART) goals for the year was for 100 percent of its students to demonstrate proficiency on all common assessments, Tom utilized FLEX 2.0 to help the ten other students. He emailed the principal with his request, requesting FLEX 2.0 for the following Tuesday. The principal then emailed teachers who were not teaching during FLEX time on Tuesday, seeking one volunteer. Rose Larsen, a Spanish teacher, was off during the Tuesday FLEX period and agreed to support Tom. When Tuesday arrived and the FLEX bell rang, the students who had science with Tom were directed to go to the library with their reading materials, and Rose was waiting in the library for the students. The students filed in, sat down, and began reading with Rose just as they would have with Tom in their science classroom. Meanwhile, the ten students who needed to see Tom walked into the science room and received an additional thirty minutes of support from him. If students from this group had a need for more support after this FLEX 2.0 session, Tom could replicate this process on another FLEX day.

The process just described is a testimony to a staff working together as a true PLC to support students. Once some staff members saw this plan in action, many teachers took advantage of this opportunity.

## FLEX 2.0 Option 2

Flex 2.0 option 2 was designed for either the grade-level department team or the entire department in order to give large groups of students more doses of FLEX to improve the skills of many students at a multitude of levels. At strategic times during the school year (based on our assessment calendar), our math and language arts departments used this option. Once a department or team decided to use FLEX 2.0 option 2, all they had to do was email the principal. This set in motion a special schedule for the days requested, and an entire department of teachers was able to get extra time to support specific students during extra FLEX periods.

For example, the seventh- and eighth-grade language arts departments decided that during the month of February, they wanted to run four additional FLEX sessions every Friday. These extra sessions were affectionately called "Friday FLEX" or "MegaFLEX" by the teachers involved. In early January, when the teams made this decision, they emailed me with their request, which was swiftly granted after appropriate processing through our SLT (what SLT would turn down a huge group of teachers who want to work extra time with their students?), and the planning was on. The principal communicated with the entire staff that on Fridays during the month of February, we would be using a language arts FLEX schedule. The rest of the staff knew ahead of time that their Friday classes would be a couple minutes shorter, but they also understood that this gave hundreds of students extra support. During the January team meetings, the language arts teams broke students into various groups based on area of student need and the skills being taught, and decided what teachers (language arts, special services, and bilingual all participated in this) would teach what groups of students. The team called it MegaFLEX because it was a massive undertaking that required significant amounts of planning. When all was said and done, each grade level was able to give hundreds of students, both high and low performing, extra FLEX time sessions in the targeted areas that each student needed.

This second FLEX 2.0 process was a lot of work for departments, but it was worthwhile, as teachers were able to work with many students all at once and could use all of their colleagues' strengths to support learning. Our math department heard about this plan of action and also incorporated it in future years as a part of its plan. As a principal, it was exciting to see the passion and creativity of our school's educators spread like wildfire!

## FLEX 3.0

Using FLEX simultaneously during the 2010–2011 school year was a large success, shown by the fact that scores in both our state testing (based on attainment) and our local testing (based on student growth) reached their highest levels in school history. Additionally, the feedback from the staff was incredibly positive, with some staff requesting FLEX schedules four times per week! As we went through the 2011–2012 school year, we tweaked all of our FLEX 1.0 and FLEX 2.0 processes. We made improvements in the way we electronically communicated and tracked students, and we made our large intervention sessions, like MegaFLEX, more systematic in multiple content areas. In February, we went through our annual 3–2–1 process. The positives of FLEX were highlighted by staff, but now the staff had some new ideas. It was from this annual process that the FLEX 3.0 idea was born—to give students options and choice for FLEX sessions. We decided to pilot the FLEX 3.0 process during the month of May. A memo was sent to the staff explaining the vision for FLEX 3.0, which was to provide our students with three or six FLEX sessions of enrichment "clubs." An enrichment club could be any extension activity that a staff member would like to do to support students. Teachers could develop whatever they wanted, but each FLEX 3.0 session had to be approved by the SLT. I promised our staff that any participation by teachers would be completely at the teacher's discretion. They could choose to run a FLEX 3.0 session, or they could choose not to. Because several teachers had expressed interest during our brainstorming sessions, we were confident that we would have some clubs to offer students during this time. In the end, we ended up running about twelve different clubs for students, including:

- Introduction to Shakespeare
- Trebuchet science kits
- Creative writing
- Orchestra sectionals
- Band sectionals
- Movie maker

- Walking club

- Civil War

- Drawing club

- Japanese club

The caveat for students was that they could participate only if they had no missing homework and no major disciplinary issues. In a sense, we created these options for students as a reward for their hard work over the entire school year. At all of our student lunches over the course of the school day, I reviewed the FLEX 3.0 expectations, the options, and the process for students to get involved. I then ran sign-ups at lunch, and students participated in either three- or six-session clubs during the month of May.

For example, Jan Lundeburg, a seventh-grade language arts teacher, had noticed that our core curriculum lacked any exposure to Shakespeare. As a teacher sending many students on to high school who would be in the honors/AP track, this concerned her. Jan was very excited to have the opportunity to provide a FLEX 3.0 Introduction to Shakespeare club to any interested students. A total of twenty-eight eighth-grade students chose to go to six FLEX 3.0 sessions on consecutive Tuesdays focused on the works of Shakespeare. Jan raved about the experience of teaching this FLEX 3.0 session, as the students were highly motivated and wanted to be there. This was a great example of FLEX 3.0 meeting the needs of our higher-level students.

FLEX 3.0 happened at the same time as FLEX 1.0 and 2.0, so it did not require any additional time or a new schedule in order to make it happen. Students who qualified and chose to participate in FLEX 3.0 did so in place of their reading time during May. Additionally, FLEX 1.0 and 2.0 always took priority over FLEX 3.0, so no student was denied getting the support or intervention that he or she needed.

## FLEX Autonomy and Next Steps

One of the reasons that the FLEX schedule was received so well by our staff is the autonomy it gave them. Individual teachers worked collaboratively with their fellow content-area team members to determine what students would get the FLEX support. Our FLEX schedule was given to our staff in advance each semester, so they could align their common formative assessments with their FLEX schedules for extra time and support. As you read in the summary of FLEX 2.0, teaching staff were not just limited to the twice-per-month FLEX sessions if they took advantage of the FLEX 2.0 process.

Typically, our students would continue to get support (FLEX 2.0 or an after-school study session) if they were not able to demonstrate the expected progress or knowledge base. Progress monitoring for FLEX (which we would define as being in the Tier 1 to Tier 2 range) was done at the teacher-team level. It is important to note that the work of creating assessments and monitoring individual student progress took place during the school day in the collaborative team meeting.

A student who continually struggled through our FLEX 1.0 and 2.0 supports could potentially be referred to one of our more intensive Tier 2 or Tier 3 interventions as part of his or her school schedule. These interventions were forty minutes daily and in smaller groups in a more intensive setting. The student still had his or her eighty-minute language arts course but would also get an additional forty-minute period (one could call this "core plus more"). For example, if we identified a specific student as having a comprehension issue that was not getting solved through our FLEX process, that student could be taken out of an elective class and placed in a forty-minute Tier 2 reading intervention. These interventions were focused on building the foundational reading skills for our most struggling reading students. If a student was referred to a more intensive Tier 2 or Tier 3 intervention, that student would be part of a more systematic progress-monitoring system coordinated by his or her intervention team, comprising the intervention teacher, our school psychologist, and a case manager when appropriate. Additionally, the student would still have access to the FLEX schedule as our FLEX schedule never discriminated; it was inclusive and available to all who qualified.

## The FLEX Results

Jane Addams is very proud of the results we were able to achieve from 2008 to 2013. Over that time period, our assessment focus shifted from the ISAT to the NWEA's MAP. We valued MAP far more in our school and district, as it focused on individual student growth where our state assessment mostly evaluated how we did with our most struggling students. We measured two data points in relation to MAP.

1. Percentage of students who reached their target goal in math and reading from fall to spring

2. Percentage of students who doubled their target goal in math and reading from fall to spring

Both of these data points are significant, because not only is it imperative that all students grow, but that they grow in ways that maximize their potential. Table 7.3 shows how we progressed as a school in MAP over several years.

As you can see, our students grew considerably between fall and spring each year. In the area of reading, we saw consistent growth, putting us in the top 6 percent in the nation. The most dramatic growth was seen in the area of math, as we grew from being in the 50th percentile to being in the top 2 percent in the nation. Additionally, we were ecstatic as a staff to see that we grew to consistently have over 50 percent of our students double their growth.

**Table 7.3: MAP Progress From 2009 to 2013**

|  | **2009–2010** | **2010–2011** | **2011–2012** | **2012–2013** |
|---|---|---|---|---|
| **Percent Reaching Reading Growth Target** | 63 percent<br><br>89th percentile nationally | 65 percent<br><br>91st percentile nationally | 65 percent<br><br>91st percentile nationally | 67 percent<br><br>94th percentile nationally |
| **Percent Reaching Math Growth Target** | 57 percent<br><br>50th percentile nationally | 71 percent<br><br>85th percentile nationally | 71 percent<br><br>85th percentile nationally | 81 percent<br><br>98th percentile nationally |
| **Percent Reaching Reading Double Growth** | 31 percent | 49 percent | 48 percent | 51 percent |
| **Percent Reaching Math Double Growth** | 46 percent | 51 percent | 47 percent | 56 percent |

It's important to note that we didn't achieve the results we did solely because of a few interventions like FLEX 1.0, FLEX 2.0, and FLEX 3.0. Instead, it was the cumulative nature of being strategic in supporting students in the most effective ways possible. This strategic focus was never done because we thought something might work or because we liked something. Conversely, we learned together and collaboratively sought out ways to incorporate best-practice and research-based concepts in order to improve our student achievement through systems of student support. I dedicate this chapter to all of those staff members at Jane Addams Junior High School who made a great difference in the lives of their students.

# Resources

Allington, R. L. (2001). *What really matters for struggling readers: Designing research-based programs.* New York: Longman.

Buffum, A., Mattos, M., & Weber, C. (2009). *Pyramid response to intervention: RTI, professional learning communities, and how to respond when kids don't learn.* Bloomington, IN: Solution Tree Press.

DuFour, R., DuFour, R., & Eaker, R. (2008). *Revisiting professional learning communities at work: New insights for improving schools.* Bloomington, IN: Solution Tree Press.

DuFour, R., & Fullan, M. (2013). *Cultures built to last: Systemic PLCs at work.* Bloomington, IN: Solution Tree Press.

Fullan, M. (2010). *Motion leadership: The skinny on becoming change savvy.* Thousand Oaks, CA: Corwin Press.

Fullan, M., & Hargreaves, A. (2012). *Professional capital: Transforming teaching in every school.* New York: Teachers College Press.

Heath, C., & Heath, D. (2010). *Switch: How to change things when change is hard.* New York: Broadway Books.

Marzano, R. J. (2003). *What works in schools: Translating research into action.* Alexandria, VA: Association for Supervision and Curriculum Development.

Wiliam, D. (2007). Changing classroom practice. *Educational Leadership, 65*(4), 36–42.

**Jack Baldermann** met Richard DuFour in 1996 and was one of the first principals to implement professional learning communities' (PLC) concepts while at Carl Sandburg High School in Orland Park, Illinois (serving 3,500 students). The team at Sandburg used PLC to attain significant gains in student learning, test scores, and graduation rates. At Riverside Brookfield High School in Riverside, Illinois, Jack and his team used PLC concepts to propel the school to become one of the most improved and top-performing high schools in the nation. As director of secondary schools in Hartford, Connecticut, Jack worked with a talented group of educational leaders to implement PLC and response to intervention (RTI) in several urban schools.

Today, Jack serves as principal at Westmont High School in Westmont, Illinois. After two years of implementing PLC and RTI concepts, Westmont has become one of the most improved high schools in the country. It has earned a graduation rate of 99.2 percent, built the most improved Advanced Placement program in Illinois (2014), made adequate yearly progress for the first time in seven years, and achieved double-digit score increases on the state-mandated exams in reading and math.

Jack has presented to schools in over forty U.S. states and in Canada.

To book Jack Baldermann for professional development, contact pd@solution-tree .com.

8

# Building and Sustaining a Culture That Supports Learning for All

Jack Baldermann

**Editors' Note** Besides the exceptional results, many aspects of the Riverside Brookfield High School story impress us. One unique element is the school's proactive use of summer school to extend time and support student learning. Most secondary schools offer summer school. Unfortunately for struggling students, however, this extended time is used to make up courses a student has already failed. As we have often said, allowing incoming students to fail before providing help is like shutting the barn door after the horse has escaped. At Riverside, students deemed at risk entering ninth grade are required to attend summer school *prior* to the start of school, providing key remediation before they have the opportunity to fail. Besides strengthening their academic skills, this preventive support sends these students a powerful message: we care about you, and we are not going to let you fail! What a great first impression for an incoming student.

Equally important, this support did not end with summer school. Ongoing support was provided, primarily coordinated by the academic-support person. This example captures perfectly the concept of tiered interventions. Because one particular intervention cannot meet the needs of every student, a school must be prepared with targeted levels of support. As shown in figure 8.1 (page 168), Riverside created a pyramid of interventions that made it exceedingly difficult for students to fail.

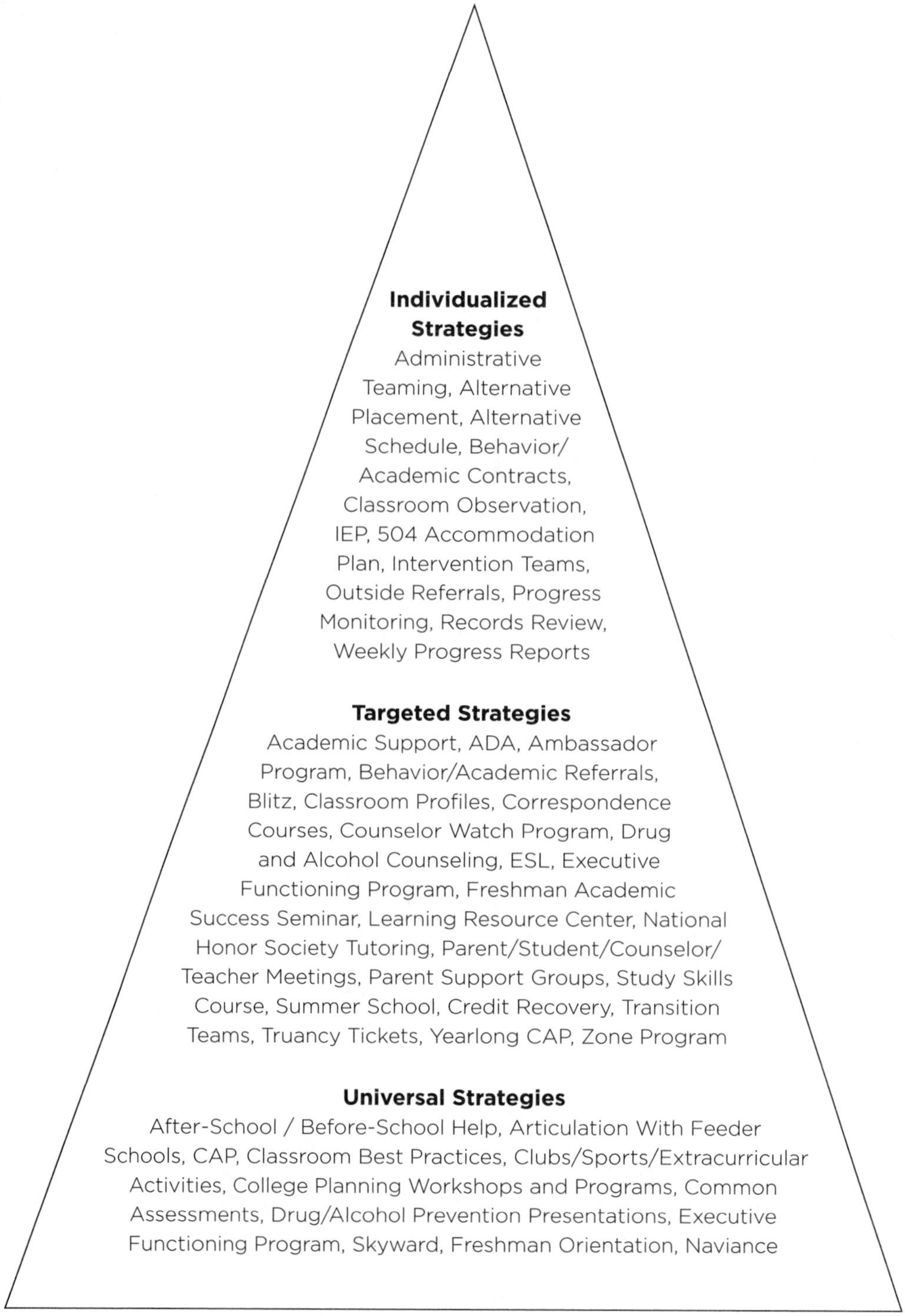

**Individualized Strategies**
Administrative Teaming, Alternative Placement, Alternative Schedule, Behavior/ Academic Contracts, Classroom Observation, IEP, 504 Accommodation Plan, Intervention Teams, Outside Referrals, Progress Monitoring, Records Review, Weekly Progress Reports

**Targeted Strategies**
Academic Support, ADA, Ambassador Program, Behavior/Academic Referrals, Blitz, Classroom Profiles, Correspondence Courses, Counselor Watch Program, Drug and Alcohol Counseling, ESL, Executive Functioning Program, Freshman Academic Success Seminar, Learning Resource Center, National Honor Society Tutoring, Parent/Student/Counselor/ Teacher Meetings, Parent Support Groups, Study Skills Course, Summer School, Credit Recovery, Transition Teams, Truancy Tickets, Yearlong CAP, Zone Program

**Universal Strategies**
After-School / Before-School Help, Articulation With Feeder Schools, CAP, Classroom Best Practices, Clubs/Sports/Extracurricular Activities, College Planning Workshops and Programs, Common Assessments, Drug/Alcohol Prevention Presentations, Executive Functioning Program, Skyward, Freshman Orientation, Naviance

Figure 8.1: Riverside Brookfield High School response to intervention (RTI) strategies.

At times, it seems crazy and irrational to pursue the ideal of learning for all. Certainly, in the pursuit, one can feel at times incompetent and frustrated. Yet anything less than learning for all means allowing students who might have found success to remain in a state of failure. That is unacceptable.

We teachers, administrators, counselors, and support staff members entered this profession to make a powerful difference in the lives of our students. When our students learn despite numerous obstacles, ridiculous challenges, and consistent self-sabotage, then we know we are in the right battle. This is where we will make our mark: our commitment to and passion for our students will overpower all that stands in our way. This is why we are educators.

At Riverside Brookfield High School (RB) starting in the winter of 2001, our team of faculty, administration, and staff committed to the concept of learning for all with a whatever-it-takes attitude. RB was a good suburban school just outside of Chicago, serving approximately 1,500 students. While the demographics of the student body changed over time, on average 20 percent of the student body was Latino, 8 percent was African American, 13 percent had an individualized education program (IEP), and 15 percent qualified for the free and reduced-price lunch program.

A "good school," yes, but as noted expert Jim Collins (2001) writes, "good is the enemy of great" (p. 1). To become a great school—which is always possible but never a final feat—the RB staff would need to create a mindset of never giving up on a student regardless of what we faced. Our goal was to build a high-functioning professional learning community (PLC) dedicated to all students where we could measure significant increases in student achievement. As a core group of leaders, including the principal, assistant principals, and department chairs, we felt it was our responsibility to get our team to believe that greatness was possible and then to make that belief our reality.

Many of the members of the leadership team at RB had previously worked in an effective PLC at Carl Sandburg High School (3,500 students) and had worked with Richard DuFour to implement those concepts as outlined in *Professional Learning Communities at Work: New Insights for Improving Schools* (DuFour & Eaker, 1998). Drawing on its PLC experience, the RB leadership team and faculty focused on (1) learning for all; (2) shared mission, vision, and values; (3) collaboratively built and agreed-to SMART (Specific, Measurable, Attainable, Results-Oriented, and Timebound) goals; (4) collaboratively examining student performance information identifying specific student learning gaps, collaboratively addressing these deficiencies, and using formative assessment data to determine if student learning had increased; and (5) a commitment to continuous improvement.

## Building a Passionate Consensus

The leadership team wanted RB to be genuinely committed to PLC concepts and dedicated to learning for all. The faculty and staff were professionals who were willing to follow a lead, but compliance was not the goal of our leadership team. We wanted a passionate consensus and a team that believed deeply in and would fight for and protect the mission, vision, and SMART goals, not because it was expected but because the faculty and staff believed in their minds and hearts it was the best thing to do.

To go beyond compliance and energize the RB faculty and staff required creating a culture of collective inquiry that encouraged and supported honest dissension. We had to build a trusting environment and an atmosphere where all members could express their thoughts freely and share questions and problems in open meetings. If team members with lingering doubts or concerns could not share them and have them addressed in a respectful manner, they would return to their work with students unconvinced, and this would prevent us from functioning at peak effectiveness.

To create the environment for peak effectiveness, leaders facilitating group discussions stated emphatically and repeatedly that passionate consensus and distributed leadership were the goals. Dissension and critical questioning were expected. Our team spent months inviting counterpoints during staff discussions before moving forward. In many instances, as both superintendent and principal, I tried to articulate the thoughtful and genuine concerns that members of the staff might be hesitant to voice so we could get them out in the open.

One prime example of a genuine concern was whether committing to learning for all meant teachers were being asked simply to pass students regardless of the quality of their work. These earnest teachers were fearful that we would enable students and not hold them responsible for doing hard work and meeting learning standards. Connected to this question was another fear: being responsible not only for teaching but also for learning when some students put forth no effort or often would not even attend school.

Our leadership team responded with a principle that is ever-present in the work of Richard DuFour, Rebecca DuFour, and Robert Eaker (2008) and Austin Buffum, Mike Mattos, and Chris Weber (2009, 2012)—namely, that students who are disengaged, unmotivated, immature, or irresponsible need us to be more present in their lives, not less; that the challenges presented by these students are too difficult to deal with on our own and require a collaborative and collective team response; that the work with all students, especially those who are struggling the most, is sacred and requires the efforts of a cohesive team.

The teachers who were concerned about letting students off too easy had a good point. Learning for all meant holding students accountable. Our high school would be more serious than ever about expecting more from our students. To this end, our team supported the following measures: More home visits, better relationships with parents and students, building a series of interventions that guaranteed additional time and practice for learning, collaboratively examining student performance information, and creating a program that provided an intense, team-focused approach for students most in need.

When our staff understood that we would be more proactive and that together we would hold our students accountable to be more productive, most of their apprehension disappeared. Although some skepticism remained, it was understood and appreciated that only when they witnessed quality results would they truly believe. In the meantime, we discussed the importance of all of us setting aside skepticism and putting our full efforts into doing whatever it would take to see that all of our students would achieve. We put the question of whether teachers were willing to commit to the idea of learning for all as we discussed in faculty meetings to an anonymous vote run by the teachers' union. We had a nearly unanimous positive consensus and were ready to develop a way to see if we could measure success.

## Specific, Measurable, Attainable, Results-Oriented, and Timebound (SMART) Goals

I love SMART goals, and they were one of the most powerful components of our PLC work at Riverside Brookfield High School. The goals provided focus and, when attained, a true source of pride and accomplishment. It is important to mention a few thoughts about SMART goals.

Being *specific* is crucial because the more specific the target, the clearer the steps to reach it. What is *measurable* is achievable, and if a goal is important enough to reach, then it is imperative that we know whether or not we have done it. Some educators struggle to find the perfect measurement. It does not exist. Begin by leading yourself each day. I recommend getting up in the morning with a commitment to one of your SMART goals and finding a fair way to measure your progress toward that goal. Do not beat yourself up because the measurement is not perfect. *Attainable* does not mean the goal should not be ambitious. In fact, if as a leadership team you wish to develop passion, create something exciting to accomplish. When a team is excited and passionate about its goals, those qualities can contribute toward their attainment. A goal that is *results-oriented* offers a sense of purpose and meaning, and people will commit to work that has purpose. We must bring the work in for a landing so we can measure if we have made any progress, and that is why the goal must be *timebound* so we can monitor (and hopefully celebrate) our work.

## Building the SMART Goals

The process of creating and agreeing to the SMART goals was collaborative and central to their eventual success. The entire staff started by examining the data on the school's graduation rate. From 1991 to 2001, the average graduation rate was 90 percent. This was good but not great. We posed the following questions: Should we commit to achieving a great graduation rate (one that reflected learning for all)? What would we need to do to make it happen?

All administrators, teachers, counselors, support staff, and school board members collectively looked at the data on high school dropouts and the impact that not graduating had on individuals, communities, and the country. The administration gathered the photos of the 10 percent of students who had not graduated from the previous year and put them on a big screen for all faculty and support staff to see, and in doing so highlighted that there were real people behind these numbers. On several occasions, the administration assembled an entire grade into the auditorium with the faculty present and sectioned off 10 percent of the students to give a visual example of how many students RB had been losing each year. The administration included the students in this conversation, talked about how RB and its students could not afford to continue to have such failure, and communicated that as a high school we needed students to support their peers and be part of the solution. At a few faculty meetings, the administration would bring in the local police blotter with the names of recent nongraduates circled to drive home the point we had read about in the dropout research: students who did not graduate were more likely to commit crimes and face incarceration. We once made copies of an actual letter from a person who had attended our high school, dropped out, was soon to be released from prison, and was now requesting help in obtaining a diploma so he could have opportunities in the future.

The SMART goals came to life. They were more than just numbers. But while we were building a sense of urgency and a more passionate commitment, members of our team still had concerns and reservations, along with questions about how exactly we would support this goal. In some quarters, the people asking these tough questions might be looked on as dissenters. However, we viewed them as critical friends who needed answers before they could passionately commit to the goal and vision.

We spent hours discussing how we would make sure we were not just passing students and how to ensure that the diploma would represent quality learning from all our students. To address these legitimate concerns, we needed to build a systematic approach and a series of interventions to support teachers and their students who were not achieving learning. Part of our work centered on answering the critical questions of a professional learning community. We had to reexamine exactly what we expected students to learn and how we would know if students had actually learned. Much of our continued work focused on how we were responding when students did not learn.

One of the best examples of how we worked as a collaborative team was evidenced in the way we processed SMART goals and linked them to learning for all. We shared the extensive research on the power of SMART goals but then went through a series of discussions before we came to a consensus. We took a page from Richard DuFour and Adlai Stevenson High School (Lincolnshire, Illinois) and limited our goals to three. Three seems to be the "magic number" that allows us to concentrate on achieving them. We also maintained the same goals, with very minor revisions, for seven straight years.

## SMART Goals, 2002–2009

We formulated three SMART goals for our school.

### Goal 1: Graduation Rate

Goal 1 was to improve the graduation rate from a ten-year average (1991–2001) of 90.5 percent to 95 percent or higher for each graduating class. Our team at RB knew that the ten-year average of 90.5 percent was good but not great. After our first year, we just missed the mark of 95 percent. For the next six years, we averaged a four-year 98 percent graduation rate, which included classes where 100 percent of our African American and Latino students graduated, and two years when we had a four-year 99 percent graduation rate for all students. RB went from having a just barely above-average graduation rate to being in the top 1–2 percent in the state.

### Goal 2: State Standards

Goal 2 was to improve the percentage of students meeting and exceeding state standards (as measured by the Prairie State Achievement Examination—the Illinois version of the federal No Child Left Behind [NCLB] exam—which included a full ACT test) from failing to make the top 10 percent in Illinois to being in the top 5 percent or higher. The test scores would fluctuate over the next seven years, but RB increased the percentage of students meeting and exceeding state standards by an average of over 16 percent. For several years, RB was ranked in the top 3 percent of high schools in Illinois using this measure. Over this seven-year period, RB ranked in the top 5 percent of high schools for both improvement and overall performance. The school made adequate yearly progress (AYP) every year but one. In 2008, the school did not make AYP for the first time due to low reading scores for our Latino students. The administration, faculty, students, and parents used that setback as inspiration to redouble our efforts. In 2009, Latino students at RB scored in the top 1 percent for all Latino students in the state, had the most improved reading scores in Illinois, and outscored 96 percent of all schools, and RB once again made AYP.

### Goal 3: Advanced Placement

Goal 3 was to build the most improved Advanced Placement program in Illinois, as measured by iterations of Jay Mathews's *Challenge Index*. Although RB was not in 2002 ranked among the top forty high schools in Illinois, our goal was that by 2006 RB would rank in the top five high schools in Illinois, triple the number of students passing Advanced Placement exams (from 80 to 240), triple the number of passed exams (166 to 498), and triple the number of Advanced Placement scholars (from 18 to 54).

The students and faculty at RB surpassed all of these ambitious Advanced Placement goals. By 2006, the high school had the most improved AP program in Illinois and one of the top-ten most improved programs in the nation, whether measured by the *Challenge Index*, the increase in students taking and passing exams, or the increase in the number of AP scholars.

Some of the highlights included a national ranking of seventy-six (2006); prior to the SMART goal and the AP initiative, the school had not ranked in the top thousand schools in the country. RB had improved from not ranking in the top forty high schools in Illinois to number two of 650 schools, and it remained in the top five for four more consecutive years. In 2005 and 2006, RB ranked in the top-ten most improved AP programs in the nation as measured by the *Challenge Index*. In a ten-year period, RB's overall school enrollment increased by 35 percent, but the number of passed exams increased from 112 to 738 (an increase of over 600 percent). The number of individual students passing exams went from 80 to 346 (an increase of over 400 percent), and the number of Advanced Placement scholars increased from 16 to 144 (an increase of over 700 percent).

Keeping the SMART goals consistent for seven straight years made it easier to maintain focus and keep track of positive growth.

## Dramatic Progress

The attainment of these SMART goals was instrumental in Riverside Brookfield passing a major referendum to rebuild the entire high school curriculum, being able to recruit and retain high-quality teachers, and attracting a significant increase in families moving to the district so their children could attend the school. The culture at RB changed dramatically. Many schools from throughout the state and from different parts of the country visited RB, and teachers, students, and parents started to think of the school as one of the best in Illinois. The SMART goals had a high impact on morale and achievement. However, RB could not have realized these gains without first establishing the commitment to learning for all and being dedicated to a PLC culture. The way the SMART goals were established and agreed to was also inextricably linked to the success and accomplishments that were attained.

## Putting Practical Supports Into Place

Our commitment to learning for all was building, but we needed practical supports in place when students were not successful. After our administration, teachers, support staff, and school board guaranteed that students who did not learn would be supported with additional time and practice; we put our team's commitment to a test. Our teachers' union conducted a poll that asked teachers if they supported the concept of learning for all, as had been discussed over the previous months, and the SMART goals we had collaboratively built. While collective results were to be made public to the entire staff, students, and parents, individual teacher responses would remain anonymous. Even though we were establishing a culture of trust, we wanted the faculty to express their commitment to these goals with no one feeling forced to say they agreed. The results from the union poll were that 100 percent of the faculty expressed support for the graduation rate SMART goal and the commitment to learning for all.

The other SMART goals that we pursued did not enjoy 100 percent agreement or support. We moved forward with 75–80 percent agreement in these initiatives, explaining that the vast majority of the faculty was enthusiastic and that we would closely monitor progress, remain open to concerns that had been raised about these goals, and reassess at the end of each year. Most of the teachers who objected to these goals did not like the focus on standardized testing. However, it was explained that the ACT (50 percent of Illinois's NCLB assessment) was a gate-keeping exam that affected our students and we wanted to maximize their opportunities. The administration also discussed how individual departments and teams within departments could set SMART goals that measured the kind of learning they valued most. Those who initially did not agree with the Advanced Placement goal believed we were including too many students. In time, as we monitored the results of the initiative and celebrated the success of the work that had been done, more faculty members supported the goal.

There was concern about the faculty who had not been behind some of the goals. We argued that if the vote had not been so overwhelming, we would not have pursued these goals, but since it was, all members of our team had a responsibility to put their best efforts into attaining the initiatives. Consensus does not require unanimity. As called out in Richard DuFour, Rebecca DuFour, Robert Eaker, and Thomas

Many (2010), "A group has arrived at consensus when: 1. All points of view have been heard. 2. The will of the group is evident even to those who most oppose it" (p. 166).

To maintain the momentum and strengthen the consensus, we listened to dissension, adjusting to critical input, welcoming concerns, taking action, and making changes that demonstrated that we took our faculty's ideas seriously. Some teachers were concerned that the standards in the summer credit recovery program, which allowed students to stay on track for graduation even though they had failed classes during the year, were not on par with what students were expected to learn in regular classes. A group of department chairs and teachers reexamined the summer curriculum and instituted a series of upgrades that improved the quality of the curriculum and instruction. By responding with action, we increased the quality of learning for the students in the credit recovery program and reassured members of our faculty that our graduation standards and graduation rate were legitimate. Effective leaders do not just listen. They follow through by taking action on the issues raised by the faculty, especially the concerns that are focused on student learning. It is in the follow-through that trust is reaffirmed.

Adrian Gostick and Chester Elton (2008) point out that positive, specific, and genuine feedback is more powerful than money in motivating people. We committed to the concept of offering ten positive pieces of feedback for every one critical suggestion. A common practice would be to walk the halls asking students which teacher helped them learn that week or in which class were they challenged in a positive way. Specific, positive answers from students about their teachers would be shared immediately with the appropriate teacher or broadcast in front of the entire staff at the next faculty meeting. We were constantly sharing stories about the great things our teachers were doing for students—adopting the whatever-it-takes attitude toward their work.

### Celebrating Success

We also celebrated our success and recognized the excellence in the work being done. When our high school was ranked in the top hundred in the country by a national magazine, we purchased polo shirts for every member of the staff to wear. When our school reached some ambitious SMART goals, we purchased hundreds of T-shirts with the mascot on the front and all of the accomplishments of the faculty and students on the back. All around town, our students and staff would wear these shirts as a symbol of our shared success. The goals were examined and celebrated at the start of every school year, documented continuously in publications sent to our school community, and always present in the upper right-hand corner of meeting agendas. We celebrated and made sure the whole building knew when a parade of schools from our area and from different parts of the country would visit to see how we were making a difference for our students and getting results. A six-foot by ten-foot placard announcing the SMART goal success was hung in a prominent place in our main gymnasium.

After several years of struggle, hard work, success, and the recognition that always followed, our teachers' union president sat in my office to praise the success, capping it by saying that our "teachers really believe they are the best." That was the point. We wanted to overwhelm our staff and students with appreciation and positivity. We wanted them to feel like nothing could stop them and that any problem we faced was no match for their collective intelligence and amazing compassion.

In this atmosphere, it was easier to ask staff to chase goals and take risks. When it became necessary to approach a teacher about going above and beyond for a student who was in danger of failing, our teachers responded with additional time, instruction, and positive energy, because they knew their efforts would make a difference and be appreciated. As each year progressed, momentum was building, and there were results that showed that our collective efforts were leading to student achievement gains. Our administration made it a constant focus to recognize all that the staff and students had accomplished.

### Fresh Challenges

Our faculty was committed to learning for all with a whatever-it-takes attitude, but to achieve the best results, systemwide support was needed, and the administration and teacher leaders had to take action to address several issues that were getting in the way of our work with students.

When we had established our SMART goals, the staff asked that we (1) create meaningful and impactful articulation programs with our sender schools; (2) address the issue of students arriving at our high school well-below grade level in reading and without necessary academic skills, especially in mathematics; (3) more closely monitor student-performance information (and in a more proactive manner, especially for the students most in danger of failing); (4) provide additional time and practice for students who were not mastering essential learning targets; (5) provide intense daily support to address the academic and social-emotional needs of students; (6) build time into the schedule for students who needed second-chance opportunities to demonstrate success through formative assessments; (7) provide staff time to meet with their PLC teams; and (8) extend the concept of collaboration to include departmental and grade-level teams.

We implemented a systematic approach and a series of interventions that addressed these concerns of the faculty. Along the way, we addressed all eight of the aforementioned concerns and many others that arose. We started by working with students and their teachers before they ever entered our high school.

### *Partnering With the Sender Schools*

Often, high school teachers will blame middle schools and junior highs for not adequately preparing students for the high school experience. We knew that complaining would not increase learning for our students, so we set aside time for a series of meetings with the goal of building partnerships with our sender schools. We wanted to make certain that these meetings were more than talk, so seventh- and eighth-grade teachers from the sender schools and ninth-grade teachers from the high school were released from their teaching assignments to meet for a few hours every other week for three months. The meetings built eighth-grade exit and ninth-grade entrance assessments that we could use to measure student learning. With the learning targets clearly established and assessments for measurements in place, the sender schools knew what they were responsible for teaching.

After establishing the targets and building the assessments, the middle schools concentrated on making sure that the students would learn the essential skills and content that the seventh-, eighth-, and ninth-grade teachers had mutually agreed on. When the first round of assessment results came in around January (the traditional placement and registration time), the teachers from the sender schools and the high school together looked at the student-performance information. The results were used to make preliminary placement decisions and to give teachers feedback about achieving the learning goals; the data could also be used in a formative way to attack learning gaps in the final months of school and in the summer program that would serve as a bridge between middle and high school.

Often the specific skill sets or content knowledge that determine whether a student is placed in a remedial class, a regular class, or an honors program are not clearly defined, and placement is left to test scores and teacher recommendations. In our program, we had clear demarcations, and the learning gaps identified through the exit and entrance exam that would have placed students in a remedial class were addressed instead throughout the remainder of eighth grade and in a mandatory summer school session. If students wanted to be in an honors class, they would work during the remainder of the eighth grade and in a summer jump program on meeting the standards they were missing.

Thus, we really had two major goals as we examined the exit and entrance data. We wanted as many students as possible in the honors classes, and we wanted all students prepared for our regular program, since we had eliminated remedial classes. We used the student-performance information from the exit and entrance exams and were aggressive and proactive. Traditionally, schools will use the information from entrance exams to sort students: the scores will dictate placement. Sometimes, students are restricted from participation in the more rigorous classes or are placed in remedial courses. We had a very different approach.

### Outreach

We used the data to actively recruit students who had just missed the cutoff scores. We talked to these students and their families about how with a little more instruction and support they would be ready for success in our school's most rigorous classes. We shared the research from Clifford Adelman's (1998) *Answers in the Toolbox: Academic Intensity, Attendance Patterns, and Bachelor's Degree Attainment*, which stated that the number-one factor in determining bachelor's degree completion was the rigor of the high school curriculum. Opening wide the admission gates to our honors and Advanced Placement courses was not enough. Our administration met with parents, sat down to pizza with small groups of students we were recruiting, talked about how college admission counselors would be impressed, attempted to inspire them, and made presentations with teachers who explained that they were behind the initiative to include more students and would be there to support students who started to struggle. Teachers also helped to create peer-mentoring teams, and most AP teachers added after-school and Sunday-night extra-help sessions for any student who was interested.

Some critics claimed that all we had done was have more students take the classes and exams. We countered with the data that showed that there was an almost 300 percent increase in the number of passed exams and the number of students passing exams, and a 300 percent increase in the number of Advanced Placement scholars. The Chicago Area Directors of Curriculum and Assessment (CADCA) ranked our school fourth in Illinois using an index that examined how many passed exams each high school had per 100 students. Our high school's performance on the excellence and equity rating (a scale created by the College Board that determines the percentage of the graduating class that had passed an Advanced Placement exam) also more than doubled during this time frame.

Beyond all the data, the reputation at the school had improved. While difficult to measure, confidence and pride increased within the walls of RB. They became a part of our culture, and there was a general expectation that students would take rigorous schedules and that teachers would support them. The RB reputation spread outside its walls, too. Many schools visited to learn about the RB Advanced Placement program and commitment to *learning for all*. Many adopted our practices and programs and realized significant achievement gains of their own. In addition to the significant increase in the number of exams that had been passed, we also believed there was great value for the students who would have been excluded in the past. Although some of these students did not pass the exams, they had been challenged and exposed to a more rigorous curriculum.

Jay Mathews, the journalist behind the *Challenge Index*, and the person who has probably spent the most time in American high schools, argues throughout his work the importance of giving students the opportunity to take the most rigorous courses. His thinking is echoed in *The Toolbox Revisited: Paths to Degree Completion From High School Through College* (2006), Clifford Adelman's follow up to *Answers in the Tool Box* (1998). We took to heart the report's directive to students: "Take the challenging course work in high school, and don't let anyone scare you away from it" (p. 103). In fact, a full class of students who under the old system would have been placed in remedial classes ended up taking Advanced Placement courses at RB before they graduated.

Supporting a record number of students to find success in rigorous classes was a priority. Perhaps our greatest passion, though, was preparing the students who had significant learning gaps for success in our regular curriculum. We examined information regarding the students who had dropped out and not graduated in the previous ten years, and it came as no surprise that a disproportionate percentage of these students had entered high school with low entrance-exam scores, poor grades, and serious learning gaps. Just because we had eliminated the remedial courses did not mean that the learning deficiencies would no longer exist.

### Mandating Summer School

We were expecting our teachers to close learning gaps, make up lost ground, and maintain a rigorous learning pace. They made it clear that they would need more time. In addition to working with our colleagues at the sender schools in true professional learning community fashion by (1) establishing clear learning targets, (2) examining students' performance information from collaboratively built assessments aligned with the learning targets, (3) strategizing together in implementing successful reteaching and reassessing measures, and (4) measuring growth from second-chance learning opportunities, we also mandated summer school for all students who were entering high school below grade level in reading or math. We knew very well the students who were coming to us behind in their learning. They could not afford to lose more ground by not attending school for three months, and we could not allow them to take the summer off.

Yes, there was a cost involved in maintaining a summer school program. However, for the price that equaled less than two coaching stipends, we were able to present data that showed how integral this program was in catching students up in their learning and keeping students on track for graduation. The summer school teachers would compare pre–summer school to post–summer school data, clearly demonstrating that some of the learning gaps were being closed. In time, our school also had the increased graduation rate information, and we explicitly made the case to the board of education that the summer school program was essential to the graduation rate increases. The administration and faculty demonstrated that the district's investment was leading to more student success.

I will not pretend that all students were up to grade level after the summer session, or even that all students were at grade level by the time they finished high school. However, by the time this class reached senior year, our school had a graduation rate of 99.1 percent. Students who transferred to another high school were not counted for or against our rate, but we were accountable for the students who transferred into our school even if they arrived in tenth, eleventh, or twelfth grade and were deficient in credits. Furthermore, Riverside Brookfield's student-achievement scores (as measured by the previously mentioned Prairie State Achievement Examination) ranked in the top 5 percent in the state for both performance and improvement. During this time, the percentage of students identified for the free and reduced-price lunch program increased, while spending per pupil adjusted for inflation remained the same. The mandatory summer school intervention was crucial to this success.

The summer session, which ran Monday through Thursday for three and a half hours a day for five weeks, gave the students and teachers a running start as they began their high school experience. We used the specific learning target data culled from the articulation efforts to focus the curriculum. It was a valuable chance to start to close learning gaps and build relationships.

John Hattie's (2009) research points to the significant impact teacher-student relationships have on student achievement. We believed that having students and teachers staying together for over three years would establish powerful bonds. Teachers would have a greater knowledge of their students and their students' learning styles. We specifically recruited teachers who were willing to commit to this concept and be held accountable for their students' success. The goals set for this team (and our high school), including graduation rate, test scores, and Advanced Placement participation increases, were all exceeded. It started with building relationships and addressing learning gaps in the mandatory summer session focused on getting students ready for success in algebra, building literacy skills with an emphasis on improving students' reading, and sending the message that with effort they could succeed in school.

Many people have asked how we made summer sessions mandatory. We held orientation and registration presentations in February and invited all students who would be starting in ninth grade to attend the summer session so the targeted students would not feel stigmatized. We talked about how top student athletes would never take the summer off from practice. We cited research about learning loss for certain students who took the summer off. We asked the coaches, club sponsors, and fine arts sponsors to support our efforts and encourage their students to attend, and we had them build summer practice schedules to accommodate the summer learning session. If students needed financial help, they received it. If they had a family vacation, time off was excused. If they had 95 percent attendance, they would receive a 50 percent rebate on a very low $125 tuition fee. Students would also receive 0.5 elective credits that would give them a jump start toward the credits they would need for graduation.

We also explained to students and their families about how most thirteen- or fourteen-year-olds were not very productive during summer mornings, that they would still have a few weeks after eighth grade and before ninth grade during which there was no class, and that every week would still be a three-day weekend off from school.

Some of the students who really needed the summer program were still not convinced. We identified these students, made phone calls, and met with the students and their parents, family by family. As principal, I personally called the families and students who remained resistant or were nonresponsive and asked for a meeting with the family and student. I would sit down, face to face, at whatever time in the morning, afternoon, or evening worked for the family and outlined the learning gaps and skill deficiencies that had been identified and talked about how we would address these gaps during the summer session so the students would be better prepared for success once the school year started. The one-on-one family meetings usually worked. Seeing that we could use information from the entrance or exit exam in a formative way to address specific learning needs made a difference.

We would problem solve with families on any issue. Our driving argument was not only that our work with students is sacred but also that students themselves are sacred. Our students were only going to go through high school once, and we wanted them to be successful; we emphasized that this was not a punishment, and that the students had done nothing wrong. We cared about every student too much to ignore learning gaps that were only going to get worse without being directly addressed.

Of course, there were students who did not want to give up part of their summer. We tried to use humor, talked about how they would still have afternoons, three-day weekends, and two weeks before the summer session and two weeks again before school started. We shared how the teachers were planning cookouts and fun activities during and after the session. We pulled out all the stops to let them know how important they were to us and how important this session was to their future success.

In the end, only a small handful of students had poor attendance. We made sure to show those who did attend, through formative assessments linked to the learning targets we had identified, that their time in the summer session had led to some increases in learning. Some of their skill deficiencies had been addressed, and the teachers had a chance to build relationships and better understand individual student's learning styles and needs. We also sent the message that we cared about them deeply and that together we were going to be successful at Riverside Brookfield High School.

### Systematic Tracking

When school started in the fall, we implemented a systematic and more intense approach to tracking student progress. To more closely monitor student performance, we took our cue from *Professional Learning Communities at Work* (DuFour et al., 2008) and changed our progress reports from once every five weeks (the midpoint of every quarter) to weekly updates on every student.

For years, eligibility reports were required for every athlete on a weekly basis. If it is important to track the progress of our athletes, then why not monitor every student? We asked our teachers to identify every student who had a grade of D or F on a weekly basis. When our programs were fully implemented, teachers would review the specific progress of their students in mastering learning targets in their department meetings (these teams met during the forty-five minutes we set aside each week as PLC time); teachers would review student performance as part of their grade-level meetings (we built the schedule so teachers on the same grade-level team had the same prep period so they could meet to plan and discuss); and teachers, administrators, and members of the guidance team formed a data team that would review the weekly progress reports to make certain that students who were not making the grade would receive the appropriate intervention.

The interventions were determined by the team and focused on doing whatever was needed to see that our students were successful. This would include but not be limited to adding an academic support period for students in need; making schedule changes if necessary; providing additional tutoring; calling for a parent meeting or a full staff meeting initiating classroom observations of the student to learn more about the particular situation; setting up one-on-one meetings with the counselor, assistant principal, or principal; or providing social work services or other interventions available through our intervention pyramid.

## A Team Approach to Academic Support for Students in Need

As a school, we knew we wanted to provide additional time and practice for students who were not mastering essential learning targets; to make certain that there was intense daily support to address the academic and social and emotional needs of these students; and to build time into the day so they could be provided with second-chance learning opportunities to demonstrate success through formative assessments. The academic support center and class, the academic support position, and the interdisciplinary transition team were created and implemented to follow through on these concerns and meet the needs of those of our students who were struggling.

### The Interdisciplinary Transition Team

The teachers on the transition team were part of an interdisciplinary team that included a core group of students they had in common. However, the teachers also participated in department work, where teachers would use information from common formative assessments to learn from each other and improve their instruction, curriculum, and assessments in their content area.

The students benefited from this coordinated team. The team members were constantly communicating with each other about the progress of the students they had in common. They could problem solve together and support and reinforce each other's work. In the vast majority of high schools, teachers have no idea if they even have students in common, let alone conversations about students they might share. When a teacher had a challenge with a particular student, that teacher could often rely on a team member who might enjoy a better relationship with this student to help improve the situation.

### Academic Support Center

One of the most impactful interventions was an academic support center, staffed by an academic support person. This educator was expected to be a big brother or sister, advocate, mentor, tutor, and liaison between teachers and students and between home and school, and someone who would be dedicated to the whatever-it-takes philosophy, so all students would reach their full learning potential and graduate. (Examples of overviews that explain the class or position created by academic support educators and distributed to the students are provided in figure 8.2, pages 186–187.) The academic support period was built into the students' schedules so they would receive support services from the academic support center educator on whatever basis was needed.

### The Academic Support Person

This position was vital to the interdisciplinary transition team success. The person selected for this responsibility had to possess strong interpersonal and organizational skills. His or her primary focus would be on helping students stay on track for graduation and support them in reaching their full potential in their academic courses.

The academic support person received training in executive functioning, goal setting, study skills, and time management and taught the students in the academic support class all of these skills. While building positive relationships with the students in the program, the academic support person was in regular contact with parents and guardians. The person who had this position took pride in being proactive and consistently would call home with specific, positive feedback about student performance. In addition to developing positive relationships between home and school, this educator was charged with helping to teach better organization skills to students who were forgetful, inattentive, or having a hard time juggling all of their classes and responsibilities. The academic support person also helped to facilitate the formative assessment process by working closely with teachers to coordinate additional time and practice for students. The classroom teachers still took the lead on formative assessments, but the academic support person helped with coordination, reteaching at times, and whatever the team and student needed to master essential learning.

This academic support person started working with his or her group of students in the summer before ninth grade and would meet with them every day during the academic support center time through the end of the students' junior year. Even the most diligent and concerned counselor would find it impossible to meet with every individual student every week, let alone every day. In this program, the academic support person would see his or her students *every day for three years*. The student load for the academic support educator would run from seventy-five to eighty-five students. This educator was also a member of a team that would stay with its core group of students for the first three years of high school. The team would share a planning time and a lunch period, and communicate every day throughout the day through email, letters attached to assignments and assessments, and hallway conversations.

## Monitoring

This coordinated effort was intense and provided constant monitoring of student progress. If a student missed an assignment or needed additional time and practice on a skill or concept during a class period, the teacher could email this information to the academic support person, who would be waiting and ready to follow through and support the student later in the day (or the next morning), having full knowledge of the student's learning needs.

Figure 8.2 shows how academic support educators described their responsibilities and the academic support class in the handout that was given to all students in the program.

**Academic Support, Riverside Brookfield High School**

Renee Ramsey

Student Name: _____

### What Is Academic Support?

Academic support is a program created to provide students with additional help they may need on any homework, papers, or projects assigned in their classes. As a student in the academic support program, you are at a great advantage over the other students at RB. I am here to be your tutor, helper, go-to person, or whatever you want to call me for one class period a day. Other students at RB have to find additional help through a variety of teachers, while you already have a class embedded in your schedule to receive this help. This means that your time spent in academic support should be used wisely and never wasted. I will also be available for help before school from 7:00 a.m. to 8:00 a.m. and after school from 3:05 p.m. to 3:25 p.m. Please use this extra help when needed.

### What Is Miss Ramsey's Role?

I am your advocate. What does this mean? I am here to support and defend you. Throughout the school year, I will provide you with help in your studies, make sure you are staying on track with your homework assignments, provide you with confidence and any support you need to succeed in your classes, and be there if you ever need someone to talk to. You should feel comfortable to come see me, in or out of class, if you need to talk or if you ever need help.

### How Should My Time Be Used in Academic Support?

This is not a class set up for you to talk to your friends, listen to headphones, run around, or do any other nonschool-focused activity. In this class you will do work. Work is defined as homework, catch-up or makeup work, reading (classroom-assigned reading), retaking a test or quiz, writing an outline or essay, doing research for a paper or project, and getting some help from me. That is the reason I am here. If you insist that you have nothing to work on, then I will find something for you to complete.

### What If You Have No Homework?

This situation may come up occasionally. When it does occur, then you have to complete an "I Had No Homework Form." You will need to take this form to every one of your teachers and have them sign it. The form must be returned to me the next day with signatures from every teacher confirming that you had no homework in your classes. I expect you to come prepared every day and ready to work. If you complete your work, then you are responsible to keep busy and quiet. Our classroom is located in the library, so it will not be hard for you to receive reading material. Please do not disturb your classmates who are working.

*Source: Riverside Brookfield High School.*

Figure 8.2: Handout describing academic support.

*Visit **go.solution-tree.com/rtiatwork** for a reproducible version of this figure.*

The positive effects of the tight-knit nature of these teams, the immediate and specific follow-through, and the deep relationships among teacher-team members and between teachers and students cannot be overstated. The teachers and academic support person met during the summer to build a game plan for the upcoming year. They shared learning targets and assessments. The content-area teachers would help build the skill set of the academic support person. The team was very clear about what it was attempting to accomplish during the school year and what the students needed to learn.

Almost every morning, the team (consisting of the academic support person, a math teacher, and an English teacher—and in later years a science teacher or counselor might have been included) would meet for twenty to thirty minutes before school to discuss the learning targets for the day and the assignments, assessments, and needs of individual students. This team often would have a daily common planning period to further strategize and address student learning, and team members would also share lunch together. Throughout the day, they would phone each other, email important communications, staple a quick message to an unfinished assessment or incomplete homework assignment, and perhaps even visit each other's rooms.

As soon as a student started to struggle, he or she was provided follow-through and support. If a student failed to turn in an important homework assignment, this was communicated immediately to the academic support person. Often, the support person had the student fish a crumpled up, semi-completed homework assignment out of a book bag or locker, or provided the student with a new assignment, helped with the work, and had the student turn it in within twenty-four hours, so there was no missed assignment.

### Immediate Intervention

The team was dedicated to mastery learning, formative assessment, and a grading system of A, B, C, and "Not Yet" ("Not Yet" replaced F and served almost as an incomplete and required additional work from both the student and teacher) in pursuit of learning for all. When a student failed an assessment, the team would insist that the student retake or redo the exam, quiz, test, essay, or project. Social and emotional needs were also addressed. I have often thought what I would not give to have someone in my life whom I could meet with on a daily basis to help answer questions when I got stuck, support me to improve the quality of my work, and kick me in the butt when I was procrastinating. This is what the academic support person did for our students.

The academic support period was built into the students' schedule and served multiple purposes, depending on the need of the students on a particular day. The seven-period schedule allowed each student on the team a full academic load of six classes plus the academic support center class. The additional time and practice that our students needed was guaranteed every day. This use of the time was flexible and met several learning needs for the students. On one day, they might be retaught a concept they were struggling with. The next day, they might receive extended time on an assessment. The following day, they might retake an assessment. If students had failed to turn in homework, they completed the assignment during this time, or on certain days, they might just complete their homework under the watchful supervision of a caring advocate who was in constant contact with most of their teachers.

At times, students still needed to attend before- and after-school tutoring sessions with their teachers. However, every day, there was a guarantee that students would receive additional time and practice so they would remain successful in school.

## Strategies for Creating Time

Where did we find time to make this happen? Here are a few of the ways.

- Retakes and redos: Teachers would allow for these in their classroom when possible and advisable.

- Academic support class: Each day there were fifty additional minutes for reteaching, learning, and retakes, and for students to demonstrate mastery through second-chance learning and assessment opportunities. Students who were up-to-date in all of their work would use the time to read and study.

- Retake Fridays: Teachers in the program would allow students the opportunity to retake quizzes and tests. On occasion, teachers would allow for retakes on an as-needed basis throughout the school year.

- Blitz sessions: Twice a quarter, we held an extended work session lasting three hours, where we would buy the students pizza and they would stay after school, complete work to demonstrate mastery, and retake assessments to show they had met standards. For students who had been sick and needed to catch up, these sessions were most helpful. For students who transferred into our school in the middle of the semester, the sessions provided needed additional time.

- Intelligent Summer School: In our Intelligent Summer School program, students were told that they had to meet the learning standard. It might take the students all of the regular school year, or it might take the school year and a day, or the school year and a week, or an additional month. It depended on the pace at which the students could learn. When the student met the standard, he or she was done with the course. As an example, if the C grade meant mastering seven out of ten standards and the student had mastered five at the end of the school year, that student would focus on the two standards he or she had not completed and would be finished with the course when he or she had demonstrated mastery on the additional two standards.

- Looping: The teachers who were a part of this program met their students in summer school prior to ninth grade and remained with this common group of students until the end of junior year. This meant that the students would have the same math teacher for algebra, geometry, and advanced algebra. They would have the same English teacher for English 9, 10, and 11. They would also see the same academic support person every day for three years. This concept, sometimes called "looping," is rarely used at the high school level. However, it should be noted that during the six-year period of time that this model was fully implemented, only 1 percent of the students in the program dropped out of high school or did not graduate. Keep in mind that the program targeted the students who were at highest risk of dropping out and not graduating. The graduation rate during the implementation of this program/intervention was in the top 1–2 percent of all high schools in Illinois.

- Because one teacher had focused on preparing students to meet the standards they were expected to reach at the end of junior year, gaps in curriculum were minimized. The teachers knew their students well, and many powerful relationships were formed.

## Financial Costs

One potential obstacle to implementing this intervention program was the cost. In the end, this intervention, with all its benefits, turned out to be cost neutral. However, it took some work to get there. For the academic support center to work, the student load in every class had to be limited. We were asking an educator to fulfill all of the responsibilities we have described (from tutor to advocate to liaison and more), and so class size had to be reduced for teachers to be effective. Early on, each team had approximately seventy-five to eighty students. We wanted to limit each period of academic support to no more than fifteen students (which in itself presented some challenges). However, this proved to be a manageable number.

One way to afford this additional and very valuable support was to hire the academic support person on a lesser pay scale than the faculty salary schedule. We found many highly qualified and dedicated people who received about 65 percent of what a full-time faculty member would have been paid. Almost all of these educators remained on the team for the three-year duration.

Most of those who took on this position were fully certified teachers who could not find full-time teaching jobs. Some were transitioning from another profession to teaching, and this was an ideal position for those who wanted experience in the education world but still needed to gain their certification. A few were teachers who were seeking their certification as counselors, and this was a great learning opportunity as they transitioned to their new role.

The excellent news is that most of the educators who stayed in this role for the three years not only found it extremely rewarding but were also hired in full-time and full-paying faculty or counseling positions. Most, in fact, ended up at Riverside Brookfield High School, while several used the high-quality and unique experience to gain full-time teaching jobs in other schools.

The students took what is certainly a full load with six classes, but their seventh class might have been an additional elective. Instead, they took academic support, which made sense because the trend data indicated that many students who had similar test scores and grades in middle school took six or seven classes but often only passed less than five (sometimes only one or two, which led to dropping out). Did it not make more sense for students to take six with academic support and pass six rather than take seven and pass five or less?

## Protecting the Electives

Another obstacle was that elective teachers feared that this approach would harm their programs and enrollment. We showed how, if these students stayed on track for graduation, more students would not have to retake core classes, and more would be around to take electives in eleventh and twelfth grade. We also made sure to maintain extra core and elective classes during the implementation of this program. In the end, we were able to provide our students tremendous, daily academic support, increase student learning, and protect our electives, all while not increasing costs.

There was concern about how one person could be trained to tutor in a variety of subjects and implement the interventions in a high-quality way. We had to remember that in the first year, a college graduate was asked to tutor in algebra, English 9, biology, and an introductory social studies course. They were not tutoring Advanced Placement calculus or physics students. The academic support person would often have to do some refreshing or learning from team members in certain content areas to become proficient in the skills and content he or she was being called on to tutor.

## Logistics of Support

Every day, the student was guaranteed fifty minutes of intervention that could be used for whatever need arose. We had seven periods that were fifty minutes each. Once a week, on PLC days, the classes ran forty-five minutes to make time for teachers for PLC work (the teachers also came in fifteen minutes early on these days). A full academic schedule was six classes. Students could take a study hall or early release, they could volunteer in the building, or they could take a seventh class. The students in this program took the academic support as their seventh class. Thus, this fifty-minute class was used for additional time and practice on a daily basis. It was used for tutoring, reteaching, completing assignments, or retaking assessments. The team would decide which intervention was most appropriate for each student on each day. Often, the academic support person would have to work with students to prioritize what work needed to be addressed first. On the same day that a student might need help with a concept that he or she did not understand in math class, he or she might also need to complete a homework assignment in science and revise a paper for English. The academic support person would help organize the student's time and direct him or her to stay after school to ensure that all work was completed. The presence of support meant that a young, sometimes disorganized, and perhaps challenged student would not have to juggle this all alone.

At the macro level, the academic support person checked overall student performance in all of the student's six classes. He or she had access to all of the student's grades and could communicate with all of the student's teachers. Every teacher at Riverside Brookfield High School was responsible for completing weekly grades, so at a glance, the academic support person could check to see how successful students were in their classes at any given time.

At the micro level, teachers used formative assessments on a regular basis to monitor progress. As soon as a student struggled with a concept, the teacher would intervene. If there was not ample time to address the learning need during the class period, the specific learning gap would be communicated to the academic support center, and remediation would begin. If even more time was needed, the academic support center person and teacher could collaborate to provide additional interventions to meet the student's learning need.

There were a few times when the team (including the academic support person) could not problem solve and offer interventions that would lead to student success. When these times did occur, the student's counselor would be consulted. At times, the administration was called on to offer ideas. Outside agencies, including social workers and psychologists, would also be brought to the table.

While this intervention proved to be very successful, there were several problems that arose requiring adjustments along the way. The first three teams (who ended up staying together for three years) had a disproportionate number of academically challenged students (as determined by Explore and Stanford scores and recommendations from the sender schools). This, of course, led to a more homogeneous group than we desired. We were getting results, but some of the students felt stigmatized, and the English teachers were stating they were burned out after the three-year loop. The sentiment from the English teacher who had just completed the experience was that this was a success, he was glad he had been a part of it, but he would not do it again. The second English teacher expressed a similar opinion. The math teachers in the first two teams each gladly signed up for and completed a second three-year loop.

The English teachers said they felt that their subject, especially interpreting literature, involved teachers offering personal opinions and that students would benefit from hearing different perspectives during their high school years. Our administration struggled with this issue, and in time we compromised and had one teacher who was designated as a team ninth-grade teacher still working as a member of the interdisciplinary team, while a different teacher would stay with the team and students for tenth and eleventh grades.

Another adjustment was to create a second team at each grade level. Instead of having eighty students (or approximately 20–25 percent of the class) on a team, we built two teams of ninety each, so over half the class was experiencing the team concept. The negative association or stigma with being in a team setting was removed, because over half the grade was *on* one of the teams. The teams were also more heterogeneous, which led to several positive outcomes; the stigma was removed, and more students were benefiting from the team concept. With so many of the students now part of this program, there were students on each team who did not have and did not really need the daily intervention of the academic support center and the academic support person. But they were still part of the culture of achievement.

Students who would have been placed in remedial classes without the changes that had been made were now sometimes having success in AP courses. The teams started creating honors sections, and students on the team were participating in Advanced Placement classes in their senior year.

## The Results of PLC

The Riverside Brookfield High School success story owes to PLC principles. As one can tell from this account, implementing PLC took dedication, commitment, and passion. The results track closely against the three SMART goals on which the team collaborated.

First, from ten years prior to the development of the program to the six-year mark during implementation, RB experienced an 8–10 percent improvement in the graduation rate. Second, the school achieved significant student learning gains as measured by the state's NCLB-mandated exam. Third, by 2006, the school had the most improved AP program in Illinois and one of the top-ten most improved programs in the nation.

In addition to meeting the collaboratively built SMART goals, RB increased its standing in several nationwide rankings, and ranked fourth out of 148 suburban high schools for growth in the ACT from demographic expectations.

Statistics tell a great story, but all of us on the team know what lies behind the numbers and growth.

The most powerful and rewarding aspects of the work done at Riverside Brookfield involved being a member of a cohesive team that pulled together, dreamed big, and remained committed to the idea that all students are sacred and capable of doing quality work. No doubt we saw the best in each other. However, dissent and team conflict helped us see something important about each other and working together. With a philosophical commitment to *learning for all,* and interventions that brought this commitment to life, the team at Riverside Brookfield High School made a powerful difference in the lives of our students.

I wish you the best on your journey to be a part of a team that has a positive impact on the lives of your students. All of us in education will face troubled students who do not see the value of their education and have lost hope—but we can be the champions of hope and give support to those most in need. I cannot think of a better way to spend a lifetime.

Visit **go.solution-tree.com/rtiatwork** for a full list and description of the many RTI strategies at Riverside Brookfield High School, as well as a look at how the principles that succeeded at RB are now helping to make a difference at Westmont.

# References

Adelman, C. (1998). *Answers in the tool box: Academic intensity, attendance patterns, and bachelor's degree attainment.* Washington, DC: US Department of Education.

Adelman, C. (2006, February). *The toolbox revisited: Paths to degree completion from high school through college.* Accessed at https://www2.ed.gov/rschstat/research/pubs/toolboxrevisit /toolbox.pdf on August 25, 2014.

Bailey, K., & Jakicic, C. (2012). *Common formative assessment: A toolkit for professional learning communities at work.* Bloomington, IN: Solution Tree Press.

Bain, K. (2004). *What the best college teachers do.* Cambridge, MA: Harvard University Press.

Ben-Shahar, T. (2007). *Happier: Learn the secrets to daily joy and lasting fulfillment.* New York: McGraw-Hill.

Black, P., & William, D. (1998). Inside the black box: Raising standards through classroom assessment. *Phi Delta Kappan, 80*(2), 139–148.

Buffum, A., Mattos, M., & Weber, C. (2009). *Pyramid response to intervention: RTI, professional learning communities, and how to respond when kids don't learn.* Bloomington, IN: Solution Tree Press.

Buffum, A., Mattos, M., & Weber, C. (2012). *Simplifying response to intervention: Four essential guiding principles.* Bloomington, IN: Solution Tree Press.

Burke, D. J. (1995). Connecting content and motivation: Education's missing link. *Peabody Journal of Education, 70*(2), 66–81.

Chapman, C., & Vagle, N. (2011). *Motivating students: 25 strategies to light the fire of engagement.* Bloomington, IN: Solution Tree Press.

Csikszentmihalyi, M. (1990). *Flow: The psychology of the optimal experience.* New York: HarperCollins.

Deci, E., Koestner, R., & Ryan, R. M. (2001). Extrinsic rewards and intrinsic motivation in education: Reconsidered once again. *Review of Educational Research, 71*(1), 1–27.

DuFour, R., DuFour, R., & Eaker, R. (2008). *Revisiting professional learning communities at work: New insights for improving schools.* Bloomington, IN: Solution Tree Press.

DuFour, R., DuFour, R., Eaker, R., & Karhanek, G. (2004). *Whatever it takes: How professional learning communities respond when kids don't learn.* Bloomington, IN: Solution Tree Press.

DuFour, R., & Eaker, R. (1998). *Professional learning communities at work: Best practices for enhancing student achievement.* Bloomington, IN: Solution Tree Press.

Dweck, C. S. (2006). *Mindset: The new psychology of success.* New York: Random House.

Frymier, J. R. (1970). Motivation: The mainspring and gyroscope of learning. *Theory Into Practice, 9*(1), 23–32.

Gallagher, K. (2004). *Deeper reading: Comprehending challenging texts, 4–12.* Portland, ME: Stenhouse.

Goodwin, B., & Hubbell, E. R. (2013). *The 12 touchstones of good teaching: A checklist for staying focused every day.* Alexandria, VA: Association for Supervision and Curriculum Development.

Gostlick, A., & Elton, C. (2011). *All In: How the best managers create a clture of belief and drive big results.* New York: Free Press.

Gray, T., & Madson, L. (2007). Ten easy ways to engage your students. *College Teaching, 55*(2), 83–85.

Hattie, J. A. C. (2009). *Visible learning: A synthesis of over 800 meta-analyses relating to achievement.* New York: Routledge.

Hattie, J. A. C. (2012). *Visible learning for teachers: Maximizing impact on learning.* New York: Routledge.

Hidi, S., & Harackiewicz, J. (2000). Motivating the academically unmotivated: A critical issue for 21st century. *Review of Educational Research, 70*(2), 151–179.

Lepper, M. R. (1988). Motivational considerations in the study of instruction. *Cognition and Instruction, 5*(4), 289–309.

Levine, M. (2003). *The myth of laziness.* New York: Simon & Schuster.

Marzano, R. J. (2000). *Transforming classroom grading.* Alexandria, VA: Association for Supervision and Curriculum Development.

Marzano, R. J. (2006). *Classroom assessment & grading that work.* Alexandria, VA: Association for Supervision and Curriculum Development.

Marzano, R. J., Norford, J. S., Paynter, D. E., Pickering, D. J., & Gaddy, B. B. (2001). *A handbook for classroom instruction that works.* Alexandria, VA: Association for Supervision and Curriculum Development.

Marzano, R. J., Pickering, D. J., & Pollock, J. E. (2001). *Classroom instruction that works: Research-based strategies for increasing student achievement.* Alexandria, VA: Association for Supervision and Curriculum Development.

Milton, O., Pollio, H. R., & Eison, J. A. (1986). *Making sense of college grades: Why the grading system does not work and what can be done about it.* San Francisco: Jossey-Bass.

O'Connor, K. (2009). *How to grade for learning: K–12* (3rd ed.). Thousand Oaks, CA: Corwin Press.

O'Connor, K. (2011). *A repair kit for grading: 15 fixes for broken grades* (2nd ed.). Boston: Pearson.

Pink, D. H. (2009). *Drive: The surprising truth about what motivates us.* New York: Riverhead Books.

Porter, E. (2013, June 25). Dropping out of college, and paying the price. *New York Times.* Accessed at www.nytimes.com/2013/06/26/business/economy/dropping-out-of-colle-and-paying-the-price.html?_r=0 on March 4, 2014.

Raffini, J. P. (1993). *Winners without losers: Structures and strategies for increasing student motivation to learn.* Boston: Allyn & Bacon.

Reeves, D. B. (2006). *The learning leader: How to focus school improvement for better results.* Alexandria, VA: Association for Supervision and Development.

Reeves, D. B. (Ed.). (2007). *Ahead of the curve: The power of assessment to transform teaching and learning.* Bloomington, IN: Solution Tree Press.

Ripley, A. (2013). *The smartest kids in the world: And how they got that way.* New York: Simon & Schuster.

Schlecty, P. C. (2001). *Shaking up the schoolhouse: How to support and sustain educational innovation.* San Francisco: Jossey-Bass.

Schmoker, M. (2006). *Results now: How we can achieve unprecedented improvements in teaching and learning.* Alexandria, VA: Association for Supervision and Curriculum Development.

Stone, D., Heen, S., & Patton, D. S. (1999). *Difficult conversations: How to discuss what matters most.* New York: Viking.

Tileston, D. W. (2005). *10 best teaching practices: How brain research, learning styles, and standards define teaching competencies* (2nd ed.). Thousand Oaks, CA: Corwin Press.

Wigfield, A., Eccles, J., & Rodriguez, D. (1998). The development of children's motivation in school contexts. *Review of Research in Education, 23,* 73–118.

Wolk, S. (2007, May). Why go to school? *Phi Delta Kappan, 88*(9), 648–658.

Wormeli, R. (2013). *The collected writings (so far) of Rick Wormeli: Crazy good stuff I've learned about teaching along the way.* Westerville, OH: Association for Middle Level Education.

Zeidner, M. (1998). *Test anxiety: The state of the art.* New York: Plenum Press.

**Rich Rodriguez** was principal of Charles W. TeWinkle Middle School (TMS) in Costa Mesa, California, for three years, 2010–2013. During that time, he led the implementation of an effective professional learning community (PLC) and response to intervention model (RTI). Comparing TMS to other middle schools with 85 percent of the student body receiving free or reduced lunch, TMS ranks in the top 10 percent in academic performance and is in the 60 percentile when compared to all middle schools in the state of California. Prior to serving at TeWinkle, Rich Rodriguez was the principal at Newport Coast Elementary School in Newport Coast, California, and led that school in the successful implementation of a PLC / RTI model. During his four years at Newport Coast, he also helped guide the school to a 2010 California Distinguished School Award and raised proficiency rates to the 90-percent level, while raising the Academic Performance Index from 901 to 949 (out of 1,000 points). Most significant was the focus on enrichment. Thirty-five percent of the students scored advanced in 2006; in 2010, that number was 65 percent. Only 2 percent of the students—eleven students—were below basic. The same PLC / RTI model was implemented at both schools. Today Mr. Rodriguez serves as the principal of Newport Elementary School located in Newport Beach, California, where he is implementing the same model that was successful at his previous schools.

To book Rich Rodriguez for professional development, contact pd@solution-tree .com.

# The Power to Change Lives: Creating a Secondary Intensive Reading Intervention Model

Rich Rodriguez

**Editors' Note**

We know that for a student to learn at grade level, that student must be taught at grade level. We also know that some students will enter secondary school lacking foundational literacy skills that should have been mastered years prior. Finally, many of our most at-risk students come from homes in which English is not the primary language, requiring the school to also address this need. This common scenario creates a difficult dilemma: how do we provide some students access to grade-level language arts, remediation in foundational literacy, and targeted English language-development instruction? The detailed example provided by TeWinkle Middle School demonstrates exactly how these three critical learning outcomes can be accomplished within the school day. Equally important, the results the TeWinkle staff achieved demonstrate that, when provided the right intensive supports, secondary students can improve their reading skills by multiple Lexile levels within one school year.

Another important takeaway from TeWinkle's example is how the school used reading programs. Too many schools think that the key to providing intensive reading support begins with buying the "right" program. Honestly, we wish it were that easy. Unfortunately, we currently do not know of a silver bullet, all-inclusive secondary reading program that can meet all the needs of struggling readers. This is because reading is a complex cognitive process, and every struggling reader does not struggle for the same reason. We are not suggesting that there are no effective, scientifically research-based reading intervention programs available. We are suggesting that none of them is a cure-all, but rather all should be seen as additional tools in your intervention toolbox. TeWinkle's intensive reading support is not based on a single reading program but instead consists of a variety of instructional supports to meet the individual needs of each student. Equally important, the school has identified the essential grade-level standards that all students must learn and has embedded them into its intensive reading support to ensure that these students still have access to grade-level curriculum.

Finally, we suspect that some readers, by focusing on the additional support staff that TeWinkle uses to support its reading interventions, might determine that its program cannot be replicated at their school due to a lack of equivalent staffing. Having led schools that had significant categorical funding due to a high number of at-risk youth and schools that were extremely limited due to few categorical funds, we can say with confidence that making the staffing work in both situations is difficult but possible. While schools like TeWinkle might have a few more resources, they also have hundreds of students who need this level of support. At schools with less funding, there are usually far fewer students who demonstrate this level of need. In other words, the resources are usually proportional. As we consistently recommend throughout this anthology, one must instead look at the process TeWinkle used to create its intensive English language arts supports and determine how the same thinking can support your school's efforts to achieve similar results.

---

During the 2011–2012 school year, TeWinkle Middle School served approximately 725 seventh and eighth graders. Its demographic information was as follows.

- Approximately 85 percent of students were on free and reduced lunch.
- 80 percent were Hispanic.
- 45 percent were English learners.
- 55 percent, or 368 students, read at or above grade level.
- 15 percent, or 86 students, read one to two grades below level.
- 30 percent, or 209 students, read three to five grades below level.

Prior to 2010, the school established a number of effective interventions. It opened a before-school and after-school tutoring program with certificated teachers. Transportation was provided in the form of an early bus and a late bus to take the students to and from the tutorials. Teachers agreed to retest students in order to give them additional opportunities to show mastery. The school also opened a mandatory

ZAP (Zeros Aren't Permitted) program. During the day, if students did not complete homework from the previous night, they would be assigned ZAP and would then phone home and let their parents know they would be staying after school to finish their homework. An after-school homework club was also established for students who chronically did not complete their homework. During the school day, two elective sections of reading intervention were opened, during which a basal reading program designed for students reading more than two grades below level was used.

Prior to the beginning of the 2010–2011 school year, the state of California suffered a severe budget crisis, and the following resources were cut from TeWinkle: one security guard, two counselors, the school resource officer, one assistant principal, the money for before- and after-school tutorial teachers, and the cost of bus transportation before and after school. This is the year I became the principal. There comes a time when the results of the changes that have been implemented flatten, and this school was at that stage in 2010. Teachers were working extremely hard, resources were cut, and the Academic Performance Index (API) results remained flat. Because their efforts were not producing the results they once did, many of the staff felt discouraged.

## The Purpose

The staff agreed that about half of our students did not have the reading and writing skills necessary to master the grade-level standards. Thirty percent—209 of our students—read three to five grades below level. These students needed to learn to read! As you can imagine, the needs of students reading at a first- or second-grade level are different from those of students reading at a fourth- or fifth-grade level. It was no wonder that our reading intervention elective classes were not producing the results we hoped; every low reader was placed in the same program.

Our staff knew we needed to create a schedule that would provide additional time for intensive support for our lowest readers. This extra support needed to take place during the school day in small groups, and we knew technology could assist in lowering group size. Flexible grouping was extremely important, because we knew students would progress at different rates. Thus, we needed the ability to move students based on their progress.

Our desired outcome was to increase student reading levels at a rapid rate, in a targeted and systematic manner, as we continued to teach the core curriculum and the grade-level essential reading and writing standards. It is extremely important that the agreed-on essential learning standards are described in student-friendly language, contain agreed-on examples of rigor, identify prerequisite skills and substandards, and determine pacing. Common formative assessments must also be created so the data can be used to revise instruction, and enrichment must be described for students who have already learned the material (Buffum, Mattos, & Weber, 2012). Having this information would provide us the opportunity to align intensive reading intervention to the core instruction, giving the students a double dose of reading.

## The Research

What does an intensive reading intervention model look like, and how do we implement it at our site? Our staff conducted collective inquiry to answer these two questions. We assembled a research team consisting of the principal, a reading coach, teachers from the content areas and special education, and our guidance counselor.

Our research quickly concluded that our school needed to improve our response to intervention (RTI) practices, according to what we referred to as the RTI model, as described in *Pyramid Response to Intervention: RTI, Professional Learning Communities, and How to Respond When Kids Don't Learn* (Buffum, Mattos, & Weber, 2009). Our team used this model as a guide to address the needs of our school and develop a plan to strengthen core instruction. Once this plan was in place, we were ready to build supplemental and intensive interventions for Tiers 2 and 3. The staff appreciated the guidance of the research team and committed to focus on improving core instruction. All content teams spent collaboration time identifying essential learning standards that had endurance, leverage, and readiness (Ainsworth, 2003). This process clarified what was essential: rigor, prerequisite skills, common assessments, and pacing. This was the foundation for the tiered intervention we were about to build. This essential learning chart in figure 9.1 shows the process that all content teams used to determine essential learning (Buffum et al., 2012). This gave us a focus—reading comprehension and writing across all content areas—around which we could collaborate.

Our research team also determined that the following questions needed further research in order to design a plan.

1. How do English learners (ELs) acquire the language and learn to read?

   Our research discovered that planning effective reading instruction and interventions for ELs includes building decoding skills through explicit and intensive instruction in phonological awareness and phonics, vocabulary development, explicitly teaching reading strategies necessary to comprehend narrative and informational text, improvement of oral reading fluency, providing opportunities to engage in discourse, and increasing engagement

**Instructions:** Working in collaborative teams, examine all relevant documents, Common Core State Standards, state standards, and district power standards, and then apply the criteria of endurance, leverage, and readiness to determine that standards are essential for all students to master. Remember, less is more. For each standard selected, complete the remaining columns. Complete this chart by the second or third week of the instructional period (semester).

**What Is It We Expect Students to Learn?**

| Grade: | Subject: | Semester: | Team Members: | | |
|---|---|---|---|---|---|
| **Description of Standard** | **Example of Rigor** | **Prerequisite Skills** | **When Taught** | **Common Summative Assessment** | **Extension Standards** |
| What is the essential standard to be learned? Describe it in student-friendly vocabulary. | What does proficient work look like? Provide an example, description, or both. | What prior knowledge, skills, or vocabulary are needed for a student to master this standard? | When will this standard be taught? | What assessment(s) will be used to measure student mastery? | What will we do when students have already learned this standard? |
| | | | | | |

Figure 9.1: Essential learning chart.

*Visit **go.solution-tree.com/rtiatwork** for a reproducible version of this figure.*

through independent reading (Francis, Kieffer, Lesaux, Rivera, & Rivera, 2006).

2.  How do we foster a culture to support interventions?

    We took a team of six teachers to a two-day RTI training based on *Pyramid Response to Intervention* (Buffum et al., 2009) to help us understand how to develop a structurally sound RTI model.

3. How can we use technology to support student learning?

   Some teachers received training from the Ware Group, a reading software company. This company supplied our district with a research-based reading intervention program called Lexia, which is designed for children and adolescents reading below the third-grade level because it is rich in phonics. They also supplied another reading program called Reading Plus. This was designed for students reading at or above the third-grade level and focused mainly on comprehension skills and reading words per minute. This program was available to schools in our district.

4. How do we design our master schedule to accommodate blocks of time for core and reading remediation?

   The team looked at various master schedules to get ideas as to how we could begin the intensive intervention process with our current master schedule. We also were looking for ideas to design the master schedule for the following year.

5. How do we use curriculum-based measurements to screen and diagnose reading deficits?

   We learned we needed a screening and reading diagnostic assessment component in order to determine the exact levels of the students and areas of need for each student. There are a number of publishers who provide curriculum-based measurements for reading screenings and diagnostic assessments (for example, AIMSweb, DIBELS, easyCBM, and Intervention Central). Our site used *Assessing Reading: Multiple Measures for Kindergarten Through Twelfth Grade (Second edition)* (Consortium on Reading Excellence, 2008). Professional development was necessary.

6. How do we implement a balanced reading intervention model that addresses phonics, vocabulary, fluency, and comprehension to align with our core curriculum?

   Because approximately 30 percent of our students were three to five grades below reading level and we could not place this number of students in intervention classes, we needed to change our approach to teaching in Tier 1 and Tier 2. We took twelve of our teachers to a one-week CORE (Consortium on Reading Excellence) training on the teaching of reading to at-risk adolescents. This knowledge led us to research the teaching of word study and look at how the developmental stages directly correlate to our reading intervention model (Invernizzi, Johnston, Bear, & Templeton, 2009). This became an important intervention tool that helped our students in phonics study and decoding.

All of this research and training became the foundation for our reading intervention model. Our model was based on the identified reading and writing essential learning standards determined by the teaching teams at grade level. We used the diagnostic tools to determine what each child needed and determined the appropriate targeted intervention to administer. Our plan called for small-group, targeted instruction; more time with a trained teacher; additional student engagement with frequent progress monitoring; and support with a computer-based reading program.

## The Obstacles

We faced two major obstacles. The first was, How do we create a master schedule that will provide ELA classes for our at-risk readers to receive Tier 1 access to grade-level curriculum, as well as classes to provide Tier 3 intervention? The second concern was, Who would teach the core and intervention sections?

The first issue was difficult to solve, given that we had so many students reading below grade level and could not create enough intervention with a traditional master schedule to address the needs of this many students. Our research team found a way to create additional intervention time within our current traditional schedule—we would use our intervention support team. The team consisted of the reading coach, special education teachers, two hourly support teachers, the librarian, two aides, and the ELA and intervention classroom teachers. This team would push into one or more classroom sections to systematically work with our low readers. Specifically, we analyzed the reading diagnostic data for every at-risk reader. These data allowed us to group students by need and approximate reading grade-level equivalency. We then designed flexible groups specific to our intervention curriculum and created an intervention rotation two to three days a week when our intervention team could implement the reading curriculum during a traditional period. The small groups were based on student needs. Consider the following example, a first-period, eighth-grade English language arts class met from 8:40 to 9:41 a.m., led by teacher number one. There were thirty-five students in this class, eight of whom were enrolled in a reading intervention class as an elective and twelve of whom were reading at or above grade level. Two days a week, Tuesday and Thursday, an intervention team would push in and work with small reading groups based on students' diagnosed needs. Students received thirty minutes of targeted small-group instruction and thirty minutes of computer-based intervention.

The staff group assignments and student-to-teacher ratios are shown in table 9.1.

**Table 9.1: Staff Assignment and Student-to-Teacher Ratios for Reading Intervention**

| Assigned Staff | Group and Reading Grade-Level Equivalency | Student-to-Teacher Ratio |
|---|---|---|
| Reading coach | Group 1, fourth-grade level | 6:1 |
| | Group 2, fourth-grade level | 5:1 |
| Hourly support teacher | Group 1, fifth-grade level | 7:1 |
| | Group 2, sixth-grade level | 5:1 |
| Teacher 1 | Group 1, at grade level (whole period) | 12:1 |
| Librarian | Reading Plus | 10:1 |
| | Reading Plus | 13:1 |

Students in group 1 received thirty minutes of small-group targeted intervention and then went to the computer lab to practice the reading strategies using Lexia or Reading Plus. Group 2 started in the lab for thirty minutes, then went to small-group targeted intervention for thirty minutes.

The key to success is in the planning of the curriculum. Because two days of the week were used for intervention in foundational reading skills, these intervention core classes could not cover all required grade-level curriculum. All students received the essential grade-level curriculum during the three days they did not rotate for reading-intervention groups. Instead, these classes focused exclusively on the grade-level standards that our school's language arts teacher teams deemed essential.

Our second concern was determining who would teach the core and reading intervention courses. We assembled our reading support team, teachers working with our at-risk readers, with the intent of providing them with training in the teaching of reading and training in PLC and RTI. Some of these positions were paid for with Title I, Economic Impact Aid, or Program Improvement funds. Alone, this team could not fix the reading issues on our campus. We concluded that the best way to improve reading was to have a schoolwide focus. This cultural shift would complement our reading intervention sections and provide our students with strategies to help them succeed at the next level. We had to break the practice of teachers sending our students to intervention to be fixed. We all needed to be part of the solution.

Anthony Muhammad (2009) describes transforming school culture as a foundation to support and sustain collaborative teams. He states that toxic cultures do things *to* students and healthy cultures do things *for* students. He is very successful in describing the types of resistance schools face when implementing change. Some schools resist changing long-held practices because the vision is simply unclear. Others resist because there is a lack of trust with the site leadership. Others resist because they need more time and support in order to implement change. Lastly, some reject the change outright, because they philosophically do not agree with it (Muhammad, 2009). In our situation, there was a lot of fear, because our teachers did not have the appropriate experience and training to meet the reading needs of the students on our campus. They simply needed additional time and support. However, they were all very open to professional development and accepting of their roles in changing the entire school culture. It became clear that in all our content areas, including physical education, there existed the opportunity to teach reading and writing skills. This was a major schoolwide accomplishment.

I am a firm believer people can be successful when placed in a supportive environment with the tools necessary to be successful. Our staff members were collaborating and supporting each other to bring about student success. This was the moment we broke the long-held attitude that we send our students to intervention to be fixed. Our staff came to consensus that we would provide weekly lessons in all content areas revolving around close-reading strategies (Schmoker, 2011). This is described as reading with a purpose, annotating, note-taking, discussion, and writing. We sent some staff members to close-reading training and focused on how to implement the strategies schoolwide.

## The Strategy

Our staff spent collaboration time learning how to model close-reading strategies (Schmoker, 2011). We used content articles and textbooks and agreed to implement this instruction on a schoolwide basis at least once a week for fifteen to twenty minutes. Following are the strategies we used.

1. Pick a focus: Our focus when we read will be . . .

   * To infer / interpret / draw conclusions

   * To support an argument with evidence

   * To analyze and evaluate opposing arguments

   * To solve a complex problem

2. Provide background (on topic and text structure) and any needed vocabulary (can be all student generated).

3. Model (think aloud) your questions, thoughts, and connections.

4. Have students think aloud and read in pairs or groups using sentence starters (I think . . . , I agree/disagree . . . , I [don't] understand . . . , I wonder . . . , This reminds me . . .).

5. Give verbal or written reflections on the reading focus.

## The Schedule

The more remediation our students needed, the more intervention time we designed. As our research team explored various schedules and options to deliver intervention, we came to a stunning conclusion: it is not the traditional master schedule that needs to change; rather, it is what you do *within* the schedule. Our master schedule evolved over three years. The schedule for our most intensive readers—those reading four to five grades below level—looked different than the schedule for students reading two to three grades below level. We created pathways. (We purposely avoided the term *tracking* because of the connotation it has of placing low students together with little hope of moving them out of this track.) Traditionally, our honors students travel in the same pathway in order to flow into the honors sections. Similarly, our most recent English learners traveled in a pathway in order for them to access sheltered instruction, which is an approach to teaching language learners that integrates language development and mainstream grade-level content. We simply created a reading pathway for our intensive and strategic readers with built-in flexibility.

The group composed of students reading two to three years below grade level would access a core English language arts and history or intervention elective course pathway. The difference between this pathway and a traditional honors or mainstream path is that we built intervention time into these courses. Table 9.2 shows how we reached students for intervention during fourth period. The support team entered two classes, ELA 7 and ELA 8, serving sixty-eight students, three days a week for thirty minutes. Twenty-six of these students read at or above grade level, thirty-two were strategic (that is, reading between fourth- and sixth-grade level), seven were intensive (that is, reading below the third-grade level), and two left the school. This intervention was designed in addition to the previously described first-period schedule. As we gained experience, we added students to our model.

**Table 9.2: Staff Assignment and Student-to-Teacher Ratios for Reading Intervention**

| Assigned Staff | Group and Reading Grade-Level Equivalency | Student-to-Teacher Ratio |
|---|---|---|
| Librarian | First- and second-grade level | 7:1 |
| Reading coach | Fourth-grade level | 7:1 |
| Special education teacher | Fifth- and sixth-grade level | 8:1 |
| Hourly support teacher | Guided study (students already enrolled in an intervention class) | 14:1 |
| Teacher 1 seventh grade | At grade level or above | 14:1 |
| Teacher 2 eighth grade | At grade level or above | 12:1 |
| Tech aide computer lab | Reading Plus | 4:1 (open as needed) |

These students received their small-group targeted instruction. As they gained levels, they would access the next group level. As you can see, regardless of a student's reading level, he or she can progress to full time in the core. This cohort of students would also get additional reading instruction in their history class, which came in the form of close reading, guided instruction, and leveled passages in the history content. They also received sessions in the computer lab in Lexia or Reading Plus.

Our most intensive students, reading four to five grades below level, followed a similar pathway: they were in a core language arts class with extra support and a reading-intervention elective in which most of the intensive intervention was provided.

Two important factors contributed to the effectiveness of this intervention model.

1. We collected reading diagnostic data—curriculum-based measurements—to properly determine exactly what the at-risk readers needed.

2. We developed a highly targeted intervention curriculum via our CORE training that proved to be very effective.

This intervention was effective because it was designed to support the core curriculum providing extra support in comprehension, vocabulary, fluency, discourse, and phonological skills. In other words, it was not an isolated program (like fluency instruction that is not related to the core).

In developing our 2012–2013 master schedule, our goal was to simplify the reading pathways to make the groupings more effective (that is, to group our most intensive and strategic readers into similar pathways). We created two double-block sections, ELA 7 and ELA 8, to serve our sixty most intensive students reading four or more grades below level. We had our most experienced reading teachers in these four sections and pushed in our intervention team for one of the two periods. Our strategic readers, two to three grades below level, were placed in a core ELA class and took a study skills elective or history class where they received intervention from the team. The reason we pushed extra support into a history or study skills class was that we did not have enough of the appropriate single-subject language arts credentialed teachers to keep our reading intervention classes open. This schedule worked very well, because the pathways were simplified. In order to push the intervention team into the appropriate pathways, we had to hand load and lock the students in to the master schedule based on our reading diagnostic data. Although this was very time consuming, it was the key to building a schedule conducive to our intervention efforts.

## The Identification Process

In fall, winter, and spring, we administered a STAR reading test by Renaissance Learning. This is a universal screener that told us which students appeared to be two or more grades below in reading. Three times per year, we also administered a comprehension reading screening test in the form of CORE Reading Maze Comprehension. This is a silent reading test to determine if readers understand the syntax of the text. The passage is based on the students' grade level. The score is determined as benchmark (at grade level), strategic (in need of supplemental support), or intensive. If students were at benchmark, we did no further diagnostic testing. If students were below benchmark, we administered a series of diagnostic assessments until students scored at benchmark. This was how we determined the skill deficits and prescribed the targeted intervention. Next, we would administer the MASI-R Oral Reading Fluency Measurement. This is considered a curriculum-based measure. The score is calculated as words correct per minute. We would also administer the CORE Vocabulary Screener. If the student was still not achieving benchmark scores, we administered the CORE Phonics Survey, which indicates whether a student needs instruction in selected phonics that should have been mastered by the end of third grade. These include letter names, consonant sounds, vowel sounds, short vowels, consonant-vowel-consonant (CVC), consonant blends with short vowels, digraphs, *R*-controlled vowels, long vowel spellings, variant vowels, low-frequency vowel and consonant spellings, and multisyllabic words. These are the essential decoding phonetic skills a student needs. If a student still was not successful with this assessment, we administered the CORE Phoneme Segmentation diagnostic. This assessment was useful in providing information for older students who were experiencing delays in reading and spelling that are not attributed to limited English.

All of these assessments can be scored as benchmark, strategic, or intensive. These assessments are from *Assessing Reading (Second Edition)* (CORE, 2008). Together they give data points for phoneme awareness, phonics, vocabulary, fluency, and comprehension. We administered an orthographic inventory (Invernizzi et al., 2009). We also had our students take a computer software reading assessment developed by the Ware Group in the form of Lexia or Reading Plus. Together, this provided us with multiple data points to help determine a level of rigor and grade-level equivalency. All of these data points provided enough information to group the classes into groups with the same needs. Our reading coach, with the assistance of our hourly support teacher, administered and charted the reading assessment data.

## The Determination Process

Our research indicated that schools achieving 90 percent proficiency rates with a student body comprising 90 percent free and reduced lunch and 90 percent minority (the 90/90/90 schools) achieved great success without utilizing publisher programs. The techniques these schools used were replicable. They used consistent practices in instruction, diagnostic assessments, and teacher-created interventions. Although the details varied from school to school, the implementation was consistent with regard to reading and writing, performance assessment, collaboration, and targeted instruction (Reeves, 2004). This gave us the confidence to design reading intervention curriculum based on our training by CORE, which included instruction in comprehension strategies, vocabulary, oral reading fluency, phonics, discourse, and writing, as well as practice on researched-based computer software for reading intervention. In each small group, the students were exposed to the essential learning standards of the grade level as well as any remediation they needed. The appropriate level of rigor was determined by the multiple measures we used to diagnose each struggling student (figure 9.2, pages 213–214); the page references in the table refer to *Teaching Reading Sourcebook: For All Educators Working to Improve Reading Achievement* (Honig, Diamond, Cole, & Gutlohn, 2008).

## The Monitoring Process

The reading coach, hourly support teacher, and intervention and core teachers monitored the students' progress from the reading software program reports along with the fluency and comprehension assessments. The teacher team met during their preparation period to discuss the data and regroup the students. The teachers also took time during the intervention period to meet with students on a weekly basis to review their progress compared to the goals they set for themselves. The students were involved in charting their progress and received assistance in achieving their goals. All of them knew their reading levels and understood why they were receiving extra support.

## The Revision Process

Our teaching and intervention support teams gained experience in making adjustments to improve results. Since we had leveled intervention groups, we had the capacity to move a student to the appropriate group. Sometimes students were moved for behavioral reasons, such as being off task or disruptive to the group. We simply retaught the desired academic behaviors, changed groupings, and monitored and rewarded the desired behaviors. Because our students were getting the instruction they needed, schoolwide behavior improved. Our strategic students, approximately seventy in all, showed that only one gained less than one year's growth, eleven gained one level, and the remaining students gained between one and a half to three grade levels. Our observations indicated that students who were not progressing showed growth as we placed them in different groups to target their needs. Some students did not show growth because they left the school; others had the skill but not the will. Two students were referred for psycho-educational testing by our student study team (SST) to determine if the student qualified for special education services. The purpose of the referral was to help the student receive additional services in high school, since he or she would not receive the same type of intensive support. A majority of our special education students in the intervention model showed growth; some did not show growth; and only a handful showed minimal progress. I knew all of them. They had heartbreaking stories, and academic progress was not a priority. I simply admired how they came to school every day. There were nine altogether. We worked with a district grant program and  placed them in intensive group and individual behavioral counseling. Three stayed in school the whole year.

| Days | Day 1 (Phrase Cues) | Day 2 (Phrase Cues) | Day 3 (Phrase Cues) | Day 4 (No Phrase Cues) | Day 5 (No Phrase Cues) |
|---|---|---|---|---|---|
| Possible comprehension focus | Teacher modeling-monitoring (think-aloud or close reading) Purpose: interpret conclusions | Connecting to main idea Purpose: connections, draw conclusions | Authors' purpose (analysis) or important supporting ideas, text structure Purpose: analysis, evaluation of opposing arguments | Visualization or how to write outlines, notes, graphs, diagrams, and so on Purpose: inference, solve a problem | If easyCBM passage, do comprehension, quiz, writing |
| Possible writing focus | Think write, anticipation guides, story impressions, summary | Compare, contrast own connection or conclusion with text's | Write own argument about text with evidence | Discuss a scene Write a problem-solution Come up with own QAR questions | Any genre of writing or what I learned this week, what I did well, what goals are for next week |
| Fluency focus | Teacher reads aloud after silent read, pausing | Teacher-assisted choral reading by paragraph (phrasing) | Teacher-assisted echo reading (intonation, prosody) | Peer-assisted partner reading, duet reading (accuracy) | Charting on progress chart easy CBM cold read |

*Source: Compiled by Laurel Zwilling, TeWinkle Middle School.*

Figure 9.2: Weekly study curriculum map.

Continued on next page ↑

| Vocabulary strategies | Words that fit theme outside of text or within text: Know-don't-sort of | Quick activity: word map, definition map, or pave map | Quick activity: categorize it, draw it, compare, contrast | Quick activity: word games, antonym scales, poem | Write possible sentences for the words, quiz |
| --- | --- | --- | --- | --- | --- |
| Decoding word sorts or core | New sort: explicit instruction using academic language | Write sort in notebook | Use manipulative | Dictation on paper or whiteboards | Spelling assessment |

# The Results

During the 2011–2012 school year, our intervention team decided to begin planning for the following year. We also needed to report our findings to the district in order to continue to receive its support. The reading comprehension scores are based on our reading software assessment from Reading Plus. The following are results from the six-month period of September 2011 to February 2012.

- This sample contained 122 students. Fifty students were in the strategic range (that is, fourth- through sixth-grade reading level), and seventy-two students were intensive (that is, first- through third-grade reading level).

- Thirty-eight students gained one grade level; thirty-one gained two grade levels; and twenty gained three to four grade levels. The remaining thirty-three students showed less than a one-year grade-level gain. Many of them were added to the program and did not spend enough time in the interventions to show better results.

- This same sample gained levels as follows: in September 2011, seventy-two students read between the first- and third-grade level; in February 2012, only fourteen read at this level. In September 2011, only fourteen of these students read between the fourth- and sixth-grade range; in February, it was up to sixty-nine.

This data confirmed we were on track regarding our reading goal. Our intervention team conducted a spring reading universal screening and diagnosis for our incoming eighth graders and went to our elementary feeder schools to screen and diagnose our incoming seventh graders. We determined it was time to adjust the master schedule to meet the reading needs of our students for the 2012–2013 school year.

We opened a seventh- and eighth-grade section in language arts for our most intensive readers, reading between a first- and fourth-grade level. They were placed in replacement ELA curriculum. This was a district decision for third through eighth graders three or more years below reading level. Although we preferred to keep them in the ELA core, we were determined to make it work with our intervention model. The following are reading gains from September 2012 to April 2013, a seven-month period.

- For our two ELA replacement curriculum classes, fifty out of sixty-five of the students read below a fourth-grade level in September 2012. In April 2013, only five students were below the fourth-grade level.

- During this seven-month period, fifty-two of the eighty-two students in this program gained two or more grade levels. Twenty-seven students gained between three and five grade levels.

- The number of students in this cohort changed due to students leaving the school, new students arriving, students placed in this section from the English learner newcomer class, and students leaving this program to be mainstreamed.

- The newcomer class was composed of students who spoke little to no English. There were thirty-two students in September 2012; at the end of the year, fifteen were moved up to the replacement curriculum because they progressed past the third-grade reading level.

Our strategic intervention groups, reading two to three grades below level, were in a core ELA course and a study skills elective or history section, where they received reading intervention. This placement was based on the needs of the student. These students received small-group instruction two days a week. The following data are from September 2012 through April 2013, seven months.

- The original forty-nine students who started in September 2012 were reading between the third- and sixth-grade level. In April 2013, forty-six of the students were reading between the sixth- and tenth-grade level. Throughout the year, some of these students were regrouped out of this intervention, and some were added.

- In this same group, fifty-three students were in it long enough to show the following results: thirty-one students gained two or more reading levels, and twenty-four students gained three to five levels in seven months or less.

Our staff has a great amount of satisfaction in knowing our students will enter high school with improved reading skills. Looking back, we know we made the right changes for the right reasons. If I could do anything differently, I would avoid going to a replacement curriculum for our lowest readers. Rather, I would leave all students in the core so they have access to the grade-level rigor. Although they have difficulty decoding and comprehending at this level, they can still think and discuss at high levels. When we send a student to high school reading below a fourth-grade level, we know his or her future is not bright. When we send some of our most at-risk readers to high school reading within two grades of grade level, they have a fighting chance. When we send at-risk readers to high school reading at or above grade level, the sky is the limit!

This all started with a staff asking the right question. The question was not, Why are we receiving such low readers from the elementary schools? Rather, we asked, "What do our students need?" They need to learn to read at high levels! The process to achieve this is indicative of what a school can do when it has the right focus. There are too many middle schools facing the same reading issues we face at our school. We share our story to motivate and inspire others to do the same. As individual teachers, we do our best. As a school, we have the power to change lives! We encourage you to go forth and change lives.

## References and Resources

Ainsworth, L. (2003). *Power standards: Identifying the standards that matter the most.* Englewood, CO: Advanced Learning Press.

Buffum, A., Mattos, M., & Weber, C. (2009). *Pyramid response to intervention: RTI, professional learning communities, and how to respond when kids don't learn.* Bloomington, IN: Solution Tree Press.

Buffum, A., Mattos, M., & Weber, C. (2012). *Simplifying response to intervention: Four essential guiding principles.* Bloomington, IN: Solution Tree Press.

Consortium on Reading Excellence. (2008). *Assessing reading: Multiple measures for kindergarten through twelfth grade (2nd ed.).* Novato, CA: Arena Press.

Francis, D. J., Kieffer, M., Lesaux, N., Rivera, H., & Rivera, M. (2006). *Practical guidelines for the education of English language learners: Research-based recommendations for instruction and academic interventions.* Portsmouth, NH: Center on Instruction, RMC Research Corporation.

Honig, B., Diamond, L., Cole, C. L., & Gutlohn, L. (2008). *Teaching reading sourcebook: For all educators working to improve reading achievement.* Novato, CA: Arena Press.

Invernizzi, M., Johnston, F., Bear, D. R., & Templeton, S. (2009). *Words their way: Word sorts for within word pattern spellers* (2nd ed.). Boston: Allyn & Bacon.

Marzano, R. J., Pickering, D. J., & Pollock, J. E. (2001). *Classroom instruction that works: Research-based strategies for increasing student achievement.* Alexandria, VA: Association for Supervision and Curriculum.

Muhammad, A. (2009). *Transforming school culture: How to overcome staff division.* Bloomington, IN: Solution Tree Press.

Reeves, D. B. (2004). *Accountability in action: A blueprint for learning organizations* (2nd ed.). Englewood, CO: Lead + Learn Press.

Schmoker, M. (2011). *Focus: Elevating the essentials to radically improve student learning.* Alexandria, VA: Association for Supervision and Curriculum Development.

**Darin L. Fahrney, PhD,** is the high school principal at the Singapore American School and former K–12 coordinator of student support services. Before relocating internationally, Darin served for almost two decades as a teacher and high school principal in his home state of Wisconsin. His doctoral research studied student perceptions of response to intervention (RTI) at the high school level, research that gave rise to the Compassionate RTI approach to ensuring high levels of learning for all students in a nurturing supportive environment.

Darin holds a doctorate in philosophy and a master of arts degree from Marian University and master of science and bachelor of science degrees from the University of Wisconsin-Stevens Point.

You can follow Darin on Twitter @DarinFahrney.

**Timothy S. Stuart, EdD,** is the executive director of research and development and strategic programs at the Singapore American School. He is the co-author of the books *Children at Promise* and *Raising Children at Promise.* Tim's research and writing offers parents and teachers an alternative paradigm to the "at-risk" labels ascribed to children. The "at promise" paradigm suggests that both adversity and relationships are essential to creating an optimal growth environment.

Tim holds a doctorate in education from Seattle Pacific University, a masters in education degree from The College of New Jersey, and a bachelor of arts degree from Wheaton College.

You can follow Tim on Twitter @drtstuart.

To book Darin L. Fahrney or Timothy S. Stuart for professional development, contact pd@solution-tree.com.

# Maximizing Student Learning Through a Compassionate Response to Intervention Model

Darin L. Fahrney and Timothy S. Stuart

**Editors' Note**

Many high-achieving schools fall into the trap of believing there is no reason to create a system of interventions because their results are already good enough. Our experience is that these schools almost always serve students who come from highly affluent, well-educated parents who serve as their children's "system of interventions." In this case, students often succeed, regardless of—or sometimes in spite of—the school's practices. And for those students who struggle because they do not receive this level of parental support, the school's response is to systematically move them out: out of advanced placement (AP) and honors classes because they just can't cut it, out of grade-level coursework because they lack the skills, out of electives because they need academic support, and out of their school and into alternative or continuation programs because they are just too far behind.

The success of a school program should not be measured by the achievement of those students who are going to make it regardless of what the school provides, but instead by the growth of the students who make it because of your efforts. This is why we love the story of Singapore American School (SAS). Before it started implementing the professional learning community (PLC) and response to intervention (RTI) processes, SAS was one of the highest-achieving high schools in the world. Leaders at the school could have easily rested on their laurels and the efforts of their parent population and continued to solve the problem of struggling students by simply removing them from the school. But they did not settle for being a great school for most students and instead committed to being a great school for every student. They also embraced the fact that if a school can create flexible time and systematic interventions to help students who are struggling to meet grade-level standards, they can use this same process to support students in advanced coursework. In other words, RTI is not just a remediation process, but an acceleration process that can be used to maximize every student's academic potential. This additional support is provided not as a punishment but within a framework of compassion.

We would challenge every secondary school to commit to SAS's approach to student success: "Schools of excellence don't kick kids out when they don't meet the learning targets. Period." Instead of lowering expectations for struggling students, provide them a step up. Show them compassion and support, not the door.

---

The Singapore American School (SAS) is a high-performing American international school that serves the children of American and other foreign residents of Singapore. SAS operates in an environment where, as an independent international school, it has almost complete autonomy, as it makes good on its mission to provide an exemplary American education with an international perspective. In pursuit of ongoing exemplary work with students, SAS initiated a comprehensive multiyear research and development process aimed at designing the school of the future and meeting our students' learning needs in this ever-changing global environment. As a part of this process, the research and development team met with almost one hundred college representatives, visited exemplary schools around the world, and conducted a deep study of best practices in education.

After our worldwide search, one thing was evident: no other educational practice was as powerful for maximizing learning for all students as a compassionate approach to response to intervention (RTI) done in a professional learning community (PLC) structure. Many schools we visited collaborated, many schools had innovative ideas and high expectations for students, but only schools that were using RTI in a PLC structure could give a systematic guarantee that no students were falling through the cracks and that every student was being challenged at a level that would maximize his or her learning. We had freedom to choose any model for maximizing student learning, and we chose RTI.

Singapore American School is often touted as a world-class school with extraordinary academic results. SAS offers more Advanced Placement (AP) courses and exams than any other school outside of the United States. SAS offers 29 AP courses, and in 2014, our students completed 1,414 exams with 96 percent of all scores being a 3 or higher. Ninety-eight percent of our students attend four-year colleges after graduation. Though by many measures we feel we are meeting with academic success, we know we can do more to meet the needs of our students. Our vision statement, "A world leader in education, cultivating exceptional thinkers, prepared for the future," calls us to continuous improvement, and therefore we must address the needs of students who struggle academically and whose learning needs are not being met. Quite simply, we needed to rethink the way we "do" school.

## Setting the Course

Singapore American School began a comprehensive research and development (R&D) process to rethink its approach to learning and to maximize student opportunities. To achieve this end, the school superintendent and the high school principal began meeting every other week to research and ideate about what was possible for our school. What would it take for us to fully realize our vision statement? From this original thinking, they brought together twenty-two teachers and administrators, who were named the SAS R&D team. The R&D team based their school reform work on the thinking of John Dewey (1938), Ted Sizer (2004), Michael Fullan (2008), Daniel Pink (2006), and Tony Wagner (2008) and their leading change process on the work of John Kotter (2012). From this original thinking, the R&D team mapped out a plan of action.

After our worldwide exploration of the U.S., Finnish, Australian, New Zealand, and Singaporean education systems and a robust analysis of the literature, we not only discovered that RTI conducted in a PLC environment consistently demonstrated improved learning for students, but other meaningful themes emerged as well. The additional themes spoke specifically to the human side of education and reinforced how a compassionate approach to RTI can be so successful. The additional themes emphasized that relationships are the cornerstone that learning is built on and that personalizing the learning experiences for students is an extremely powerful and rewarding way to maximize their learning and access their untapped potential. When we spoke to the students participating in compassionate, nonpunitive interventions, it was apparent that they actually liked or at least appreciated the interventions in which they were participating.

## The Obstacles to Creating a New Way of Doing School

As with many schools that hold reputations of academic excellence, SAS can be traditional in its approach to teaching and learning. We knew we did things well but felt that, to be a world leader, we needed to provide structures for teachers to collaborate and learn from each other. As a result, we incorporated a PLC approach to address student learning and behavioral concerns, establish a guaranteed and viable curriculum, and create common assessment and grading standards. We knew that strong PLCs would be the foundation for any and all work that lay ahead for maximizing learning for all students. It was the first thing that we had to establish to better support our students.

Implementing the PLC structure at SAS began with a two-year process to change our schedule so we could allow for late starts for students every Wednesday morning, so that teachers could meet in their collaborative teams and work to answer the four guiding PLC questions.

1. What do we want students to know and be able to do?

2. How do we know when they know it?

3. What do we do when they don't know the material?

4. What do we do when they already know it? (DuFour, DuFour, & Eaker, 2008)

Securing this collaboration time did not come easily. When your school community views what you are doing as highly successful, there is not always a strong sense of urgency to change. Initially, the SAS High School Division proposed that students would start their day one hour late so teachers could meet with their PLCs. However, the school community was concerned about the loss of teacher-student contact time and the busing issues with high school students coming late to school. As a result, the proposed schedule change was vetoed for that year by the school board until more research could be gathered.

It was at this point that our administrative team and teacher leaders had to practice what we preach to students: grit, perseverance, and problem solving. The next year, our proposal to the school board and school community addressed the concerns they expressed about our first proposal. The new proposal readjusted when PLC time began; instead of 8:00 a.m., the start of the student day as had previously been proposed, PLC time began at 7:30 a.m., the start of teacher contract time. This saved us thirty minutes of contact time from the prior proposal. We then added a minute to each class by shortening student breaks. By adding a minute to each class period and adjusting breaks, students actually ended up with a net gain of teacher contact time while still allowing our PLCs time to meet.

We had seemingly addressed the contact time issue, but we still had to deal with student transportation. We knew we could not afford an additional bus run for high school students, so they would have to be on campus during PLC time. The end result was the creation of supervision systems that did not involve teachers. Supervision for the students during PLC time was carried out by high school administrators, central office administrators, counselors, aides, librarians, and athletic directors. But a question remained, What would we do with all those students on campus while teachers were in their PLC time? We pulled teacher leaders together again and created activities for students to do before school started. These options include peer-tutoring sessions hosted by our honor society students, career guest speakers, large-group college counseling sessions, intramural leagues, student jam sessions, open gym and weight room, library study, and a host of other activities. We also arranged for all of the assemblies that used to be held during class time to be conducted during the PLC time, so even more class time was preserved.

Our administrators and teacher leaders refused to let lack of scheduling creativity hinder our efforts to build the time to help students. As a result, our board unanimously approved the new proposal, and the new schedule was put into place and has been successful with only minor alterations to activity offerings. Getting the supervision we needed to watch twelve hundred students was challenging, but we were able to use creative supervision solutions and engaging activities to make it possible.

Although creating the time was a challenge for our school community, the impact of creating this time and providing a PLC focus to it allows our teachers to know what they are teaching, how they are assessing it, and when to intervene for students who need assistance or extensions. Creating the PLC structure built the foundation for helping our students learn.

The obstacles for creating structures to support students did not stop with our schedule. Another challenge for us was helping teachers realize they had the ability and responsibility to provide interventions to our students and to operate under the belief that every student can learn at a high level. Many of our teachers lacked experience working with underachieving students, as international schools tend to hire professionals because of their ability to challenge high-achieving students, not their ability to differentiate for all learning styles.

Finally, in what may seem like every teacher's dream, the ability to "unenroll" students who chronically struggle in our school was a significant hindrance for us. The sometimes-uttered phrase "This may not be the best school for that student to be successful" had a detrimental impact on our willingness to and belief that we could help our most struggling students learn. To challenge that long-held tradition, our administrative team and courageous PLC leaders refocused attention on something we all agreed on, and that is that we were a PLC school. We all made a collective commitment to be a PLC school, and PLC schools of excellence don't remove students when they don't meet the learning targets. Period. Instead, they make time and interventions the variables, not learning, and do whatever it takes to help students learn at high levels.

At first, this was a paradigm shift for us, and it really came down to courage in leadership, both teacher and administrator, to begin changing from an exit to a PLC philosophy. The second year of PLC implementation was when we really became tight—in other words, uncompromising—on not exiting students for being academically weak. As such, we had our inevitable test case student arise almost immediately. A new student, Lee, began the year with us, and it did not take long to discover he had severe social phobias, deprecating self-perception issues, and major transition struggles, as this was his first time in an English-speaking school. He refused to do any work. After a month of working with administration, his counselor, our school psychologist, and his mother, Lee was still floundering. The email requests from teachers suggesting that our school was not the best place for him began to roll in.

A meeting was called, and a more dire report from teachers of a student's personal and academic status could not have been delivered. Lee was in crisis, and our teachers felt that our school was too fast paced, academically demanding, and emotionally strenuous for a student in such a precarious state. They felt, as a show of kindness, not malice, that Lee should be exited from our school and enrolled in a less challenging one, as they hated to see him suffer trying to meet the high expectations that SAS demanded. The consensus in the meeting was clear about what should happen with this student's enrollment, and I can tell you that as a second-year administrator at one of the most highly respected international schools in the world, I swallowed hard and did a gut check before saying, "No, Lee stays with us, and we need to figure out how to help him." At that point my career flashed before my eyes, as I feared a massive backlash from staff for challenging this long-held practice. Then an amazing thing happened. One salty veteran teacher in the meeting nonchalantly said, "Okay, I have seen tougher than this. Here's what I think will work for this kid . . . ," and at that point the whole tone of the meeting changed from problems to solutions. The team just needed the boundaries redefined for them, and incredible professionals that they are, they rose to the occasion. And now two years and a heck of a lot of sweat equity from our staff later, Lee is earning almost all As and is an involved member of our school community. Those original teachers in that room became Lee's greatest champions, and when we speak of him today, there is a sense of pride and accomplishment in seeing Lee shine.

Lee was not the last one. The tough students kept coming, as they always do, but our intervention systems have gotten better at serving them and our teachers are now working in those systems to help all students maximize their learning. As for our school in general, we have not exited a student for academic weaknesses in two years, while at the same time we have actually increased student academic performance. Though technically our school policies still allow for exiting students who underperform, since becoming tight on this issue we have not asked any students to leave SAS for academic issues. We could, but we don't!

# Making the Time

Few things have had as large an impact on our ability to serve the needs of students than adjusting our schedule to allow for PLC time and intervention availability. It took creativity and perseverance, but the end result was great for student learning. Another large part of making the time to help all students meet learning targets is our bell schedule. The bell schedule itself has been in place for some time, but how we are using it has changed with the advent of PLC time. The schedule, shown in figure 10.1 (page 226), is essentially an eight-period rotating block schedule that has classes meeting every other day. The beauty of this schedule is that it allows ample time for interventions, planning, and student meetings.

As currently implemented, the schedule allows for subject-specific PLCs to meet for one hour per week to address the four essential questions of the PLC. In addition to teacher meeting time for PLCs, our class schedule has built in meeting times—twenty-five minutes in the morning and fifteen minutes in the afternoon when students can meet with teachers—and after school, time is blocked off from activities for forty-five minutes so students can attend help sessions with teachers without feeling like they are missing their extracurricular commitments. A series of activity buses run shortly after four o'clock to transport students home who have stayed late for clubs or additional assistance. The twenty-five-minute block in the morning has been especially helpful for teachers to arrange intervention times with students, for the office to connect with students without pulling them out of classes, and for students to collaborate on projects or meet with one of the 105 student-led clubs they may be involved in.

# Getting What You Need, When You Need It

Just having a schedule that allows for PLC time is not enough. You must have support structures available during the school day to allow teachers to intervene to help students who are struggling. To ensure that we have structured intervention classes every period of our day, we had to make some difficult decisions on how to best use our five Learning Support teachers, who serve the 109 students at SAS who are identified with learning disabilities and challenges.

| Time | A* | B | C | D | Time | Wednesday Schedule |
|---|---|---|---|---|---|---|
| 7:00 a.m. | Buses Arrive | Buses Arrive | Buses Arrive | Buses Arrive | 7:50 a.m. | Buses Arrive |
| 7:55 a.m. | First Bell | First Bell | First Bell | First Bell | 8:00 a.m.–8:35 a.m. | Flex Period Teacher PLCs (7:30-8:30 am) |
| 8:00 a.m.–9:30 a.m. | Block 1 | Block 5 | Block 3 | Block 7 | 8:35 a.m.–8:45 a.m. | Break |
| 9:30 a.m.–9:55 a.m. | Break | Break | Break | Break | 8:45 a.m.–10:05 a.m. | Block Class |
| 9:55 a.m.–11:20 a.m. | Block 2 | Block 6 | Block 4 | Block 8 | 10:05 a.m.–10:15 a.m. | Break |
| 11:20 a.m.–12:00 p.m. | Lunch | Lunch | Lunch | Lunch | 10:15 a.m.–11:35 a.m. | Block Class |
| 12:00 p.m.–1:25 p.m. | Block 3 | Block 7 | Block 1 | Block 5 | 11:35 a.m.–12:10 p.m. | Break |
| 1:25 p.m.–1:35 p.m. | Break | Break | Break | Break | 12:10 p.m.–1:30 p.m. | Block Class |
| 1:35 p.m.–3:00 p.m. | Block 4 | Block 8 | Block 2 | Block 6 | 1:30 p.m.–1:40 p.m. | Break |

*Source: Singapore American School.*

Figure 10.1: The SAS High School bell schedule.

| 3:00 p.m. | Final Bell | Final Bell | Final Bell | Final Bell | **1:40 p.m.– 3:00 p.m.** Block Class |
|---|---|---|---|---|---|
| **3:15 p.m.** | Buses Depart | Buses Depart | Buses Depart | Buses Depart | **3:15 p.m.** Buses Depart |
| **3:15–4:00** | Club and Intervention Time | Club and Intervention Time | Club and Intervention Time | Club and Intervention Time | **Club and Intervention Time 3:15–4:00** |

*ABCD days fall on different days of the week. If a day is missed due to a holiday we pick up from the letter we left off. This ensures that one day is not overrepresented.

To make the time, our Learning Support department decided that we would maximize unsupported student inclusion in the regular classroom environment. Great care was taken so that individualized education support programs (or IESPs, the international equivalent to IEPs) were written to reflect this changed approach to service for students. By eliminating some team-taught sections of courses, our Learning Support teachers were then available for intensive interventions for students. This allowed our most intensive support classes, Learning Support and reading and writing lab, to be available almost every period of the day, thus facilitating quick inclusion of students into the intervention classes with minimal impact to teacher and student schedules. This was a significant but essential shift to how we allocate resources to make intensive intervention available for students. With limited Learning Support staff, we had to rely more heavily on classroom teachers and their PLCs to intervene to help our students with disabilities and learning challenges to free up our Learning Support staff for more intensive interventions.

To mitigate the impact of removing team-taught sections, our Learning Support teachers meet with subject-area PLCs every other week (depending on the time of the year), so they can stay current on classroom work and advise classroom teachers on differentiating for and accommodating to the needs of students with learning challenges. Even though our Learning Support teachers are assisting classroom teachers and students, classroom teachers know that they can go to a student's counselor at any time if they feel the student needs additional help. We encourage the classroom teachers to over- versus undercommunicate regarding any student concerns they may be having.

One might initially think this would result in decreased outcomes for students with learning challenges, but actually the opposite has occurred. Coupled with our schoolwide move toward standards-based grading and strong implementation of PLCs and Compassionate RTI (described in the next section), our percentage of students who are failing or receiving Ds has dramatically decreased since shifting our supports. At the end of the first-semester marking period in 2010, our students registered 18 Fs and 169 Ds. At the end of the 2013–2014 school year (with increased total enrollment), our students registered 1 F and 65 Ds.

So now what? We researched best practice, we made time for teachers to collaborate in a PLC structure, and we began to challenge existing beliefs about whom we could and should teach. But we needed more than that. We now had to retool our traditional support systems in order to guarantee that all students got what they needed to maximize their learning.

# What Do We Do When Students Are Not Learning? The Philosophy Behind CRTI

From our research and our R&D work, we knew that caring relationships are essential to learning; therefore, the Singapore American School High School Division implemented a three-tier intervention system that focuses on closing student-learning gaps while at the same time addressing the hardships caused by those gaps. Tim's Children at Promise research, which suggests that both adversity and relationships are essential to creating an optimal growth environment, and Darin's research, focused on RTI-based reading interventions at the high school level, provided the framework for an approach called Compassionate RTI (CRTI). The CRTI approach addresses student gaps in academic skills and social and academic behaviors while recognizing that these gaps in many cases have themselves caused emotional distress in students and will continue to do so unless compassionate mentors are willing to "struggle" alongside and empathize with them to help them overcome their learning challenges.

Although interventions don't have to be a struggle to be effective, openly acknowledging the struggle has been a powerful tool for easing the burden on our incredibly dedicated and professional international educators. It has helped us serve a broader array of students, because it challenges the notion that every student must be an A student immediately, and if students aren't, then either we can't serve them or we have failed as teachers. Acknowledging the struggle actually gives our teachers permission to do whatever it takes to help students learn at high levels. The "struggling together" part of the CRTI approach recognizes that helping students overcome their academic and emotional struggles can be difficult and frustrating for both teachers and students, but it also signifies that we are in this together and no matter how hard this gets for teachers and students, we will never give up on each other.

The basis for Compassionate RTI was formulated as a result of Darin's doctoral study of an academically and behaviorally successful Tier 2 reading intervention at the secondary level in Wisconsin (Fahrney, 2013). The study was conducted in a large suburban high school with many of the issues of an inner-city school, using the most current RTI research and state guidelines and focused on students' perceptions of their experience in the intervention. From the results of the study, several themes emerged regarding the interactions between students and teachers, students and students, and students with themselves. The findings revealed the compassionate reality underlying the intervention—in the literal sense, since the root meaning of *compassion* is to "suffer together" or to be highly empathetic toward another's difficult circumstance. When students tackled their reading challenges in the presence of a compassionate mentor, namely their teacher, students emerged better readers with an improved self-perception. The results provide the groundwork for CRTI as implemented at Singapore American School. The three foundational tenets of quality CRTI interventions include:

1.  Deep understanding of student academic and personal history

2.  Classroom structures that build community and tailor attention to specific student need

3.  Strong consideration for the emotional status of each student

At the SAS High School Division, all tiers of intervention have been implemented using these tenets. By doing so, we address what educators already know, that behavioral and academic challenges in students, especially at the Tier 3 level, are deeply intertwined and difficult to correct in isolation. Further, we believe that the CRTI enhances the RTI interventions that are already occurring in many schools and provides that next level of extraordinary care for our most at-promise students.

At the same time as the CRTI approach is being implemented at SAS, schedules and policies are being changed to allow for student learning to be personalized and for *all* students to go deeper into studying their area of passion. As a companion to our CRTI model of intervention, a pyramid of acceleration is being created to ensure that we support students who have already mastered grade-level learning targets or have untapped strengths that they want to pursue.

At SAS, in alignment with the CRTI tenets, two separate Tier 3 intervention pathways are used to address significant student gaps in learning and behavior. The first pathway, Learning Support, focuses on addressing executive functioning challenges and gaps in academic behaviors. The second intervention, Reading and Language Arts (RLA) Lab, works to combat student gaps in reading and writing skills. Both interventions are regular classes and are offered every period of the day so students have easy access if the need arises during the course of the school year. The classes can be taken for credit or no credit depending on the time of the semester the students are added. Due to the rigor and pace of our school, most students take only seven classes each semester, which leaves a class block free for them as a study hall. This dynamic allows for easy placement of students out of study hall and into the intervention courses during the semester if the need arises.

## Guaranteeing That Students Get What They Need to Learn in a Timely Manner

Having strong intervention systems is important, but you must first identify which students need help and what kind of help they need before you can effectively assist them. To do this, SAS has multiple firewalls. The first is a proactive identification system that relies on our admissions department, the school counselor, and universal screening assessments to identify students who could potentially be in need.

The admissions office at SAS handles the application of all new students. The admissions screening process looks at cumulative folders of incoming students, transcripts, confidential reviews of student performance from two prior teachers the students have had, and any testing and psychological evaluations the students may have had. All students who are identified as potentially needing services are brought to a high school review committee consisting of administrators, counselors, admissions representatives, and the support services department chairperson to identify and plan for what services will be needed to meet the students' needs. Related to that, because we do not have a program for students who are so cognitively impaired that they will not be living independently after high school, those candidates' families are informed that we cannot meet their needs and are provided information about other schooling options in Singapore.

The counselor acts as the second line of identification for support for any new student, be it an incoming freshman from our middle school or a student new to our school. SAS has placed a significant amount of resources into the counseling ranks to ensure early screening and intervention with students. Specifically, two counselors are devoted solely to high school transition and serve approximately 150 students each. This expenditure of resources pays off in that we can provide a strong system of monitoring and proactive versus reactive assistance for students who are struggling. The role of the counselor in identifying students in need of assistance during transition includes:

- Middle school transition—Three formal transition meetings with the middle school counselors, middle school Learning Support teachers, and the high school counselor, assistant principal, and psychologist-learning support person. This meeting identifies which students will need specific accommodations and supports based on their IESP.

- Middle school file review—In alignment with CRTI tenets of building a deep understanding of the personal and academic history of students, the high school counselor will review the cumulative file of every student new to the high school and identify any and all academic, social, or emotional struggles the student may have experienced in school up to that point, so proactive discussions can be had during the difficult transition students experience attending a new school.

- Counselor interview—Each new student will participate in a counselor interview at the start of the school year. The protocol for the interview is based on three items.

  - Review of academic history based on the student's cumulative folder and the student's perceptions

  - Transition pulse check regarding how well the student is managing the move to high school or an international school

  - Social and emotional check regarding home life and expectations of parents and students, especially given that over fifty nationalities are represented at our school. The cultural integration challenges can have a significant impact on student learning.

The counselors' role does not end with these screenings. They will continue to meet with the students and teachers throughout the school year to discuss student needs, intervention progress, and academic performance. The counselors are also responsible for arranging, reviewing, and processing universal screening assessments. These assessments identify students who, on large-scale assessments, are performing in the lowest quartile compared to their SAS peers. These initial screening assessments come in four forms initially.

1. Measures of Academic Progress (MAP): This large universal screening assessment available through Northwest Evaluation Association (NWEA) is used at SAS in grades 3–9 to identify students who may be struggling in the area of reading and writing. The results are available to teachers to inform their instruction as well as to the counselor as an indicator that the student may need additional assessment or assistance to reach learning targets.

2. Math placement tests: All incoming students take a math placement test created by our math department based on our clearly defined math standards. The assessment is a sampling of specific learning standards that students must master to progress to the next math level. The results of the assessment inform the counselor regarding what level of math a student should begin in. Four entry-level options exist for students in math, with our most needy students being placed in our most basic level of math with additional assistance from Learning Support. The counselor is responsible for spearheading those initial interventions.

3. EDmin Lexile screener: SAS is exploring the use of simple online Lexile screeners. Ours happens to be through a software package that we have purchased called EDmin, which provides information about basic student reading levels to teachers and counselors. These quick indicators can provide faster red-flag data to counselors and teachers than MAP assessments can.

4. PowerSchool: As an additional safeguard, so that no students slip through the cracks in initial identification or the communication of need, all students who are identified as needing accommodations or assistance have a yellow icon located on the teacher dashboard in PowerSchool, our digital student data tracking system (figure 10.2). With one click on this nonexpiring icon, all of a student's teachers have access to the accommodations a student needs and information about his or her disability or learning challenge. The PowerSchool icon is another simple and effective way for counselors and Learning Support teachers to ensure that students are not lost in transition from grade to grade or from regular education teachers to special teachers.

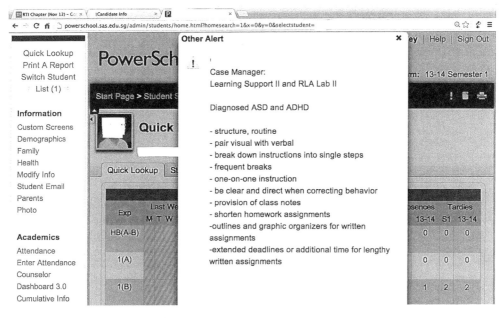

*Source: Singapore American School.*

Figure 10.2: Screenshot of digital student-tracking system.

In addition to the large-scale screening mechanisms, another student identification screener, which is more organic and functional, typically begins with the classroom teacher. Any teacher, administrator, parent, or counselor can refer students who seem to be struggling emotionally, socially, or academically to a group called the Student Services Team (SST). This team is made up of counselors, administrators, teacher representatives (special education and regular education), the support services department head and school psychologist. The SST is also the clearinghouse for arranging interventions for any student brought to its attention. A student does not need a defined disability to be referred to the SST, only a functional manifestation that impedes his or her academic ability or personal well-being. When the student is brought to the SST, pertinent cumulative folder data are reviewed, including standardized test scores such as MAP tests, Lexile scores, or educational psychologist assessments. Additional data include behavior information such as absences or discipline referrals; classroom grades, both current and historical; summative and formative assessment information; and a review of any past interventions that have been attempted by the classroom teacher that have, or have not, met with improved learning.

Meeting minutes are kept on a running Google Docs document (figure 10.3) that can be collaboratively updated as interventions are attempted. The document is based on the principle of keeping it simple. Since our SST meets only twice a week for forty minutes (before school but during contracted time), there is not a great deal of time for complex paperwork and forms in triplicate. Typically, the description of the student and the issue that student is struggling with is brief, and the desired outcome of the student discussion, the person responsible for implementing any decisions, and the time the student's progress will be reviewed are clearly defined on the document so the student doesn't end up in intervention limbo.

It is strongly preferred by the SST, but not essential, that classroom teachers attempt research-based or evidence-based interventions of a sufficient duration, intensity, and fidelity to address the student's need in the classroom with the student's peers before bringing him or her to the SST. Often, recommendations for how teachers can intervene to help students will come out of the SST process. If the evidence presented to the SST indicates that the student needs significant interventions beyond the classroom to close gaps in learning at an accelerated rate, the full measure of our support offerings can be made available all at one time, regardless of what interventions the student is currently involved with in the classroom.

| Date of Meeting/ Referral | Grade Level | Student Name | Name of Counselor, Administrator, or Learning Support Presenting | Issues | Action and Desired Outcome |
|---|---|---|---|---|---|
| 9/3 | 9 | Sam | Sue | New to SAS and has begun a pattern of school refusal. High social anxiety. Suggest Learning Support to help with homework completion. | Placement into Learning Support (LS) class for semester for emotional support and academic skill building. Weekly counselor meetings (Sue) to discuss anxiety. Desired outcome: Come to school every day, become involved in one club. (Review next week and at semester.) |
| | | | | | 9/17—Still absent but behavior is improving. |
| | | | | | 9/23—Clear expectations needed with him (admin); hold him accountable. Executive functioning assessment scores from LS average or above, move placement to Supervised Study (SS) instead of Learning Support. Will issue, not skill issue. |
| | | | | | 10/1—Saturday suspension, no further absences since. Attending school socials. |
| | | | | | 10/19—Grades improved to only 2 D+s. Keep in SS as improvement is happening. (Review at end of semester 1.) |

*Source: Singapore American School.*

Figure 10.3: SST Google Docs document for meeting minutes.

CRTI foundations of knowing the student's academic and personal history and giving strong regard for the emotional status of each student come heavily into play here. We look for supports that are appropriate to address the student's need without having the intervention cause undue stress. You have to use the available data and your understanding of a student to determine the most likely tool to get a positive outcome with minimal intrusion. These decisions require flexibility, speed, and the creative collective thinking to make things happen.

Although we empower our teachers and counselors in the SST to make most decisions related to intervening to help students, for interventions that may push the bounds of policy or involve resource allocation, an administrator needs to be involved if we are to implement the intervention within our desired time frame (one week). An administrator ensures that quick approval can be given when needed and that protocol is being followed (however simple it may be) and gives permission and encouragement to SST members to think creatively to assist students. The importance of the administrator presence cannot be overemphasized.

## Implementing the Interventions

Our initial interventions are typically driven by subject-specific teacher teams based on common formative assessment data aligned to their essential course standards and learning targets. The formative assessment data allow these subject-specific teacher teams to consider student success through a macro lens and micro lens. The macro lens considers the results of specific teachers and how their students collectively performed on the formative assessment. This allows teachers to have meaningful discussion about what is working to help students meet the learning targets and what is not. This feedback allows teachers to learn and grow from each other as professionals.

On the micro level, the teacher teams break down the formative assessment data by how individual students have performed on individual standards. Using these data, which are typically gathered on a spreadsheet, the teacher teams have created mandatory interventions during lunchtime, during break time, or after school. The responsibility for conducting these sessions is collectively shared by the subject-specific teacher teams, so no one teacher has to do all of the interventions him- or herself. Because Learning Support teachers are involved in the teacher team discussions, they can provide teachers with insights into how to effectively intervene based on student need. Having a fresh set of eyes on the issue has been extremely helpful.

Our greatest challenges with the implementation of this Tier 1 intervention system have been associated with getting the teacher teams to agree on learning targets and time their common assessments such that they can reasonably compare data. Although the Tier 1 intervention process is in different stages of development among our teams, all are making progress based on self-assessment data given at the beginning of the year.

When students fail to respond to interventions in the classroom or simply need a double dose of assistance to catch them up or to focus their academic behaviors, a more intensive intervention is available. The second tier of intervention comes in the form of a supervised study-hall program that faculty can assign a student to at any point in the school year. The supervised study hall occurs during a student's free block and is in essence a small-group (approximately one to ten students) structured study hall that can monitor students' work activities. The groups are purposefully small, so that individualized attention can be given to each student. The study hall is supervised each hour by a different teacher, who is paid a stipend for his or her work with the students. Money for paying the teachers was found by lobbying for stipend money available through our central administration. A student's assignment is not punitive in nature, and there is a declared focus or reason for the assignment, so the study hall teacher knows what an individual student should be working on. The assigning teacher must be extremely clear about this. The duration of the assignment is hinged on the students getting their work completed or tightening up their academic focus during their off time. Both the assigning teacher and the supervised study hall teacher communicate regarding the progress of the student toward addressing the purpose of the assignment. Peer tutors can also be arranged for students if they need assistance with focusing on their studies. The link to the Supervised Study Student Placement Form is given to all faculty and counselors at the beginning of the year. (Visit **go.solution-tree.com/rtiatwork** to access this link.) Because the link was created on a Google form, once the referring professional submits it, the form goes directly to the student's counselor, who then enters the student into supervised study hall. This also helps get students who may need additional assistance on the counselor's radar.

Figure 10.4 (page 238) shows the directions for explaining to each teacher and counselor the guidelines behind the placement of students into supervised study hall.

Our most intensive interventions, Learning Support and RLA Lab, are available to any student who may need them at any time. Unlike interventions described earlier, these intervention classes require placement based on admissions data described earlier, counselor transition meetings, or the SST. Students may receive elective credit for these interventions depending on the timing of their placement. Both of these interventions rely heavily on the tenets of CRTI. Each class starts out with some sort of community-building activity that is simple but does wonders for

1. **Placing teacher** explains to the student the purpose for the placement and what the student needs to accomplish to be removed from SS. Placing teacher contacts the parents to inform them of his or her concern.

2. **Placing teacher** informs student the location that he or she must report for SS and the date the student must report. Please allow two days for counselors to enter the student in the SS roster (Monday form completion = Wednesday start date). See the next section for SS locations.

3. **Placing teacher** completes this form and turns it into the counseling office (emailing the form is acceptable as well).

4. **Counselor** adds the student into the SS roster and forwards a copy of the placement form to the SS teacher. If a peer tutor is requested, counselor will attempt to arrange a peer tutor from a prearranged list of volunteers.

5. **Counselor** will remove the student from the SS roster only when the placing teacher requests an end to the placement.

### Guidelines

- Teachers have the authority to place students in Supervised Study for learning-related reasons. Learning reasons may include but are not limited to low grades, low test scores, missing homework, failure to show mastery of standards, or other learning-related needs.

- Placements cannot be related to poor student behavior.

- Teachers will determine the duration of placement (minimum two weeks).

- A new form must be created for each placement.

- The placing teacher should attempt in-class interventions before referring a student to SS.

### Supervised Study Locations for First Semester

| | |
|---|---|
| 1A = Mr. Timothy Joseph, H401 | 1B = Ms. Willa Strong, H406 |
| 2A = Mr. Percy Anderson, H101 | 2B = Mr. David Kean, H310 |
| 3A = Ms. Marion Ames Zubin, H402 | 3B = Mr. Isaac Kaplan, H323 |
| 4A = Mr. Harry Patkin, H403 | 4B = Mr. Jon Pankle, H204 |

Figure 10.4: Procedure to place student in SS.

*Visit **go.solution-tree.com/rtiatwork** for a reproducible version of this figure.*

camaraderie in the classroom; one example of this is called simply "high and low." The students begin their class time by declaring their high and low event from the last twenty-four hours. These types of simple activities have done much for fostering the CRTI approach to building community and tailoring attention to specific student need. By having to share emotions, ideas, and beliefs, the activity forces students to connect with one another and with the teacher in a way that fosters relationships. The activity further helps the teacher target his or her mentoring role to define students' needs. The activity fosters the need to give strong consideration for the emotional status of each student. Through this simple activity, the teacher can begin to hone in on the intangible issues associated with being a student who struggles academically in school, especially in a high-performing school such as SAS. As a side note to this, during progress interviews with the assistant principal at SAS, students involved with high and low have consistently cited it as something that they enjoy and find meaningful in the class.

The first intensive intervention, Learning Support, focuses on students who, through placement data described earlier, are found to be struggling in areas more closely related to academic behaviors and challenges. Students placed in Learning Support have challenges that go beyond small gaps in learning or choice behaviors about studying or homework. Those issues are typically addressed by earlier interventions. Students in Learning Support have more severe needs or gaps in their learning, such as processing issues or executive functioning deficits that inhibit their success in achieving classroom learning targets.

Regardless of when students are placed in the class, they are always given an initial executive skills assessment. The assessment used is the Executive Skills Questionnaire for Students, found in the text *Executive Skills in Children and Adolescents: A Practical Guide to Assessment and Intervention (Second edition)* by Peg Dawson and Richard Guare (2010). From these assessment data, students and teacher choose two areas that the assessment has indicated the students need help on. They then identify two strategies that they will work on to help them improve their academic performance. These areas may include, but are not limited to, such strategies as use of concept maps, use of technology inhibitors such as "self-control" software, organizational strategies, homework prioritization lists, or word-association devices. Students declare the strategies that they plan to work on, and the teacher and student monitor their progress using a daily self-reflection form (figure 10.5, page 240) and arrive at a grade based on their combined assessment of progress. At first, some of our teachers assigned the strategies that students had to work on, but it became apparent that when students were allowed to choose and change which strategies they used, they were more likely to actually use them on a consistent basis. Keep in mind that this process takes continued monitoring from the teacher. When skills are not helping the student to be more successful academically or behaviorally, they need to be changed. Students don't always have the know-how to assess what is working and what is not, and a teacher acting as a persistent but caring coach is essential to the process.

| Date | Coursework | Learning Goal 1<br><br>List and organize assignments. | Learning Goal 2<br><br>Use color layouts for all classes (add bio). | Points and Comments |
|------|-----------|------------------|------------------|---------------------|
|      |           |                  |                  |                     |
|      |           |                  |                  |                     |
| Comments: |      |             |                  | Weekly Point Totals: |

*Source: Singapore American School.*

Figure 10.5: Daily self-reflection form.

*Visit **go.solution-tree.com/rtiatwork** for a reproducible version of this figure.*

Also assessed is student progress toward meeting our schoolwide Desired Student Learning Outcomes (DSLO) of character, collaboration, communication, creativity, critical thinking, core knowledge, and cultural competence. Students typically work on academic behavior attributes related to character by choosing particular character attributes, such as work ethic or interpersonal skills, to work on. Student and teacher further define what behaviors might improve their learning in these areas and then both teacher and student measure their progress on those items daily.

Overall student progress is monitored on a biweekly basis when the teacher and students review daily self-assessments to determine their progress over the last two weeks. Students can replace the prior two-week scores if they improve in the use of their strategies. After several weeks of using the strategies, students can either switch strategies or maintain the work, if they feel it is helpful and effective. The strategies are almost always used to complete their work from other classes. This helps them use their skills in context and provides relevance to their learning. Figure 10.6 (pages 242–243) shows the Biweekly Assessment Form.

Whole-group minilessons (five to ten minutes) focusing on academic behaviors such as study, time management, or collaboration skills; test-taking strategies; or self-advocacy skills are taught throughout the school year. These common lessons not only help to move our Learning Support class away from being just a homework club but begin to equip students with skills and dispositions to leverage regardless of what class they may be in. Further, the group approach to lessons helps to develop the essential CRTI component of fostering classroom structures that build community and tailor attention to specific student needs.

After the whole-group minilesson is conducted, students and teachers break out into smaller groups to work with the teacher on more intense, targeted, student-specific interventions in areas of weakness or other subject areas that students may be working on. For example, if a freshman group of students in the Learning Support class have a biology test coming up in a week, the Learning Support teacher may review vocabulary and key biology concepts like *meiosis* with the group using the individual skills students are working on. In the case of the student who is working on questioning for understanding and self-reflection, the teacher might model quality questioning about the phases of meiosis for Student B to the whole group and then specifically have Student B use his self-reflection strategies at the end of the review to summarize the lesson. The teacher is sure to incorporate each of the participating students' individualized strategies into the context of the minilesson. By doing this, the students gain the executive functioning skills they need to leverage in all of their classes while still meeting their class-specific homework and study needs. When we speak with students in the Learning Support class about what they really like about the class, this teaching approach consistently comes up as one of the top things cited. For teachers, this approach takes a great deal of planning and significant knowledge of the individual skills the student is working on. Excellence in this strategy continues to be a work in progress for our teachers and is not something that they will ever be done developing. However, it is a worthy effort, and one that is greatly appreciated by our students and produces positive growth results in executive functioning.

| Character Development | | | | | | |
|---|---|---|---|---|---|---|
| **Work Ethic** | **Student** | **Teacher** | **Student** | **Teacher** | **Student** | **Teacher** |
| Sustains focus | | | | | | |
| Remembers and follows directions | | | | | | |
| Takes initiative | | | | | | |
| Follows through | | | | | | |
| Interpersonal Skills | | | | | | |
| **Work Ethic** | **Student** | **Teacher** | **Student** | **Teacher** | **Student** | **Teacher** |
| Asks questions for a deeper understanding | | | | | | |
| Is self-reflective | | | | | | |
| Problem solves | | | | | | |
| Executive Skills: Focus 1—Working Memory | | | | | | |
| **Work Ethic** | **Student** | **Teacher** | **Student** | **Teacher** | **Student** | **Teacher** |
| Creates checklists | | | | | | |
| Has space to work and put things; packs bag night before | | | | | | |

*Source: Singapore American School.*

Figure 10.6: Biweekly assessment form.

Continued on next page →

| Executive Skills: Focus 2—Sustained Focus | | | | | | |
|---|---|---|---|---|---|---|
| **Work Ethic** | **Student** | **Teacher** | **Student** | **Teacher** | **Student** | **Teacher** |
| Takes breaks every twenty-five to thirty minutes | | | | | | |
| Moves away from distractions | | | | | | |

1—Never

2—Rarely

3—Some of the time

4—Most of the time

5—Always

*Visit **go.solution-tree.com/rtiatwork** for a reproducible version of this figure.*

# RLA Lab

Our most intensive student intervention for students is the Reading Language Arts Lab. This intensive reading and writing intervention is accessed by students through admissions placement, eighth-grade transition meetings with counselors, or SST. Greater placement focus is emphasized on test scores and reading-related data than in any of our other interventions. Just having bad English grades is not enough to be placed in the RLA Lab. Students may have poor grades, but they must also show weaknesses in other diagnostic measures that we will describe shortly. This intervention, more so than all other interventions we offer, must have proper placement. For a high school student who has a significant challenge with reading and carries emotional strain from his or her history of that, the worst nightmare is to be placed in intervention with a student who reads well but simply has bad behaviors.

There is a two-layer approach to determining placement. First, students must demonstrate low proficiency on universal screening assessments that we offer, such as MAP, EDmin Lexile, the ACT Plan test, or classroom-based assessments that are specific to reading ability. Once a student is identified with one of these mechanisms by one of the counselors who reviews screener data or by a teacher, the SST will then review the student's history and test data collectively and not in isolation of one test. If it is determined that the student may be in need of RLA Lab, the second layer of testing occurs. The most important reading assessment tool that we have to determine student placement is the Qualitative Reading Inventory, or QRI.

The QRI test is administered to the student individually by a teacher. We have found that the individualized nature of the assessment eliminates the test-fatigue response some students with behavior issues will exhibit on tests that are high stakes for adults and low stakes for students. Quite simply, we have found that some students may blow off large-scale screeners, but we have yet to work with a student who has blown off a QRI with a caring teacher. We attribute this to the personalized nature of the QRI versus the impersonal, large-scale nature of other screening assessments; some students just need to know someone cares about them and the outcome of the assessment before they will give full effort on the test. This QRI data can then be used as a baseline for monitoring progress of students who exhibit test scores low enough to warrant RLA Lab entrance—typically, those scoring at least two grade levels below their peers. Students who post scores close to or at grade level will then be referred back to SST by the test proctor, where they will typically be placed in other interventions more focused on academic behaviors and low motivation. Placement can occur at any time during the semester, and once in, students are given the QRI. Like supervised study hall and Learning Support intervention classes, RLA Lab is available as a for-credit or not-for-credit class during every period of the day. This allows for maximum scheduling flexibility for students.

Once in the RLA Lab, the student participates in a highly structured eighty-five-minute intervention time. Because the work is so structured, it may be most helpful to describe it in agenda form (figure 10.7).

**RLA Daily Agenda Description**

- **Five to seven minutes:** Opening activity incorporating word study words (that is, high and low, response to YouTube video, news article, upcoming school events). Every two weeks, word-study words are introduced for the students to define, identify roots, synonyms, antonyms, and parts of speech. Words used are from the English curriculum (for example, *Lord of the Flies* vocabulary) and taken from word lists for grade levels.

- **Thirty to forty minutes:** Reading / writing interventions (typically 1:1 or small group). All materials are rotated through weekly or biweekly (schedule dependent and student need dependent)—

  - Timed Reading Plus (comprehension/fluency)

  - Grammar workbooks (individual skills identified)

  - Evergreen books (additional reading, grammar, or writing skills aligned with prerequisite reading standards)

- Daily oral language (sentence structure, grammar, syntax)

- Journaling (incorporation of coordination and subordination into writing and word-study words)

- Every month, data are taken during "intervention time" for both reading and writing using the Qualitative Reading Inventory or DIBELS reading passages, and writing samples are written (responses to prompts given)

- **Twenty-five to thirty minutes:** Minilesson (whole class).

  - Skills aligned with standards identified, practiced, and broken down (that is, review of logos, pathos, and ethos or review of characterization in *To Kill a Mockingbird*)

  - Incorporation of intervention strategies are also used during this time (that is, pairing a visual to the meaning of logos, pathos, and ethos or characters, mind mapping, outlining, and so on)

*Source: Singapore American School.*

Figure 10.7: RLA daily agenda description.

Biweekly during minilesson time, students are asked to rate themselves on strategies they have identified to apply to their coursework (for example, outlines, annotations, writing conferences, and color coding) and then write a reflection (metacognition) about what they are doing and identify why they aren't using some (if applicable) and how they will improve.

If there is time, typically the last ten to twenty minutes of class are used to apply strategies to coursework (that is, outlining persuasive speech, identifying literary devices in text, or practicing vocabulary words with a practice quiz).

Further evidence of our success comes from the students themselves. Once they are in the course, they don't want to leave even though they are reading at grade level. Unfortunately, most of these students have to leave the class to make way for others who are struggling, as our sections for RLA Lab are always at or surpassing the ideal target number of seven. When interventions are done in a compassionate way, students gain both emotionally and academically from the effort.

A note regarding numbers of students in this intervention: it is ideally kept as low as seven students in one class, but we have had situations where class sizes can be as high as sixteen. When demand necessitates large class numbers, difficult decisions have to be made about increasing class sizes in other sections to decrease class sizes in interventions. Another approach that has met with success is the use of reading improvement software packages, such as Empower3000, PLATO Learning, or NovaNET. By adding computers and headphones, teachers can divide the class into needs groups and focus intense intervention time with specific students based on need. Though not ideal, it does provide options when available staff are at a premium.

## Pyramid of Advancement

SAS is in the process of developing a "pyramid of advancement" that will articulate strategies and structures used to accelerate and enrich student learning at every level. Our move in this direction reinforces our commitment to providing students with opportunities to explore their areas of interest and passion beyond the limits of the curriculum. As a result of the R&D process, an increasing number of courses offer projects and applied-learning opportunities to students who demonstrate mastery of intended learning targets. One model, called the "flipped classroom," has students watching the teacher's instruction at home through an online video recording of the lecture before class starts. At the beginning of the lesson, the teacher presents a brief recap of the main ideas followed by a formative assessment to determine levels of mastery for each student. Students who are able to demonstrate mastery of the key concepts for the day are assigned authentic projects, debates, or research opportunities that go beyond the curriculum. Students who are still struggling with the key learning targets are given an opportunity to deepen their understanding through additional instruction and tutelage.

In addition to extended learning opportunities within the traditional classroom, capstone project courses are available for all of our students. A capstone project course provides time, space, structure, and advisors for students to engage in deep intellectual exploration in areas of passion. Students engaged in the capstone project course use core knowledge and competencies and apply them to real-world projects, problems, or products. Under the tutelage of a community mentor, students engage in authentic and applied learning experiences culminating in a public defense of their work and learning in front of a panel of community and industry experts.

## Results

As with any new program implementation, it is important to monitor results so that we can make course corrections if needed and celebrate successes when warranted. Here are some of the data points we have been tracking over the last couple of years.

- Our RLA Lab results indicate that 100 percent of students increased their reading level to the upper-middle-school level or higher; most students were at least two years behind their grade-level peers.

- The number of students in our RLA Labs has doubled due to students requesting to be placed there, having experienced success in their regular classes as a result of their RLA Lab experience.

- Our AP scores have increased for the third year in a row, even though SAS is in the top 1 percent of all schools, both in the United States and internationally, in numbers of students receiving a 3 or higher on their results.

- Since instituting a standards-based grading policy, RTI, and team structures, our "F" list was reduced from thirty-seven to two students.

- Since implementing the CRTI model, we have not exited any students from SAS for poor academic performance.

While our journey is far from over, initial results from the compassionate response to intervention model give us courage to continue down this path. At our core, we are convinced that a CRTI structure supported by a professional learning community framework is the single best strategy for maximizing learning for all of our students. The road can certainly seem uphill at times, and the ravines we encounter are deep and daunting, but the benefit to students is worth every bit of struggle encountered along the way.

# References

Buffum, A., Mattos, M., & Weber, C. (2009). *Pyramid response to intervention: RTI, professional learning communities, and how to respond when kids don't learn.* Bloomington, IN: Solution Tree Press.

Collins, J. C. (2001). *Good to great: Why some companies make the leap—And others don't.* New York: HarperBusiness.

Dawson, P., & Guare, R. (2010). *Executive skills in children and adolescents: A practical guide to assessment and intervention* (2nd ed.). New York: Guilford Press.

Dewey, J. (1938). *Experience in education.* New York: Touchstone.

DuFour, R., DuFour, R., & Eaker, R. (2008). *Revisiting professional learning communities at Work: New insights for improving schools.* Bloomington, IN: Solution Tree Press.

Fahrney, D. (2013). *Voice of struggling adolescent readers in a secondary school response to intervention (RTI) reading program.* Unpublished doctoral dissertation, Marian University, Fond Du Lac, Wisconsin.

Fullan, M. (2008). *The six secrets of change: What the best leaders do to help their organizations survive and thrive.* San Francisco: Jossey-Bass.

Kotter, J. P. (2012). *Leading change.* Cambridge, MA: Harvard Business Review Press.

Leslie, L., & Schudt-Caldwell, J. (2010). *Qualitative reading inventory-5* (5th ed.). Boston: Pearson.

Pink, D. H. (2006). *A whole new mind: Why right-brainers will rule the future.* New York: Riverhead Trade.

Sizer, T. R. (2004). *Horace's compromise: The dilemma of the American high school.* New York: Houghton Mifflin Harcourt.

Stuart, T. S., & Bostrom, C. (2003). *Children at promise: 9 principles to help kids thrive in an at-risk world—Turning hard knocks into opportunities for success.* San Francisco: Jossey-Bass.

Wagner, T. (2008). *The global achievement gap: Why even our best schools don't teach the new survival skills our children need—And what we can do about it.* New York: Basic Books.

**Jane Wagmeister, EdD,** is currently executive director of curriculum and instruction at the Ventura County Office of Education (VCOE) and chair of the Ventura County RTI² Task Force. The VCOE operates specialized student programs and provides leadership and service to Ventura County districts and schools, including instructional reviews and professional development opportunities. The RTI² Task Force is a multidisciplinary collaborative seventeen-member team that developed the Ventura County recommended RTI² model with aligned academic and behavioral resources.

Jane is a former K–12 administrator, previously serving as principal of a National Blue Ribbon elementary school, principal of various K–8 special education schools, and head of a private school for students in grades 2 through 12 with learning differences. She is the coauthor of the California Department of Education's *Response to Instruction and Intervention (RTI²): An Implementation and Technical Assistance Guide for Districts and Schools* (2011), has been awarded the California School Board Association's Golden Bell Award for creation of a common formative assessment for students with disabilities (2006), is a four-time California Services for Technical Assistance and Training (CalSTAT) award recipient (2010–2014) for exemplary RTI² and professional development of positive behavioral intervention and supports (PBIS), received an award for RTI² leadership from Phi Delta Kappa Ventura (2011), and has presented the California RTI² model at California's Curriculum and Instructional Leadership Conference (2011).

To book Jane Wagmeister for professional development, contact pd@solution-tree .com.

# From a Last Resort to a Model School of Choice

Jane Wagmeister

As educators, we know that academic success and proper behavior go hand in hand, since the students most at risk academically often demonstrate behaviors that are counterproductive to learning. Learning time is lost when teachers stop instruction to redirect student behavior or when the behavior becomes so disruptive that students must be removed from the learning environment. Learning time can be gained if these disruptions can be decreased. Unfortunately, most schools have not created consensus on the exact academic and social behaviors that all students must demonstrate to be successful. Even when schools have achieved this clarity, these skills are rarely systematically taught to the students, and the primary way of providing behavior interventions is to increase negative consequences.

The model described in this chapter provides clear examples and proven processes to increase student learning time by creating a schoolwide focus on teaching proper academic and social behaviors. Because most student misbehavior happens during student transition time, both inside and outside the classroom, the school clearly identified the specific behaviors each student must demonstrate at these times and then systematically taught them to every student. This positive, proactive approach to student behavior decreased behavior violations and increased student time on task.

Flexible intervention time often requires students to transition to different classrooms and work with staff who might not be their regular teacher. Many schools, foreseeing the possibility of student misbehavior during these times, fail to begin implementing an intervention period due to these concerns. Our experience is that students will be whatever you expect them to

> be. In other words, if you expect secondary students to be immature children who can't be trusted with responsibility, you're right. That is how most students will act, because that is how you treat them. But if we expect students to be responsible young adults capable of making good decisions and we teach them the positive behaviors they need to achieve these outcomes, then that is how most of them will act.

---

Gateway Community School in Camarillo, California, works with students who are at extremely high risk. These students are referred to Gateway by their home district, legal probation, or the Student Attendance Review Board.

High-risk students include those involved in continual incidents of moderate to severe misbehavior, including expellable offenses, repeated suspensions, chronic absenteeism and truancy, as well as those students who are at risk of dropping out or incarceration, those who are engaged in severe drug and alcohol abuse, and those who have criminal or gang involvement.

Gateway was established in 1980 by the Ventura County Office of Education (VCOE) to serve youth in grades 6–12 throughout Ventura County's twenty-one school districts. The school's 166-student enrollment at that time consisted of 81 percent Hispanic or Latino students, 66 percent socioeconomically disadvantaged students, 38 percent English learners, and 15 percent students with disabilities. Historically, the typical student entering Gateway Community School averaged Ds and Fs, with reading levels as low as third grade, and scored below or far below basic on annual state testing. The typical Gateway high school student was on average sixty credits deficient in core classes (math, English, social science, and science) and three or more grades behind in reading and writing skills. Before the school's transformation, approximately 30 to 40 percent of students were assigned to a Ventura County probation officer or agency due to a misdemeanor or felony crime, with approximately 20 percent on an intensive probation program for repeat or severe offenses. Formal probation mandated drug testing and counseling, frequent meetings with probation officers, and mental health support. In addition, the school culture exposed foster care and homeless youth, who already were confronted with very difficult or extreme situations, to extreme and negative experiences, making even more difficult their struggle to improve behaviorally and academically.

Complicating the environment of poor student behavior were inconsistent and ineffective staff practices and responses to student behavior, which lacked consistency and cohesion. Another obstacle was that students themselves did not want to go to Gateway. It had a reputation among parents and community members as the school where you send the "worst of the worst." Referral to Gateway, in fact, was seen by the community as more of a sentence than an opportunity, and was often used as a threat to a student who was about to be expelled. Because of the severe recidivism, low student attendance (averaging 75 percent), and ineffectual school culture, the community had lost confidence in Gateway and had significantly reduced the number of referrals, with a resulting enrollment of 125 students, and with students returning to their home districts ill prepared.

Interview after interview with returning staff suggested that curriculum and instructional strategies were not sufficiently implemented or monitored for student understanding and mastery. For example, the school employed a character-based learning (CBL) curriculum that used a series of novels that held high interest but was not standards based or designed around consistent subject content. Although a literacy course was added after CBL was found ineffective as a primary means for teaching English learners, the course had little content to develop listening, speaking, and writing practice. The weak curriculum added to the school's stigma as a poorly functioning alternative school where students are sent to "fail even further." The student pass rate on the California High School Exit Examination (CAHSEE) was 30 percent, with *no* students achieving at the proficient level.

Staffing was naturally affected by this environment. Turnover averaged 30 percent, with teachers often leaving for more desirable positions. Staff members recognized that they had a minimal amount of support in behavior intervention and lacked appropriate programs for the school's special populations (students with special education services and English learners). Gateway staff and students were in survival mode.

A typical day at Gateway would include incidents of misbehavior at the onset of the day with students being searched outside and in full view. This procedure provided an audience for the misbehavior, and the staff were in the role of "putting out fires" on a daily basis. The 2008–2009 school year included over one thousand days of suspension, five hundred individual student suspensions, and over forty fights. Due to an absence of transition support or effective screening, students would struggle even to start school at the beginning of the term. Staff lacked a system to respond to misbehavior and resorted to poorly planned and executed protocols and procedures. A lack of cohesion on how to intervene in a proactive manner resulted in discrepant strategies for addressing student discipline.

## Creating a New Model

In January 2009, the Ventura County Office of Education made the Gateway Community School a priority, identifying it as a site needing more financial, instructional, and behavioral resources and supports. In 2010, the Ventura County Office of Education created a steering committee consisting of representatives from the

VCOE, local districts, probation agencies, and other agencies invested in Gateway's success to provide input into the school's restructuring. This committee made a number of recommendations, including implementation of the academic and behavioral components of response to instruction and intervention (RTI[2] includes not only intervention but also instruction); a realignment of hiring and staffing, a new principal, Principal Koenig; and an increase in rigor and curriculum.

The task of the new principal and the administrative team—composed of the VCOE director, the principal, and representation of a counselor, teacher, and classified staff (classified staff consisted of office staff, security, and paraeducators)—was to move the school from a survival and reactionary mode to a well-trained, well-planned, proactive school with proper interventions and support and a variety of collaborative models. In practice, this would mean fewer student fights and more teaching.

After extensive review of data by the leadership team and interviews with key stakeholders (parents, former students, teachers, support staff, and district representatives), it became clear that Gateway required a tool that would not only alter the culture but give the staff a way of intervening with misbehavior. The desired model had to not only intervene but also allow staff to get ahead of the problem by using proactive measures they could rely on, and by setting long-term behavioral and instructional goals. The goals of the desired interventions were:

- Reduce incidents of discipline such as suspensions, fights, verbal altercations, and drug possession or influence

- Increase attendance

- Improve safety for students and staff on campus

- Increase CAHSEE results

- Improve the perception of the Gateway school program among Ventura County's twenty-one school districts

Once they fully understood the implications of the data and staff input, district administration and Principal Koenig formulated a set of priorities: staff would intervene collectively to fully implement the PBIS CHAMPS approach (Positive Behavior Intervention and Support along with Conversation, Help, Activity, Movement, Participation, and Success) and thereby improve the school culture and behavioral and academic performance. CHAMPS complemented with Implementation Science (Fixen, Naoom, Blasé, Friedman, & Wallace, 2005), professional learning communities (PLCs, DuFour, DuFour, Eaker, & Karhanek, 2004), the Ventura County Recommended RTI[2] Model, and PBIS research (Sprick, 2009). The Implementation

Science research was a lens to support the CHAMPS approach to ensure monitoring of effectiveness.

Principal Koenig and the administrative team believed a focus on key areas (fully implement PBIS and CHAMPS and develop programs to skillfully transition all new and incoming students into Gateway's recovery, high school, or middle school; provide more social-emotional support; decrease severe behavior and fights; and increase attendance) would bring about an alternative school culture capable of delivering quality instruction without the burden of significant and unnecessary disruption. Individual interviews with staff from Gateway, VCOE, and local school districts, along with an analysis of the budget allocation, guided the school's plan. By focusing on the steps outlined in Implementation Science research—(exploration, planning, implementation, and sustainment), Gateway trained the administrative team in CHAMPS.

The next step consisted of training a site-planning team to enact PBIS; increasing behavior services and supports, such as counseling services and specific behavioral interventions; restructuring the environment by posting guiding behavior principles in the quad and around campus; and creating schoolwide expectations for common areas. The site planning team consisted of the principal, assistant principal, director, transition specialist, and academic counselor. After several months, two teachers were added, and this team became the leadership team. One of its most important roles was to reshape the negative reputation of the school. Gateway had experienced a sharp decrease in student referrals.

In order to make the program effective, the staff had to become transparent. This meant sharing classroom management and instructional strategies and accepting administrative, district, and peer input. The Gateway program received daily and weekly visits from paraprofessionals, administrators, counselors, and probation officers. The site and district administrative team took every opportunity to meet and present to feeder districts, community partners, and local and state events and organizations. To further address the school's negative image, the leadership team invited representatives from local districts and outside agencies to visit the "new Gateway."

### Transition Program
Principal Koenig spent his first weeks focusing on the current state of the school. He read hundreds of prior student reports, reviewed the behavior data, spoke to each and every returning staff member, and familiarized himself with the site, protocol, culture, and procedures of the school. It soon became clear that there were only minimal systems in place to deal with everything from simple tasks like office duties to more sophisticated systems that monitor student progress. Often, staff were not

clear about who had been designated to handle key tasks. In response, teams were formed to follow up and guide staff members in collaboration with the administrative team.

All students need some sort of transition upon starting a new school. This is especially true for an at-risk student who has rarely or never been successful. Gateway's transition program started out as a two-week-long program combining high school and middle school students. After the first couple of weeks, the transition teacher and leadership team determined that two weeks was too long and to maximize the program's impact, the middle and high school students should be separated. The program was scaled back to five then four days for high school students and one day for middle school students (table 11.1). The refined transition class model was referred to as the "warm fuzzy," because students were provided a very low affective filter to lower the level of anxiety and frustration that they experienced when confronting a new learning task, and were given extensive support and opportunities to talk through past issues and express their hopes for attending Gateway. Second in priority was to take inventory of every student's academic ability, behavior status, needs, and risks, resulting in a record of students' future goals and interests. The transition program administered and reviewed diagnostic assessments and performed observations of student behavior. Follow-up came from student conferences, interactions between students, and input from teachers and counselors. (Due to lower numbers and higher level of support, middle school students and students in more specialized programs didn't require as much time to prepare for entering class.)

**Table 11.1: Transition Weekly Schedule**

| Transition Weekly Schedule | | | | |
|---|---|---|---|---|
| Monday | Tuesday | Wednesday | Thursday | Friday |
| HS transition starts | Day 2 of HS transition | Day 3 of HS transition | Day 4 of HS transition | MS transition |

Learning more about individual students helped Gateway staff to arrange seating and to determine if counseling was needed, if there were gang issues, and if a focused behavior plan was necessary. This information not only provided an academic portrait and a list of interests and skills, but gave insight into students' ability to improve behaviorally.

Upon student completion of the transition, the transition teacher compiled the data, observations, and information and emailed the summary of each student's results to those staff members who would be working with the student. Counselors, teachers, and administration determined appropriate program placement, specific strategies, differentiation needs, and interventions. Students were targeted and grouped for interventions by a variety of student data points, including mathematics and English assessment scores, past academic progress, CAHSEE results, EL supports, and social, emotional, and behavioral needs. The school determined which staff member would take responsibility to lead specific intervention groups based on teacher requests, credentials, expertise, and current courses taught. The counselor used the results of the universal screening along with the student's academic history to determine whether he or she ought to be placed in an intervention course or could take an elective (for example, leadership, career development, credit recovery, internship, or a program designed to train and certify students in specific trades such as welding, dental assistant, or florist). Each student had a personalized portfolio with diagnostic assessments, transcript analysis, graduation planning, and terms for returning to the district from which he or she was expelled or referred. In addition to reviewing academic and behavioral expectations, the transition teacher exposed students to lessons on social skills and character building.

During this time, students were welcomed by and met with the majority of Gateway staff to ensure they knew whom they could go to in order to get their questions answered and needs met. Another key component of transition class consisted of projects designed to introduce students to CHAMPS and provide them with a basis from which to develop goals for and after their time at Gateway. Students were asked to create the guidelines in their own words using PowerPoint. They also interviewed each other and discussed and presented similarities and differences. The goal was to break down barriers between students, particularly those who were gang entrenched or self-isolated. This provided a vehicle for them to better understand each other and ensured that activities were rooted in the CHAMPS philosophy of training and encouraging desired behaviors.

At the conclusion of the transition program, the Gateway transition team made a recommendation for placement of students in one of three available programs: high school daily, middle school, or independent studies. Each student began his or her regular schedule on Friday; for middle school, it started at lunch, and for high school it began in the morning. This was intentional. If for some reason the staff members missed something on the risk assessment, they had the weekend to adjust programs as well as give the student a "cooling off" period (time to remove him or herself from a conflict and begin to think about choices).

The independent studies program was highly regulated, and the only students able to enter this program were those unable to be transported to school. This included, for example, students with severe medical conditions or family hardship and students who were in the process of giving birth or recovering from giving birth.

## Academic Foundation

In the middle of the 2010–2011 school year, the steering committee reaffirmed that Gateway would undergo restructuring to evolve into a learning community that relied on continual collaboration, communication, and refinement as it adjusted to the new model. In implementing the goals of the steering committee and focusing primarily on CHAMPS being embedded in and around the school's daily operations, Gateway staff had mastered, fully implemented, and engrained CHAMPS as the PBIS model. Communication and collaboration were vital in this process, as was treating all students with dignity and respect.

Throughout the summer of 2011, Principal Koenig sought input from all levels of his staff to identify the school's greatest areas of weakness. Staff identified the poor staff development model, minimal instructional support, and poorly thought-out curriculum map. The leadership team, along with the court and community school director and assistant superintendent of student services, identified a series of instructional tools and training opportunities—for example, Thinking Maps, pacing guides, calendar models, and English learner strategies. More involved strategies, including guiding principles for schoolwide behavior or guidelines for success, common-area CHAMPS for bathrooms and the lunch area, and a rubric for defining and providing feedback on behavior were combined with positive behavior intervention training in a three-day summer retreat during 2010. The retreat was held the week before school with a whole-staff component. District VCOE instructional content specialists provided training on Thinking Maps, EL strategies, SDAIE (specially designed academic instruction in English) strategies, curriculum organization, and site planning for CHAMPS. Ongoing training of Gateway's instructional staff and leadership team on these strategies throughout the school year (during the "a.m. hour" staff development time) ensured fidelity and continuity.

## Staff Development

To address the need for a comprehensive staff development plan, Principal Koenig had to develop an intensive, five-day-a-week training schedule (though not all districts would be able to allow that many staff development days). New staff were informed and selected based on their willingness and ability to support this new model and the priorities of restructuring. The schedule detailed key categories of trainings. Mondays were for "meet ups" to check in with the staff, Tuesday was CHAMPS training, Wednesday was dedicated to technology training, Thursday was for case management, and Friday was for outside organizations and agencies (such as probation and trainings). The staff and administrative team met forty-five minutes before school to accommodate scheduling changes and would also meet occasionally in the afternoon, and all monthly hourly trainings occurred after school.

As the staff progressed each month, the number of training days required were reduced; specifically, once staff were aware of, and understood the purpose of, information shared by outside agencies like probation, and once students were properly referred for counseling or to meet with probation, we reduced and eventually removed that particular day of training (only to add it when issues or topics of importance came up). A major focus of paring down the number of staff development days was to build leadership team capacity. This would allow leadership team members to meet in more specialized teams, where they could move further along without having to wait for the entire group or work with subject areas that did not relate to them.

## Pacing Guidelines and Calendars

Another priority of the Gateway leadership team and staff was to improve curriculum organization by developing pacing guides and calendars. In this instance, one minimum-day training (once a month) was included on how to use the CHAMPS model, develop and improve curriculum, create and develop pacing guides and calendars, and learn various other teaching and technology strategies. The priority over the summer was to fully train staff in PBIS as well as key teaching strategies (Thinking Maps, EL strategies) and to foster schoolwide buy-in and implementation. After the extended training, the leadership team and instructional staff met weekly to collaborate, provide feedback, and review all pacing guides and calendars. Teachers submitted quarterly updated versions of the pacing guides and calendars to the principal.

For the first three months of the 2010–2011 school year, Gateway staff reported feeling as if they were in front of a speeding train. Principal Koenig would talk to staff members who felt overwhelmed and provide times when teachers could catch up. Along with his administrative team, he met and discussed issues staff were dealing with. Isolated situations were addressed with staff members, and Principal Koenig or the administrative team addressed whole-group concerns. On particularly busy weeks, or when the administrative team determined staff was overloaded, they would collaborate with Principal Koenig to reschedule or eliminate trainings or meetings, allowing staff to work on class-specific duties.

## Schedule Changes

The entire staff realized that a dramatic change to the instructional day was necessary. Most at-risk students struggle just to go to school, and an inordinately early bus arrival and start time (students were at the bus stop as early as six in the morning), only increased their resistance. Instructional time was not maximized, and classes were addressing too many grade levels. For example, English classes combined multiple grades (6 to 8 or 9 to 12), and as a result, teachers were not able to focus their lessons effectively. The curriculum design combined three and sometimes four grade levels into one class. This not only caused difficulty in planning but also a lack of focus in instructional delivery. Another issue was the lack of intervention, both academic and behavioral. Time in the school day to support academically low or struggling students was created by maximizing instructional minutes. The school instructional day, which had run from 7:55 a.m. to 1:05 p.m., now ran from 9:15 a.m. to 2:25 p.m. Starting school later made it more likely that students would come and provided a sixty-minute time period in the morning for staff development. Each period now extended from just over forty minutes to sixty minutes. The six-minute passing period was reduced to a one- or two-minute passing period, without bells, which placed the responsibility for ending class on the teacher. Removing the long passing period brought multiple improvements: there were fewer late students wandering in the quad; minutes were added to the intervention classes and core classes; additional intervention periods could be provided for all programs; teachers supported security by standing outside their doors, reducing possible incidents; and there was a chance for staff to check in with students as they walked in and exited classrooms. Figure 11.1, shows the new high school and middle school schedule.

Ultimately, a forty-minute intervention period was added to the recovery program (a drug and alcohol rehabilitation program) in high school and middle school. In addition, students performing poorly on the diagnostic exams were scheduled into specific interventions, such as middle school mathematics, the California High School Exit Examination (CAHSEE) interventions in math and English, and English intervention and English learner classes. The school counselor reviewed student past assessment results and current transcripts and grades. The results from the transition math and English diagnostic assessment were used to determine if the student could benefit from other elective or credit recovery courses. Students performing better on the diagnostic exams were offered a choice of electives, including social and emotional supports, leadership class, career development, and an expanded selection of career technical education courses (for example, auto body, floral arrangement, banking, and nursing).

As a result of creating a transition class (where all new and arriving students attended extended days in transition), students were assessed using Renaissance Learning's STAR math and English diagnostic assessments, the O*NET OnLine career inventory, and observations by the transition teacher and administrative team. The administrative team composed a risk assessment in order to create a profile of each student (figure 11.2, pages 263–264) and trained students in the ways of Gateway. The assessments in math and English gave each teacher a baseline for entering students as well as a list of areas of interest, such as mechanical, organizational, health care, art work, and so on, based on insights into students' behavior and personality.

**High School Full Day**

| | | | minutes |
|---|---|---|---|
| 8:00 | 9:00 | Staff Time | |
| 9:00 | 9:15 | **Student Arrival** | 15* |
| 9:15 | 9:17 | Passing | 2 |
| 9:17 | 9:57 | **Period 1 / Intervention** | 40 |
| 9:57 | 9:59 | Passing | 2 |
| 9:59 | 10:57 | **Period 2** | 58 |
| 10:57 | 10:59 | Passing | 2 |
| 10:59 | 11:57 | **Period 3** | 58 |
| 11:57 | 12:27 | Lunch | 30 |
| 12:27 | 12:28 | Passing | 1 |
| 12:28 | 1:26 | **Period 4** | 58 |
| 1:26 | 1:27 | Passing | 1 |
| 1:27 | 2:25 | **Period 5** | 58 |
| 2:25 | 2:30 | **Student Departure** | 5 |
| 2:30 | 3:30 | Staff Time | |

**High School Minimum Day**

| | | | |
|---|---|---|---|
| 8:00 | 9:00 | Staff Time | |
| 9:00 | 9:10 | **Student Arrival** | 15 |
| 9:10 | 9:12 | Passing | 2 |
| 9:12 | 9:59 | **Period 1 / Intervention** | 47 |
| 9:59 | 10:01 | Passing | 2 |
| 10:01 | 10:48 | **Period 2** | 47 |
| 10:48 | 10:50 | Passing | 2 |
| 10:50 | 11:37 | **Period 3** | 47 |
| 11:37 | 12:07 | Lunch | 30 |
| 12:07 | 12:09 | Passing | 2 |
| 12:09 | 12:56 | **Period 4** | 47 |
| 12:56 | 12:58 | Passing | 2 |
| 12:58 | 1:45 | **Period 5** | 47 |
| 1:45 | 1:55 | **Student Departure** | 5 |
| 1:55 | 3:30 | Staff Time | |

*minutes

*Source: Gateway Community School.*

Figure 11.1: Gateway high school and middle school bell schedule.

Continued on next page ↓

**Middle School Full Day**

| Start | End | Activity | Minutes |
| --- | --- | --- | --- |
| 8:00 | 9:00 | Staff Time | |
| 9:00 | 9:15 | **Student Arrival** | 15 |
| 9:15 | 9:20 | Passing | 5 |
| 9:20 | 10:00 | **Period 1** | 40 |
| 10:00 | 10:03 | Passing | 3 |
| 10:03 | 10:51 | **Period 2** | 48 |
| 10:51 | 10:54 | Passing | 3 |
| 10:54 | 11:42 | **Period 3** | 48 |
| 11:42 | 12:12 | Lunch | 30 |
| 12:12 | 12:15 | Passing | 3 |
| 12:15 | 1:03 | **Period 4** | 48 |
| 1:03 | 1:06 | Passing | 3 |
| 1:06 | 1:54 | **Period 5** | 48 |
| 1:54 | 2:25 | **Period 6—P.E.** | 31 |
| 2:25 | 2:30 | **Student Departure** | 249 |
| 2:30 | 3:30 | Staff Time | |

**Middle School Minimum Day**

| Start | End | Activity | Minutes |
| --- | --- | --- | --- |
| 8:00 | 9:00 | Staff Time | |
| 9:00 | 9:15 | **Student Arrival** | 15 |
| 9:15 | 9:18 | Passing | 3 |
| 9:18 | 9:58 | **Period 1** | 40 |
| 9:58 | 10:01 | Passing | 3 |
| 10:01 | 10:46 | **Period 2** | 45 |
| 10:46 | 10:49 | Passing | 3 |
| 10:49 | 11:34 | **Period 3** | 45 |
| 11:34 | 12:04 | Lunch | 30 |
| 12:04 | 12:07 | Passing | 3 |
| 12:07 | 12:52 | **Period 4** | 45 |
| 12:52 | 12:55 | Passing | 3 |
| 12:55 | 1:45 | **Period 5** | 50 |
| 1:45 | 1:55 | **Student Departure** | 240 |
| 1:55 | 3:30 | Staff Time | |

**Students entering the daily program for Friday, September XX.**

**Student Name: B.L.**

Tenth grade, expel until January, wants to return to XXXX High

**Assessments:**
Math—27/29 (math is B.L.'s strength, does most math work in head)
Reading—37/40, 1130 Lexile, grade 10
Writing—On a scale of 0–4, I would give her a 3

**Behavior:** Can be talkative, moves a lot, easily sidetracked, impulsive, friendly, but does not like having behavior addressed. Some days B.L. is mellow, focused, and completely on task, and some days B.L. is a completely different person: uncontrolled outbursts, squirming in seat, and so on. I have spoken with dad.

**Interests:** Basketball, wrestling, old cars, and wants to be a marine.


**Student Name: G.J.**

Tenth grade, expel until January, wants to return to XXXX High
Has IEP for vision impairment, G.J. does not wear glasses or contacts. Should sit toward front of class.

**Assessments:**
Math—20/29
Reading—27/40, 705 Lexile, grade 4 (I think G.J. would've scored higher if test had been read to G.J.)
Writing—2/3 (needs a lot of help with revision/editing, but great starting point).

**Behavior:** On task, respectful, reflective, and insightful. G.J. is willing to work with others. Is also very honest with his peers, which sometimes is misinterpreted as G.J. is "talking smack."

**Interests:** Video games


**Student Name: S.T.**

Tenth grade, expel until January, wants to return to XXXX, but overall expresses an extreme dislike for any school

**Assessments:**
Math—14/29 (did really well on the first half of assessment and then got distracted)
Reading—34/40, 960 Lexile, grades 6–7
Writing—2/3

**Behavior:** S.T. goes from zero to ten in a moment. Is extremely sensitive, hyperaware of people looking at or talking about him, intense, explosive, dramatic, and often rude. S.T. uses excess profanity. Is more responsive if you try to talk to him without an audience. Needs space to calm down when angry. Seems to respond to compliments. Is quick to give up on an assignment, but totally has the capability to complete work. Is currently dating M.R.

**Interests:** Wants to be a veterinarian

*Source: Gateway Community School.*

Figure 11.2: Sample student profile.

Continued on next page →

**Student Name: J. G.**

Twelfth grade, eighteen in January, district referral, extremely credit deficit

> **Assessments:**
> Math—15/29 (did well on the first 15 questions)
> Reading—35/40, 1010 Lexile, grades 7–8
> Writing—2/3 (reluctant to write)
>
> **Behavior:** Pleasant, smiles/laughs a lot, but has little interest in school.
>
> **Interests:** Likes to doodle. Wants to be a tattoo artist.

*Visit **go.solution-tree.com/rtiatwork** for a reproducible version of this figure.*

These baseline data translated into an instructional program addressing more of students' individual needs as measured via benchmarks and post-assessments that identified, for example, poor basic skills, difficulty writing, or low reading scores. The students' grades, attendance, behavior, and amount of counseling received were tracked by the office clerical support and school counselor, and all data were placed in a student portfolio or file and used to demonstrate student improvement at district and individual education plan meetings, or for alternative placement (adult school, trade school, and so on).

## Special Education and English Learner Support

A subset of the goals was to improve Gateway's special education and English learner (EL) supports and services. The priority was to ensure that special populations were prioritized in the master schedule. In order to accommodate these students, instructional minutes were adjusted to provide an EL course and math and English intervention. This intervention period, accomplished by reducing each period by ten minutes, offered CAHSEE intervention in math and English as well as an EL intervention to focus students on their reading, writing, speaking, and listening skills. It was particularly important to the district director and Principal Koenig that Gateway provide EL teachers with specific curriculum instruction, versus offering curriculum designed only for reading and not for ELs. As the master schedule developed, students with IEPs were moved into general education classes to augment their exposure to general education core content.

The progress and pace of academic interventions required that Gateway create opportunities to reassure staff and students of progress. To do so, Gateway developed a series of incentives to recognize students for good behavior, attendance, and grades.

Each month, a student was selected from each program (recovery, high school, and middle school) and acknowledged. The student received a certificate, his or her name was posted on the marquee, a photo of the student appeared in the monthly newsletter, and the student received a small treat. A point sheet (figure 11.3) tabulated students' behavior and classroom performance by period into a weekly average that determined who earned an incentive. The point sheets provided consistent data on student behavioral progress and were effective for feedback on behavior. At the end of each quarter, all students with good behavior (positive point sheet data and no suspensions), 90 percent or more attendance, and grade point averages of 3.0 or above were recognized with an extended lunch, a certificate, and a small treat. The incentives helped the school sustain momentum.

| Behavior Point Sheet | 2 Excellent | 1 OK | 0 Needs Improvement |
|---|---|---|---|
| Name: _____ Today's date: _____ | Behavior 1: Student follows directions given by staff | Behavior 2: Student completes all assignments | Behavior 3: *A specialized behavior if needed* |
| Period 1: | 2    1    0 | 2    1    0 | |
| Period 2: | 2    1    0 | 2    1    0 | |
| Period 3: | 2    1    0 | 2    1    0 | |
| Period 4: | 2    1    0 | 2    1    0 | |
| Period 5: | 2    1    0 | 2    1    0 | |
| PE: Teacher notes: | | | |

*Source: Gateway Community School.*

Figure 11.3: Daily and weekly behavior point sheet.

*Visit **go.solution-tree.com/rtiatwork** for a reproducible version of this figure.*

## Building a Multitiered System of Supports

Principal Koenig was a strong proponent of the CHAMPS model and approach. As an assistant principal at a comprehensive high school, he had previously relied on disciplinary consequences and referred to himself as the "hammer." He soon realized the "at-risk" population within Gateway Community School would improve not by force but through support and well-thought-out behavior training. He carried this message to staff and students in every meeting, communication, and interaction; he and his staff adopted the term *annoyingly consistent,* a term used in the CHAMPS model.

Understanding the need for high-quality preparation, the staff requested using a trainer-of-trainer model for the PBIS CHAMPS pilot to build staff capacity. The purpose behind a PBIS model is to use tools and strategies to highlight positive or desired behavior in such a way that you can train students and staff to use those intended strategies over time, thereby supporting improved behavior. In the summer of 2011, VCOE supported a core group of Gateway staff to become PBIS CHAMPS trainers for the entire Gateway staff. This Gateway training team provided a three-day staff development before the start of school. The staff created a statement of beliefs, also known as the Guidelines for Success, which eventually became part of the school logo. The words on the logo, "We are respectful, positive, productive, proud," were also displayed in the school common eating area (figure 11.4).

Figure 11.4: The Gateway logo.

The Guidelines for Success worked as the filter through which Gateway made decisions and developed behavioral expectations, or CHAMPS. These guidelines were in a sense the vision of what behavior should be at Gateway. The staff understood Gateway could not create an environment of high performance academically if it didn't first improve everyone's attitude or behavior. Common areas (such as buses, bus stops, and drop-off areas; the student search area; quad and lunch areas; and bathrooms) previously were ravaged by misbehavior. The bathrooms and buses were of particular concern. The bathrooms were shared by high school and middle school students, and there was a schedule for middle schoolers to enter the high school campus to use the bathrooms. This schedule was not only complicated, it also interfered with movement in the high school. There were also incidents of drug use and damage to bathroom facilities. The buses were also regularly damaged, with drivers constantly complaining of inappropriate behavior and the bus having to return to the school after departing due to student violence, drug use, or extreme disruption affecting the safety of the bus and students. CHAMPS or "Schoolwide CHAMPS" (expectations) were developed for the buses as well as the bathrooms (figure 11.5). Another obvious improvement was to add bathrooms to the middle school. After doing so, staff immediately noticed a decrease in interruptions in both high school and middle school.

| Bus Rides | | |
|---|---|---|
| **C** | Conversation | Controlled, low volume, appropriate words |
| **H** | Help | See bus driver or staff while at campus |
| **A** | Activity | Sitting calmly in bus seat |
| **M** | Movement | Sitting only |
| **P** | Participation | Sitting calmly in seat |
| **Success!** | | |

| Welcome Room | | |
|---|---|---|
| **C** | Conversation | Respectfully and quietly with neighbor or staff |
| **H** | Help | Ask nearest staff respectfully |
| **A** | Activity | Turn in all items not allowed, put on ID and loaner clothes |
| **M** | Movement | Stay in line, waiting and walking responsibly |
| **P** | Participation | Positively and patiently interacting with staff and peers |
| **Success!** | | |

| Before and After School | | |
|---|---|---|
| **C** | Conversation | May speak to your friends at a reasonable volume |
| **H** | Help | See staff for assistance |
| **A** | Activity | Entering and exiting and staying in assigned areas |
| **M** | Movement | Walk |
| **P** | Participation | Minimal and quiet conversation with friends and quiet as you enter and exit class |
| **Success!** | | |

| Going to the Bathroom | | |
|---|---|---|
| **C** | Conversation | None, speak only with staff |
| **H** | Help | Wait for security or administration |
| **A** | Activity | Use and respect restroom |
| **M** | Movement | Walk |
| **P** | Participation | Only speak with staff |
| **Success!** | | |

| Lunchtime | | |
|---|---|---|
| **C** | Conversation | Speak in controlled and moderate volume with no profanity or inappropriate language |
| **H** | Help | See security or administration for assistance |
| **A** | Activity | Seated at lunch tables and benches in quad |
| **M** | Movement | Walk |
| **P** | Participation | Mingling with your friends or staff |
| **Success!** | | |

Figure 11.5: Schoolwide CHAMPS.

*Visit **go.solution-tree.com/rtiatwork** for a reproducible version of this figure.*

The bus drivers were trained by Gateway's administrative team and introduced to how to positively enforce these expectations. As a result, students heard a common vocabulary and were given consistent practices to follow from all staff with whom they interracted. Students were also trained in the CHAMPS expectations, and through follow-up on bus incidents, further disruptions were curbed. There was a strict expectation that if a student were written up, he or she would receive a warning for a minor issue; anything major resulted in a bus suspension, in order to avoid endangering the students and driver. The bathroom CHAMPS similarly detailed how students were expected to act in and out of the bathroom.

The staff developed CHAMPS at the first year of restructuring and taught these expectations to all students. Principal Koenig reviewed the expectations and the common-area CHAMPS with all new and incoming students, and introduced key rules to reduce unnecessary movement around campus (for example, no bathroom breaks during passing period and no bathroom breaks the first ten and last five minutes of class). By the end of the first semester, unnecessary movement was reduced by more than half, bathrooms were in better condition, and middle school traffic causing interruption and misbehavior on both campuses was reduced.

## Schoolwide Goals

Use of the safe and civil expectation and behavior model, CHAMPS, suggested that a common schoolwide set of goals should be developed to focus PBIS. Over the three-day summer retreat of 2011, the entire staff (this was strategic, in order to have everyone working at the school together) gave input, posted ideas, met in groups, and debated what our top behavior priorities or goals were and came to consensus on the message and direction of its behavior model. (The staff didn't wait for unanimous agreement, but wanted to ensure all staff could be on board and feel good about the outcome.) Principal Koenig and the staff adopted and embraced the most important aspect of CHAMPS—treating students with dignity and respect. By focusing on proactive strategies and explicit high-behavioral expectations, both staff and students generated staggering academic and behavior results. After year one, Gateway reduced individual suspensions and suspension days over 30 percent, attendance increased from below 75 percent to almost 80 percent, fights were reduced from over forty to under twenty within the year, and staff, students, and stakeholders alike commented on how much more calm and positive the school campus and environment was. Simple strategies like asking students to do what you expect of them, versus telling them what you *don't* want them to do, created a significant and positive shift in behavior. Additionally, Principal Koenig and the staff worked to adjust their own attitudes; he made sure the school staff were modeling the behavior they wanted to see in students. Staff greeted all students, took an interest in them, sat with them at lunch, and smiled, and all leadership team members made sure they knew every single student. Principal Koenig met with the new students, reviewed expectations and CHAMPS for the common areas, and discussed the characteristics of a successful Gateway student. Both new and returning staff and the administrative team were trained to deliver and model a culture of collaboration and communication, and "dignity and respect" permeated the school.

## Classroom CHAMPS

In year one, Gateway staff weekly meetings focused discussions on how they wove CHAMPS further into *all* aspects of the school (not just in the classrooms and common areas but in meetings as well) and used it to help students improve their own ability to improve behavior. Each week, a follow-up training was focused on the various chapters of the CHAMPS book. It was important, after the initial staffwide training on CHAMPS and prior to first implementation in the fall of 2011, to ensure that the staff moved into the more advanced stages of CHAMPS, including creating CHAMPS in individual classrooms. The idea was simply for teachers to create classroom CHAMPS around their strengths and expectations.

The teachers generated their own set of interventions and expectations according to their personal style, rather than copying them from a manual. In other words, they made the CHAMPS model their own when it came to their classroom expectations and the delivery of instruction. Teachers also made inquiries into the organization of the classroom environment—for example, where to place their desks so they had the greatest student access and students knew they could approach the teacher. A desk positioned as a barrier, for example, could be a hindrance to building relationships. Even more fundamental were the relationships that needed to be fostered. Teachers had been selected, trained, and encouraged to take complete and genuine interest in their students while getting to know them. Students who are at risk are particularly good at sniffing out someone who is not sincere. Gateway staff took these tools, made them their own, and confirmed that everyone was implementing the model.

## A Model for Other Schools

Gateway has made great gains. The focus, constant refinement, and regular collaboration among staff altered the once tumultuous and unstable campus into a highly effective school. Various behavior and academic data (suspensions, student reports, and CAHSEE results) have exceeded initial goals. What started out as a need to improve Gateway eventually became a model that other schools used—a hybrid RTI[2] model for at-risk youth. This model, based on a multitiered system of supports, is shown in figure 11.6 (page 272). Principal Koenig and his leadership team regularly would hear other school leaders report, "If Gateway can do it, then we can do it."

The multitiered model provides a comprehensive, inclusive, and integrated framework to assure consistency of service delivery. The three-tiered approach to instruction and intervention supports the academic as well as the social and emotional behavioral needs of students. The three tiers provide a continuum of increasingly intense, targeted instruction and intervention with respect to frequency and duration of services. Tier 1 employs both first-quality, effective, research-based instruction and research- and evidenced-based positive behavioral support.

The expanded intervention progress team (IPT) meets to review data and to consider referral for assessment for special education assessment after sixteen to twenty-four weeks of tiered intervention.

**TIER 3**

**Intensive**  **Indicated**

*Core + Supplemental Intensive*  *Indicated Program*
*Intervention Program*

Culturally and Linguistically Responsive Instruction

General Educator or Specialist    Counselor or Specialist

Reading or Learning Center—Extended    Time Consulting Center

Forty to Sixty Minutes Only    Designated Time

Individual / Small Groups / Additional Class Period

Continuous Progress Monitoring
PLC / IPT Determines Tier Interventions
Duration: Six to Eight Weeks

Approximately 5 Percent

**TIER 2**

**In Addition to Tier 1**

*Strategic/Targeted*    *Selective*

Core + Supplemental Program    Core + Selective Program

Culturally and Linguistically Responsive Instruction

General Ed or Specialist

Classroom or Learning Center    Classroom or Counseling Center

Thirty Minutes Daily    Designated Time

Small Groups / Secondary Lower Class Size or Shadow Class or Preteach Class
Progress Monitoring Weekly or Bimonthly
PLC / IPT Determines Tier Interventions
Duration: Six to Eight Weeks

Approximately 15 Percent

**TIER 1**

**Benchmark/Core    Universal**

Core With Differentiated Research-Based Instructional Strategies
Culturally and Linguistically Responsive Instruction
Coordinated, Effective High-Quality Instruction
Positive Behavioral Strategies
General Educator or Teacher
Classroom: Universal Screening and Intervention = Preventative and Proactive
Time Variable

Large Group / Individual / Small Group / Progress Monitoring
Duration: Six to Eight Weeks

Approximately 80 Percent

**Academic**    **Social and Emotional / Behavioral**

Figure 11.6: Ventura County RTI$^2$ multitiered system of supports.

## Tier 1: PBIS Implementation

Teachers displayed dignity and respect and practiced a ratio of 3:1 positive to negative interactions with every student. Regular administrative, leadership team, county, and CHAMPS trainer visitations observed classrooms to provide simple and immediate feedback, as shown in figure 11.7.

**PBIS/CHAMPS Observation:** Things we would like you to look for are listed here. For any yes/no question feel free to write in your input.

*We will be visiting our common areas (Welcome room (inside/outside), quad/lunch area, office, and other common area (halls, and so on).

*Identify middle school (MS) or high school (HS) when writing observations please.

Supervision and Safety:

1. Did you see the support staff continuously scan the area?

   _____ yes   _____ no

   Notes: _____

2. Did support staff circulate throughout the area?

   _____ yes   _____ no

3. What did you observe support staff saying? _____

   _____

   CHAMPS aligned? _____ yes   _____ no

4. What did you observe in the common areas? (lunch area, PE area, hallways, and so on) _____.

   Are CHAMPS needed in particular area? _____ yes   _____ no

   Which locations? _____

5. How would you characterize the general nature of the interactions between supervising staff members and students?

   _____ primarily positive   _____ primarily negative (explain)

   Notes: _____

   *Answer only if you observed supervising staff members correcting student behavior:

6. How would you characterize staff behavior when correcting students?

   _____ calm   _____ respectful   _____ instructional   _____ emotional

   _____ disrespectful   _____ accusational

   Notes: _____

Students:

1. How would you characterize the student response to being corrected by supervising staff members? _____ compliant _____ respectful

   _____ noncompliant _____ disrespectful

   Notes: _____

2. How would you characterize the general nature of interactions between students? _____ primarily appropriate _____ primarily inappropriate

   Notes: _____

3. How would you describe the appropriateness of student attire in relation to school expectations/dress code?

   _____ All students were dressed appropriately (none in violation of dress code)

   _____ A few students were dressed inappropriately (less than 5 percent were in violation of dress code)

   _____ Many students were dressed inappropriately (more than 5 percent were in violation of dress code)

   Notes: _____

   _____

4. About how many students would you say were engaged in an activity appropriate to the setting?

   _____ 100 percent of the students

   _____ About 95 percent of the students

   _____ Less than 95 percent of the students (explain)

   Notes: _____

5. About how many students would you say left the setting at the designated time? _____ 100 percent _____ 95 percent _____ less than 95 percent (explain)

   Notes: _____

Common Areas:

1. Would you say the materials, equipment, and structure of the setting seem adequate for its intended purpose? _____ yes _____ no  (explain)

   Notes: _____

2. Overall, how would you rate this common area in the following categories?

   a. Are the MS staff members using CHAMPS effectively? _____ yes _____ no (explain)

      Notes: _____

   b. Are the HS staff members using CHAMPS effectively? _____ yes _____ no (explain)

      Notes: _____

Continued on next page →

   c. Are the MS students' participation and activity matching the CHAMPS?

   _____ yes  _____ no  (explain)

   Notes: _____

4. Are the HS students' participation and activity matching the CHAMPS?

   _____ yes  _____ no  (explain)

   Notes: _____

*Source: Gateway Community School.*

Figure 11.7: PBIS/CHAMPS observation form.
*Visit **go.solution-tree.com/rtiatwork** for a reproducible version of this figure.*

When these teams noticed a staff member who was either ineffective in using the model or unwilling to use it, the leadership team or principal would meet privately with him or her or provide small-group practice. At times, the team would provide a substitute so the teacher could observe Gateway teachers skilled in CHAMPS and classroom management or give specific strategies to use and share in follow-up conferences. Principal Koenig would work with staff members who were unwilling to or incapable of managing the classroom according to the standards set by the Guidelines for Success and VCOE. By addressing group, individual, and program needs, the leadership team and staff supported staff morale and sustainability. This support included regular discussion of how to reduce issues between classes or in the common areas, and it was in these meetings and teams that key interventions, like the behavior rubric, point sheet, and office CHAMPS, were developed. Anything that impeded the school going forward was moved or thrust to the side.

The Gateway behavioral expectations were the filter through which all CHAMPS and behavior planning and implementation went. It was imperative, therefore, to keep those guiding principles alive; they were embedded in all documents, conversations, and staff development and engrained in the students' awareness. These behavioral expectations were reviewed with students during testing, group work, transitions, and independent work, and included in students' weekly feedback on behavior(s). As teachers grew more comfortable with CHAMPS, they could apply it more and more in their classrooms. Teachers created CHAMPS for direct instruction, for group work, for independent work, when with a presenter, when watching educational clips, and so on.

An important nuance of creating CHAMPS is to maintain consistency while allowing teachers to adapt it to their own classrooms. As part of the model design, teachers determined their comfort level—how little or how much organization there would be, how much or little noise and movement was permitted in the classroom, how they wanted to be addressed by students, which misbehaviors were considered minor, and which were considered severe. Once they had determined a broad idea of how to adapt CHAMPS and had established a range or scale for misbehavior, they could determine which procedures they needed to train and develop a CHAMPS for. Typically, teachers developed CHAMPS for direct instruction and group work.

When writing the CHAMPS, they kept the statements simple and clear. For direct instruction, they named the conversation, help, activity, movement, participation, and success for that activity. An example for group work would look like the following: *conversation*—low voices / appropriate language; *help*—ask partner first and teacher second; *activity*—work on assignment; *movement*—sit with group at table; *participation*—listening and taking notes; *success*—completing assignment or project. The key was to keep language simple, train students before the activity, and monitor how well they do to determine reteaching or directing as necessary.

It was equally important to create a way to display the CHAMPS—for example, using a PowerPoint, coat hanger, or whiteboard. By properly planning their classroom, explicitly writing and teaching CHAMPS, and displaying them in a way that saved time and effort, misbehavior was addressed effectively with minimal interruption and misbehavior.

### Computer CHAMPS

A further illustration of these CHAMPS, or expectations, is in the high school and recovery programs where students often use computers to work independently on projects, essays, or online courses or to catch up on failed classes; teachers created and posted the CHAMPS for computers at each station (figure 11.8), then taught all the students their expectations. As with any good behavior training model, the result is that students work with less interruption to the general class and cause less damage to the computers. In the past, it was almost impossible to get a typical student to work independently on the computer, let alone do so without damaging something.

### Physical Education in Middle School

The middle school implemented a structured exercise and physical education (PE) program framed in the CHAMPS PBIS model. Traditionally, students were relegated in PE to playing a handball activity; it was simple and easy to do, and the students could self-segregate. However, it did not teach team building, develop enough PE skill, or keep students interested over time. It was often viewed by students as a prison yard or juvenile hall activity.

During several trainings, CHAMPS models from other schools were shared. From those presentations, Gateway developed CHAMPS for recess time. This CHAMPS detailed the expectations and rules of games and were posted throughout the play area. Middle school staff expanded this idea to the PE class period (figure 11.9).

| Computer Work | |
|---|---|
| **C** Conversation | Whisper. |
| **H** Help | Raise your hand. |
| **A** Activity | Complete assignment. |
| **M** Movement | Stay in your seat. |
| **P** Participation | Read, research, write. |
| **Success!** | |

*Source: Gateway Community School.*

Figure 11.8: A computer work CHAMPS.

| Physical Education Class | |
|---|---|
| **C** Conversation | Outside voice, be positive and encouraged! |
| **H** Help | Ask staff for help. |
| **A** Activity | Change into PE clothes and stand in stretching area. |
| **M** Movement | Go directly to basketball court. |
| **P** Participation | Prepare for stretches. |
| **Success!!** | |

*Source: Gateway Community School.*

Figure 11.9: Physical education CHAMPS.

A designated teacher wrote out the CHAMPS, shared them with staff, and drafted a final version to be posted and used daily. Teachers addressed the CHAMPS and rules of the game in each class before students came out to PE. Teachers also taught and reinforced for students how they were to behave during the transition and as they exited class to the PE area. When students exited class, they sat at their designated tables; the students then went to the center of the PE basketball court, lined up in a circle around the paraeducator and teacher, and prepared for PE. Staff planned out weekly sporting events, and provided staff training in how to deliver physical education. As a result, student participation increased from 50 to over 90 percent. A strategic component was for students to be properly transitioned onto their buses after PE, which was the last period of the day.

### Other CHAMPS

Additionally, teachers created CHAMPS for entering and exiting class and for independent work. A middle school team found that by adding CHAMPS to the testing time, they reduced the interruptions and number of students removed from the testing area. The staff posted the CHAMPS or expectations on the students' desks, and at various time intervals provided students feedback—for example, "Johnny, you sat down on time and got to work; keep it up." They made sure to do this at a minimum each thirty minutes, or more or less often depending on the students' capacity for attention. This provided immediate feedback to the students and taught them how to behave during testing. In all, teachers were making CHAMPS their own or internalizing the model, to such an extent that students always knew what was expected of them and didn't have to guess what to do. The approach was so "annoyingly consistent" that students would habitually respond, "Oh, CHAMPS again!"

As each year progressed, Gateway refined, added, and removed strategies and programs within each program or "tier." Each was essential to the needs and performance of the students and the programs and interventions in which they participated. It was determined in 2011 that no program would ever be developed in isolation and staff members had to develop mutual trust when a team responded with a suggested strategy, model, or intervention.

### Low-Level Misbehavior

A basic CHAMPS philosophy is to address low-level misbehavior in the classroom effectively through a positive approach that treats students with dignity and respect. Teachers had to fundamentally learn to contain all mid- to low-level misbehavior, from students not bringing materials to class to minor to moderate interruptions, such as talking out of turn, indirect vulgarity, off-task conversation, and so on. This keeps the power in the classroom, with the teacher, and ensures the students are in class, further improving their education and behavior management.

With guidance from the leadership team, teachers typically used a set of interventions and procedures. They arranged for brief conferences with students at the start and end of class and met them in the quad at lunch before and after school to relate and address issues of misbehavior. Teachers agreed that they would address these behaviors as a team during the a.m. hour, during preparation period or collaboration time, or in meetings with the administrative team, and agreed to CHAMPS training.

### Implementation Issues

One initial implementation problem was how to fully believe in and implement the PBIS model. In order to garner staff buy-in, leadership met with each staff member, including those who were not going to return the following year, to hear their perceptions of what was and was not working. Everyone also had an opportunity to voice an opinion at an all-staff day retreat. This increased the likelihood of affecting positive change and building ownership and resulted in all staff being on the same page with respect to Gateway's model. This was especially effective for developing the Guidelines for Success. However, other areas required attention. The school had to train and provide follow-up support for several new staff members and inspire new systems and procedures, including transitions, a personalized portfolio to map student progress toward academic and personal goals, developmental asset assessments, exposure to academic and behavioral expectations, and a new handbook to define academic and behavioral outcomes and expectations.

The design for staff development was created by Principal Koenig and the district administrator in order to sustain capacity and trust. As noted previously, capacity meant that once staff had the ability to work and improve independently on CHAMPS and other initiatives, they met less often. Trust was a key factor, meaning the leadership team and principal would trust staff to continue on their own or in teams to hone and develop their skill in CHAMPS and other initiatives. Truly, this was a key aspect of Gateway's staff development over a two-year period of time, and it was applied not only to PBIS but to all of Gateway's staff development. A quarterly meeting was added to provide support staff (paraprofessionals and security) opportunities to discuss schoolwide issues such as common areas and CHAMPS supports.

Meetings always had an agenda and a designated person to take minutes and focused on the main goals of restructuring and site-based goals. Members of the administrative team made sure to open their doors, heard every piece of input, and invited and welcomed all staff to come and see them when they had an idea or needed support. This open-door policy, coupled with constant interaction and collaboration, evolved into a campus that was not only highly communicative and collaborative but one in which, at all levels, Gateway staff were taking ownership of their roles.

## Tier 2: PBIS Behavior

Unlike Tier 1 interventions, Tier 2 interventions were designed for specific and more severe behaviors and were to be implemented if the Tier 1 interventions didn't work. Examples of Tier 2 interventions are the behavior rubric and office CHAMPS.

Staff gauged all student behavior using a behavior rubric (figure 11.10).

Student Name(s): _____

Teacher: _____    Time: _____    Date: _____

|  | **Four (A)** Going Above and Beyond | **Three (B)** On Track | **Two (C)** Basic | **One (D)** Need Improvement | **Zero (F)** Unacceptable |
|---|---|---|---|---|---|
| **Conversation and Help** |  |  |  |  |  |
| **Activity and Movement** |  |  |  |  |  |
| **Participation** |  |  |  |  |  |

Teacher Comments and Description of Events: _____

_____

_____

_____

_____

_____

_____

_____

*Source: Gateway Community School.*

Figure 11.10: Behavior rubric.

*Visit **go.solution-tree.com/rtiatwork** for a reproducible version of this figure.*

The rubric was reviewed with every student during transition and again either when the student entered classes or at the start of each quarter. This was to ensure the student understood what the school defines as "good" or "best" behavior as compared to "poor" behavior. Principal Koenig explained the rubric as a scaled representation of the number of times a student could be corrected; the more corrections, the lower on the rubric the student would be. A key detail was to point out the top of the scale, where staff expected students to achieve. The bottom of the scale typically meant removal from class and possibly severe discipline (involving a parent conference or request for a parent to sit with a student in class), out-of-school suspension, or consideration of program adjustment. The Guidelines for Success, the vision and goal for behaviors, were also explicitly taught and reiterated throughout the school. This consistent deployment of the PBIS approach, infused into the content areas and class transition times, married academic to behavioral support in the school day, resulting in positive achievement in both of these areas.

### Office Champs

The office CHAMPS was a reflection handout created to address a growing issue in the office lobby and the middle school welcome room (the discipline office): after being sent to the office or welcome room, students continued to misbehave. In response, a leadership team staff member developed a middle school and high school office CHAMPS (figure 11.11).

The aim was to (1) obtain students' input about the reason they were sent to the office by providing them time to reflect on the misbehavior, and (2) reteach CHAMPS by having the students read and copy the CHAMPS for the office. Instead of simply kicking students out of class, relegating them to the office for some extended period of time, and telling them "no, no, no" and "bad, bad, bad," the issue was also addressed by having students propose a way to resolve it, state what in their opinion was a fair consequence, and meet with an administrator to discuss and enact the consequence. As an example of consequences, students' privileges were reduced or limited—no breaks and no outside access until they completed the reflection packet by copying and revisiting the CHAMPS and completing these three statements: How did you violate the Guidelines for Success? How does this impact you and others in the class? Write a fair consequence to your actions. One fundamental part of this, which was understood among staff, but not shared with students, is that if a student is working on office CHAMPS, no staff or student is to speak to him or her unless the student has an immediate health need (for example, medical attention or water). This policy of noninteraction works well. A student acting out for attention typically benefits from cooling off or calming down to a point where he or she is clear minded before communication.

As part of CHAMPS, teachers had to fundamentally learn to contain all mid- to low-level student misbehavior (materials not brought to class, off-task talking, minor vulgarity, and so on). This alone significantly reduced the number of student referrals to the office and at the same time placed authority and responsibility for correction more profoundly in the teacher's hands. Teachers learned through

Student Name: _____    Date: _____

Dear Gateway Student,

Please complete the CHAMPS page and "blank table." It is your responsibility to respect the office staff by working quietly. This work *must* be finished. You will not meet with the principal or return to class if you do not complete these assignments. If you have any questions, you can ask a staff member politely by saying, "Excuse me." Thank you.

Sincerely,

Gateway Staff

### CHAMPS Page

Directions: Carefully read "CHAMPS: Waiting in the Office." Then, complete the blank CHAMPS table.

| **CHAMPS: Waiting in the Office** | |
|---|---|
| **C**<br>Conversation | Speak quietly to staff. |
| **H**<br>Help | Ask staff politely.<br><br>Say, "Excuse me." |
| **A**<br>Activity | Finish reflection packet. |
| **M**<br>Movement | Stay seated. |
| **P**<br>Participation | Follow directions.<br><br>Be respectful. |
| **Success!** | |

*Source: Gateway Community School.*

Figure 11.11: Office CHAMPS.

*Visit **go.solution-tree.com/rtiatwork** for a blank reproducible version of this figure.*

CHAMPS such training strategies as perceived private correction, planned ignoring, and reinforcement of key CHAMPS or expectations. The strategy of perceived private correction required the teachers to address the student or students who were misbehaving or interrupting class while near them, and in a low voice, with a clear and directional but neutral tone, the teachers let them know what they wanted to see them do, being careful to avoid saying what not to do. For example, suppose

Johnny is telling another student a story loud enough for all to hear, adding all sorts of expletives. Mrs. Peters notices this, but instead of yelling from across the room, she asks the class to complete the math problem, then calmly and quietly walks over to Johnny, stands between him and the person he's talking to, and says, in a low voice, "Johnny, please write down the problem. Only talk by raising your hand, and raise your hand to ask if you can speak to your neighbor. Thank you for taking care of this."

CHAMPS is clear in stating that any correction must be short, clear, without "I" statements, and articulated with dignity and respect. The teacher, after ensuring that the message is clear, then walks away to continue the lesson, while observing Johnny to see if he corrects his behavior. When done correctly, this strategy not only corrects behavior but allows students to do so without being singled out by their peers, potentially putting them in a position where they have to defend themselves or react negatively. These strategies work best when teachers develop and refine them, adjusting to the varying student population or to the issues of the moment.

### Moderate Misbehaviors

When the behaviors were more moderate in nature, such as continually using bad language, engaging in regular off-task conversation, sleeping in class or having the head down, not completing assignments, or simply not attempting to work, teachers and staff used moderate interventions. Often, this required a conference so the students could meet with an academic counselor or mental health counselor. When misbehaviors happened more often, the student would meet with the principal or principal's administrative designee. In some cases, the probation officer or outside agency (social services) met with a student for more intensive support. Teachers and support staff (paraprofessionals and security) were trained and understood that when a student was sent to the office, it was only after the teacher's own interventions were exhausted or the behavior was interrupting the class. The probation officer's role was to deter misbehavior and provide guidance and support to all students, primarily those who were on probation. Often, misbehavior could be tied to students' circumstances: "Jenny continues to argue with the teacher, because her brother was injured the night before and hospitalized; she is not upset with the teacher or staff directly, but is taking out her emotions on staff." In cases like this, the principal or probation officer intervenes to address the behavior and provides added support or interventions. The administration might refer the student to mental health counseling that same day, call the parent, determine as a team whether or not the student should be in school, and if appropriate, plan follow-up counseling. More severe behaviors would be addressed by a crisis intervention team trained to deal with such issues as attempted or considered suicide, death, and domestic violence.

Whether a teacher, administrator, or outside agency representative was involved at this stage of the intervention, all agreed that the student must have a chance to improve, reduce interventions, and roll back privileges, but that the interventions and consequences would increase if the student continued to struggle. All interventions were embedded with this design in order to provide an opportunity to earn back privileges or increase consequences consistent with the misbehavior. Susan Isaacs, Safe and Civil Schools national trainer, best illustrates this point.

> When law enforcement gives you a ticket for speeding, the question is asked, "Does it stop you from speeding?" Invariably, the answer is no, but imagine if you regularly drove at or under the speed limit and as your reward your registration fees were reduced. Would you then stop speeding? Most people would say yes. Why? Because the positive outweighs the negative. (personal communication, April 18, 2014)

Creating an opportunity where students know they have a reasonable chance at success will generate the maximum potential for improved behavior.

### Tier 3: PBIS

As in any school, typically 5 to 10 percent of the most difficult students would be considered the most at-risk. This particular group at Gateway Community school required individualized and continuous support due to drug abuse, gang activity, social or emotional issues, severe poverty, or homelessness. Foster youth might have varying degrees of any one of these issues.

Tier 3 was Gateway's PBIS intensive scoop of extra support. The intensive intervention planning was guided by the movement of students in and out of the math and English intervention courses based on their performance. The administrative team guided teachers in determining the process by which students' assessment results and academic scores were used to determine whether they needed added academic support or would be provided with additional options, including elective or credit recovery courses. The administrative team also provided support and guidance when developing the social and emotional interventions. Student behavior progress was the barometer for adding or reducing services and supports. In year three of the restructuring, Gateway devised a plan for staff to meet weekly as a student study team (SST) rather than according to the previous "as needed" model to discuss successful students as well as those who had been struggling in academics or behavior.

The SST, consisting of teachers, the school psychologist, the academic counselor, and the transition and induction specialist, held biweekly meetings to review student achievement, note positive student success, and identify students who required additional support and interventions. The transition and induction specialist supports new and exiting students and plays a key role in providing input on students' services and supports and documenting progression. Each teacher was asked to share the names of three successful students and one struggling student to the SST. Each student was documented for follow-up as to whether he or she was progressing or struggling. If the student was making positive progress, follow-up included a positive phone call, a certificate, recognition at awards events, a mention in the school's monthly newsletter, and possibly other incentives. The student's name was also displayed on the VCOE marquee.

For students who were identified as struggling or requiring more support or intervention, the same basic principle was used. As appropriate, students might be provided with a specific goal on their point sheet, probation would meet with and counsel students on probation, administration would intervene through student and parent conferences and if necessary suspensions or referral to an agency for support (for example, one-on-one counseling or group counseling), or students' schedules might be adjusted. The principal or probation officer referrals were made if the behaviors were severe. When probation was involved, the students progressed through probation's steps of intervention, which might include admonishment by the probation officer or court official, increased probation terms (extra meetings, added counseling), or intensified probation terms, up to possible incarceration. The principal or administrators took on a slightly different role depending on the action. That role included requesting parent conferences via phone or in person, requesting that a parent sit with students in class, initiating a restorative justice conference (an idea originating from the criminal justice system that focuses on the rehabilitation of offenders through reconciliation with victims and the community; in this case, the victim is likely another student and the community is the school), and a recommendation of out-of-school suspension. Students are referred to administration when all other intervention has been exhausted and disciplinary action is necessary or seen as the last option left to consider. Restorative justice conferencing might be used in the case of verbal altercations, fights, or severe incidents involving staff. The key was to declare who was harmed, get parties to take responsibility, and agree on terms to resolve the issue. Principal Koenig has found that the results of using this system are lasting and impactful.

When these interventions did not improve behavior or if the incidents of misbehavior were severe, the student's schedule or program was changed. This change might include referral to another school or program, reduction of the student's schedule, or rearrangement of the student's courses to better match his or her needs. This was done in the most extreme cases and only when all other interventions had been exhausted.

When a student was identified as not being successful, that student's progress was shared in the biweekly SST meeting. SST meetings were used to augment current interventions—such as a smaller class size, additional targeted support; after-school tutoring or other services, including counseling for anger management; referrals to Ventura County Behavioral Health; referrals to foster and homeless services; and probation or other programs to address student needs. Students' progress was monitored by scales, rubrics, grades, the behavior point sheet, attendance records, and any other data points that could enhance the delivery and adjustment of interventions.

### Intensive Social and Emotional Supports

Middle school social-emotional supports were provided Monday and Wednesday in intervention classes. The leadership team, in collaboration with middle school teachers and mental health counselors, developed a series of lessons for these classes centered on the development of key social skills (positive choices, self-mediation, and reduction of bullying) to teach students how to operate more independently and positively. Often, the courses were centered on key programs developed by partner agencies (Palmer Drug Abuse Program of Ventura County, Clinicas del Camino Real, and Interface Children & Family Services). The teachers and leadership team developed a three-day social-emotional intervention class held at the start of each Monday, Wednesday, and Friday. The idea was to set goals and the tone for the day. If there were behavioral issues, they could be addressed in the intervention class. The difference between this model and the high school program was that these courses were provided regularly, whereas in high school, they were addressed weekly in counseling, in which the majority of students participated. On intervention class days, a counselor or therapist would teach students the needed social skills that had been identified. This was in addition to the academic intervention provided for math and English on Tuesdays and Thursdays. The staff spent more time in the social-emotional intervention classes because they believed that without addressing the behaviors and needs of the students, instruction would suffer.

Apart from middle school, the recovery program required a more intensive approach to student needs and behaviors. Previous models of treatment for addiction, counseling support, and oversight had reduced the impact on student results and performance in the program.

### Recovery and Seven Challenges

Ventura County Probation, in collaboration with Interface Children & Family Services, Palmer Drug Abuse Program of Ventura County, and VCOE / Gateway Community School, had restructured the drug and alcohol rehabilitation program, the Recovery Program, by adjusting and expanding its counseling component. The Recovery Program was a court-approved or court-ordered drug rehabilitation program held on Gateway's campus. The students were all part of formal probation and, as part of their terms, agreed to attend this program, where they continued their high school coursework, including embedded drug and alcohol counseling.

Previously, the counseling program, a twelve-step program, targeted only the various aspects of addiction with the primary intended outcome of stopping the use of drugs. After probation, along with the various agencies, including the Ventura County courts, staff collaborated and determined that a more expanded program was necessary and implemented a more intensive Seven Challenges program. This worked well with Gateway's program, as it addressed the underlying issues of addiction and assisted the students in arriving at their own understanding of why they abused drugs or alcohol. The program shared a key component of CHAMPS, which was to train students in how to manage their own behaviors.

## Results

The multitiered intervention continuum model at Gateway was developed over a three-year period. As a student moved up and down the tiered interventions, staff and leadership team members continually documented the steps via SST forms, emails, and district forms (suspension, alternative to suspension, and our student information system). What made this approach unique and possible to replicate was that both CHAMPS and the tools and strategies developed over the three years could be adapted to almost all school environments. Gateway's methods have been seen in many other schools' behavior interventions; the key to Gateway's success was that Gateway staff made the methods their own and developed them as a staff.

All of the preceding has resulted, as of this writing, in the following positive outcomes.

- Gateway experienced a two-year, fifty-two-point gain in its API.

- Attendance increased from 75 percent to 87.65 percent.

- For the first time since spring of the 2006–2007 school year, there were seven math proficient scores and three English proficient scores on the CAHSEE.

- The number of CAHSEE passing scores in eleventh and twelfth grade increased from two to fifteen.

- The community now views this alternative school as a positive choice and not as a last resort for failed students.

- This improved perception has resulted in a pupil enrollment increase from 125 to 166 students.

Table 11.2 shows the decrease in suspension days from 2007 through 2014. Table 11.3 shows the decrease in suspensions due to physical altercations from 2008 to 2014.

**Table 11.2: Decrease in Suspension Days Over a Seven-Year Period**

| Month & Year | Total Students Suspended | Total Number Of Days |
|---|---|---|
| Total Suspensions 2007–2008 | 406 | 1040 |
| Total Suspensions 2008–2009 | 326 | 1262 |
| Total Suspensions 2009–2010 | 387 | 1012 |
| Total Suspensions 2010–2011 | 321 | 837 |
| Total Suspensions 2011–2012 | 286 | 546 |
| Total Suspensions 2012–2013 | 171 | 310 |
| Total Suspensions 2013–2014 | 106 | 242 |

**Table 11.3: Decrease in Suspensions Due to Physical Altercations**

| Year | Number of Days |
|---|---|
| 2008–2009 | 597 |
| 2009–2010 | 451 |
| 2010–2011 | 200 |
| 2011–2012 | 108 |
| 2012–2013 | 80 |
| 2013–2014 | 14 |

As an unintended outcome, Gateway Community School has been recognized through grants and awards as a PBIS national alternative education visitation demonstration site by Safe and Civil Schools. In this role, Gateway hosts visits from comprehensive schools as well as alternative, court, and community schools several times a year. Additionally, the Gateway staff has presented for the Juvenile Court, Community and Alternative School Administrators of California, the Ventura County Superintendent's Cabinet, the California Judicial Branch, and the Ventura County RTI$^2$ Symposia. Gateway representatives are recognized and valued leaders and models in the Ventura County RTI$^2$ and PBIS PLC networks. In 2012, Gateway received a six-year Western Association of Schools and Colleges (WASC) approval; the WASC chair and his team gave the school high commendations, stating that Gateway should be considered a model school for the state of California. In spring of 2013, Principal Koenig was recognized for his dedicated and outstanding service to the community by the Ventura County Juvenile Justice and Delinquency Prevention Commission, the U.S. Congress, the California State Assembly, and State Senator and Assembly members.

Ventura County Superintendent of Schools Stanley C. Mantooth reports (October 14, 2013) that "the Gateway staff has been diligent in the implementation of RTI² for both academic and behavioral needs. All staff is determined to find just the right combination of strategies to reach each individual student." Randy Sprick, founder of Safe and Civil Schools, speaks highly of the work (October 18, 2013): "Ventura County Office of Education and Gateway have provided outstanding multitiered systems of academic and behavioral support and have empowered staff to provide students the support needed to survive and thrive in school." Similarly, Susan J. Isaacs, an associate with Safe and Civil Schools, reports:

> The staff at Gateway has done a remarkable job in creating an exemplary PBIS model. By starting with CHAMPS, the staff structured their classrooms to promote and teach responsible behavior, which supports learning. This foundation served as a base to move the process to all schoolwide areas. The structure that Gateway has established serves as a model for alternative schools across the country. (personal communication, October 17, 2014)

Gateway's primary goal has been to promote academic growth and remediate academic deficiencies by concentrating on core behavioral issues demonstrated by its at-risk students. Its commitment to its students, parents, community, and school districts has been to prepare them to be respectful, positive, productive, and proud young people. Gateway staff have acquired the unique ability to hold a mirror up to themselves and their students and to always view students in terms of their maximum potential, individually and collectively. They bring pride to the Ventura County educational community.

# References and Resources

Batsche, G., Elliott, J., Graden, J. L., Grimes, J., Kovaleski, J. F., Prasse, D., et al. (2006). *Response to intervention policy considerations and implementation.* Alexandria, VA: National Association of State Directors of Special Education, Inc.

Bender, W. N., & Shores, C. (2007). *Response to intervention: A practical guide for every teacher.* Thousand Oaks, CA: Corwin Press. Accessed at www.corwin.com/books/Book230947 on March 10, 2014.

Buffum, A., Mattos, M., & Weber, C. (2012). *Simplifying response to intervention: Four essential guiding principles.* Bloomington, IN: Solution Tree Press.

Chrisman, V., & Wagmeister, J. (2011) California Department of Education response to instruction and intervention, (RTI²) An implementation and technical assistance guide for schools and districts. Accessed at www.vcoe.org/Portals/VcssoPortals/cici/Technical%20Assistance%20Guide.pdf on June 25, 2014.

DuFour, R., DuFour, R., Eaker, R., & Karhanek, G. (2004). *Whatever it takes: How professional learning communities respond when kids don't learn.* Bloomington, IN: Solution Tree Press.

DuFour, R., DuFour, R., Eaker, R., & Many, T. W. (2006). *Learning by doing: A handbook for professional learning communities at work.* Bloomington, IN: Solution Tree Press.

Elliott, J. (2008). Response to intervention: What & why? *The School Administrator, 8*(65).

Fixen, D. L., Naoom, S. F., Blasé, K. A., Friedman, R. M., & Wallace, R. (2005). *Implementation research: A synthesis of the research.* Tampa: University of Southern Florida.

Fuchs, D., & Fuchs, L. S. (2005). Responsiveness-to-intervention: A blueprint for practitioners, policymakers and parents. *Teaching Exceptional Children, 38*(1), 57–61.

Gersten, R., Baker, S. K., Shanahan, T., Linan-Thompson, S., Collins, P., & Scarcella, R. (2007). *Effective literacy and English Instruction for ELs in the elementary grades: A practice guide* (NCEE 2007–4011). Washington, DC: National Center for Education Evaluation and Regional Assistance.

Sprick, R. (2009). *CHAMPS: A proactive & positive approach to classroom management* (2nd ed.). Eugene, OR: Pacific Northwest.

Ventura County Office of Education. (2013). Ventura County Recommended RtI² Model. Accessed at www.vcoe.org/Portals/VcssoPortals/cici/RtI/newNarrative2014.pdf on June 25, 2014.

Ventura County Office of Education. (n.d.). *Ventura County RtI2: Multi-tiered system of supports.* Accessed at www.vcoe.org/Portals/VcssoPortals/cici/RtI/06%20pyramid%20with%20color.pdf on August 8, 2014.

**Regina Stephens Owens** is the director of enrichment for Coppell Independent School District, Coppell, Texas, where she is working to create an international mindset and use technology to partner with others around the world. An administrator since 2000, Regina participated in designing and opening the high-performing Virtual School and the Early College Academy in Spring Independent School District. She is a highly sought after education consultant and coach serving and supporting school systems in the United States and Canada in utilizing the philosophy of professional learning communities (PLCs).

While serving as academic dean of Marshall Independent School District in Marshall, Texas, Regina led a team of educators at the campus level to develop a professional learning community. The team's efforts evolved into a districtwide PLC initiative. She is most noted for understanding and leading the change process in transforming schools, and she leads that process in establishing effective systems and structures in the online environment.

As presenter, consultant, and education coach, Regina shares what it takes to build a successful PLC and which assessment practices are most effective for sustaining this important work. Her passionate belief that a brilliant child exists inside every student fuels each presentation. With experience as a teacher, campus administrator, and district leader in rural and urban schools, Regina knows the unique challenges and opportunities faced by educators who serve youth at risk. She encourages students to partner and have a voice in their education, while working to their strengths.

Regina earned a bachelor's degree in business administration and education from East Texas Baptist University and a master's degree in educational leadership from Stephen F. Austin State University in Texas.

You can follow Regina on Twitter @Regina_Owens.

To book Regina Stephens Owens for professional development, contact pd@solution -tree.com.

# Personalizing Learning Through Online Interventions

Regina Stephens Owens

**Editors' Note**

We conclude with this chapter on the Virtual School and the Early College Academy to provide you with a vision of the future. Technology has forced retail businesses to reconsider meeting their customers' needs beyond brick-and-mortar buildings and in-person interactions. From banking to holiday shopping, customers expect access to online information and virtual services, allowing individuals to meet their personal needs on their own time schedule. Failure to provide this level of service would be a death knell to most businesses. Education, in general, has been very slow to embrace and utilize technology, both as a way to provide information and services to our customers—our students and parents—and to allow students to use personal technology at school as a learning tool.

While Spring Independent School District created an entire learning environment around technology, complete transformation is not required to begin incorporating digital tools into the curriculum. The Virtual School's and the Early College Academy's student inventory and personalized goal-setting process are powerful tools any school can use. With a smartphone, which most secondary students already possess, students have access to the world's largest library for research, an immediate feedback tool for formative assessment, a time-management tool to track assignments, and a social media tool to promote personalized communication and peer collaboration. There are also many powerful online intervention tools that can provide students with remediation and acceleration. Most schools restrict access to these tools in fear that a small handful of students might use these tools inappropriately. This is akin to prohibiting all adults from driving in fear that a few people might speed and crash. In reality, students' personal technology misuse is already happening, regardless of the schools' policies. By offering students access to these tools, schools can extend time for interventions beyond the school day.

In the end, it will be difficult to prepare our students for the 21st century if we expect them to learn in the 20th century while on campus. The programs of the Virtual School and the Early College Academy provide a real-life example of what this might look like.

---

Across the United States, programs often heap help on our schools and our students to quickly move learning forward, to close the achievement gap, to get struggling learners caught up, to ensure scores increase, and to save campuses. Many educators struggle with the multitude of initiatives and the promise that an online component of a program or technology will save us. It is not our educational community, however, that needs to be saved—it is the strength of our democracy. That strength depends on all of us who care about the next generation of elected officials, school board members, community members, school leaders, parents, and students as we embrace the moral issue that all students must learn at high levels. It is high time we educational leaders transform our thinking and good intentions from that of a deficit model of working on the students to one in which we work *with* learners to discover their strengths, voices, and potential.

With student input, we can provide a path to personalized learning that leaves the student ready to embrace all the future holds, which is the right of every student. Technology and online interventions provide access to these opportunities; online interventions allow us to partner with students in learning as the technology makes the learning tangible and transparent. Learners become knowledgeable of what they know and need to know, and can experience learning via a variety of styles, allowing them to become aware of how they learn best. We must use digital resources to help students navigate not only the *what* but the *how* of learning. *Personalization*, as the National Education Technology Plan defines it, involves using adaptive pacing, styling instruction to learning preferences, and tailoring content to learners' interests (Bienkowski, Feng, & Means, 2012).

No longer can we have our students sit in front of a computer to simply pass an assessment or increase test scores. We must use the technology to refine both interventions and the way we respond when students are underachieving—an outcome that we, administrators and staff, have taken from theory to reality at Spring Independent School District (ISD) in Houston, Texas. Spring ISD serves over 36,500 preK–12 students in a diverse and growing urban district located twenty miles north of downtown Houston. The district is working toward being recognized nationally as a leader among learning organizations and being known for exemplary student achievement; one step in that process was our creation of the Virtual School and the Early College Academy.

## Building the Virtual School and the Early College

We designed the Virtual School to provide students in the district with the opportunity to learn anytime, anywhere with flexible scheduling to meet their needs. The school serves students receiving general education, special needs, and gifted and talented services with the mission of providing an exemplary education, preparedness for postsecondary education and career choice, the use of emerging technologies, and individualized instruction that inspires while ensuring the development of 21st century skills.

The Early College Academy, another innovative school, blends high school and college work with the mission that first-generation college goers will graduate with a high school diploma and an associate degree or sixty college credit hours toward a baccalaureate degree. The school provides dual credit at no cost to students, rigorous instruction and accelerated courses online, and academic and social support services to help students succeed. In addition, it increases college readiness by decreasing barriers to college access (Texas Education Agency, 2013).

The goal for students in both of these nontraditional learning environments is to offer exemplary learning and hold students to high expectations while providing the coaching, extra time, and support needed to ensure a guaranteed and viable curriculum in which all students have the opportunity and time required to learn. More specifically, the desired intervention outcomes include students':

- Mastering grade-level essentials and being prepared for the next course of study
- Learning how to learn and how to request assistance when they are not learning
- Being taught to know how they learn best, how to work to their strengths, and how to persist until their learning needs are met
- Participating in personalized accelerated instruction utilizing online interventions

To achieve these outcomes, we established a strong intervention framework.

# Designing Belief-Driven Interventions

The evidence and research used to design both the Virtual School's and Early College's model for intervention evolved from the vision, values, and beliefs of the district and schools, which include creating capacity and leadership at all levels and working in a continual improvement culture with clarity that the student is our customer who we must prepare for both college and career. With this reality in mind, we began the intervention process by ensuring our behavior mirrored our collective commitments. In these nontraditional settings, where students and parents expect to receive not only an exemplary academic education but experiences that prepare them socially, we wanted to provide extra time and support in a manner they had not experienced in the past. Thus, the intervention system was greatly impacted by the philosophy of Yvette Jackson (2011), author of the *Pedagogy of Confidence: Inspiring High Intellectual Performance in Urban Schools*, who demands educators work to the strengths of learners, knowing that learners are each different and learn differently. In light of this, Jackson suggests we ask ourselves, "What are the operational practices that will generate high intellectual performances?" (p. 88). Simply put, what must we do to ensure our students are successful? In response to this research, we wanted students to be college ready, which is:

> the level of preparation a student needs in order to enroll and succeed—without remediation—in a credit bearing course at a postsecondary institution that offers a baccalaureate degree or transfer to a baccalaureate program, or in a high-quality certificate program that enables students to enter a career pathway with potential future advancement. (Conley, 2011, p. 4)

Thus, we designed our interventions to ensure students would attain the following college- and career-readiness skills.

- Critical thinking and problem solving
- Collaboration
- Agility and adaptability
- Initiative
- Effective oral and written communication
- The ability to access and analyze information
- Curiosity and imagination

Before receiving interventions, students learn about their personality styles, are provided a multiple-intelligence assessment and learning style survey, and participate in prescreening and goal-setting meetings. Grade-level committees conduct prescreening meetings for each student and determine a plan for additional time and support as well how to best support that individual student. During these meetings, we collect as much information and data as possible to help us design support for the student's learning as indicated in the student prescreening-interventions inventory (figure 12.1).

| Student: | Grade: | Campus: | Date: |
|---|---|---|---|
| **Courses:** | **Teachers:** | **Counselor:** | |
| Multiple intelligences | | | |
| Learning styles | | | |
| Career or college pathway | | | |
| Preplacement Concerns (Check all that apply.) | | | |
| Academic performance | | | |
| Standardized test | | | |
| Attendance | | | |
| Extracurricular activities | | | |
| Work | | | |
| Social and emotional behavior | | | |
| Parental involvement | | | |
| Previous interventions | | | |
| Additional Support or Intervention Needed (Check all that apply.) | | | |
| Teacher watch | | | |
| Peer assistance | | | |
| Student contract | | | |
| Attendance management | | | |
| Daily student accountability | | | |
| Time-management support | | | |
| Required intervention | | | |
| Level of Support Required by Area of Need | | | |

Figure 12.1: Sample student prescreening-interventions inventory.

After we conduct all prescreening meetings, we construct our master schedule for the learning needs of the students as opposed to allowing the schedule to dictate service and support. Students are scheduled in a manner that allows their needs to be met. For example, some students may accelerate in a course, completing it in a semester, while others may be scheduled in the course for a full year. Some students may be assigned mandatory interventions, while others are assigned student study groups face to face or online to provide sustained systematic support.

However, we expect *all* students to participate in a goal-setting meeting with a teacher advisor who reviews the students' multiple-intelligence report, which dictates students' innate capabilities; learning styles inventory, which dictates the way students learn best; and expectations of the learning environment and how to get assistance. That teacher then leads students in writing goals for the upcoming six or nine weeks that include measurable outcomes. During the goal-setting meeting at the beginning of the year, whether online or face to face, it is important to have an agenda, establish a goal-setting worksheet, and obtain student signatures of agreement, so that they are involved in working to their strengths, are problem solving regarding their own learning, and are empowered to take initiative to get help when needed, to learn how to communicate verbally and in writing with adults, and to imagine how their lives will be as they start to exhibit the modeled behaviors in day-to-day learning. Student-led conferences occur in the late fall at the end of the first semester to allow the students to demonstrate their participation and ownership in their learning. During this conference, students lead the discussion and share with their parents their learning goals and progress towards meeting the goals. It is imperative that students own the language and understand what they must do to succeed and what additional support is needed and that they create a plan for their success.

In *Systems Thinking in Action: Moving Beyond the Standard Plateau*, Michael Fullan (2004) states, "The best system produces a culture in which it becomes easier to accomplish more by moving beyond dependence on the heroic or martyr-like efforts of a few" (p. 8). We agree that select individuals cannot maintain systematic efforts, and therefore we agree that our students should be empowered to participate in their own learning, and that we should select online programs with adaptive learning that allow them to do so. In our schools, we design the interventions and deliver them based on our core beliefs: we allow students to become participants in their learning. This practice, in our opinion, breeds hope.

# Facing Challenges While Fueling Continuous Improvement

When a school offers interventions that include online and blended learning models with adaptive learning, there will be obstacles to overcome, such as system compatibility, access to the Internet, and use of analytics and reports. To clarify terminology, the percentage of time learning occurs in an online environment defines whether learning is *blended* or *virtual*. When instruction occurs 30 to 60 percent of the time online rather than in a brick-and-mortar building, it is considered blended. When instruction occurs more than 60 percent of the time online, it is considered virtual (Wicks, 2010). Both learning methods promise individualization; student control over time, place, and pace; and personalized learning experiences, as the research of Clayton Christensen and colleagues supports (Christensen, Horn, & Staker, 2013).

*Adaptive learning* is an educational method that uses computers as interactive teaching devices. Computers adapt the presentation of educational material according to students' learning needs, as their responses to questions and tasks indicate (Bienkowski, 2012). Realizing that we cannot achieve tailored learning on a large-scale basis using traditional approaches has partially driven our use of adaptive learning. Adaptive learning systems endeavor to transform the learner from passive receptor of information to a partner and collaborator in the educational process.

To address the concerns and challenges presented by any innovative approach to learning online or utilizing technology for intervention, we must remain focused on continuous improvement, as shown in table 12.1 (pages 298–300).

One of our greatest challenges involved evaluating online interventions or programs to ensure fidelity of implementation, so that teachers and students did not experience initiative overload. We learned to purchase online interventions with the purpose of supporting a learning goal in our school and to celebrate the learning growth that resulted from using the resource. Another constant challenge we faced involved making sure we used time wisely.

**Table 12.1: From Concerns and Challenges to Continuous Improvement**

| Concerns | Challenges | Continuous Improvement |
|---|---|---|
| Learning | Clearly identify and prioritize learners' needs for programs or online interventions to address. | During yearly planning, when teams write academic goals, evaluate the use of online interventions and programs to ensure they align with student needs. |
| | Ensure that students and teachers are aware of the essential learnings that online interventions will address. | During staff meetings, share academic data and program or online intervention data as part of progress monitoring. |
| | Ensure that teams are addressing, monitoring, and discussing learning gaps using data from online interventions during team meetings. | Expect and monitor that teacher teams are reviewing program and intervention data during data discussion and that reports and performance are a part of team Strategic and specific, Measurable, Attainable, Results oriented, and Time bound (SMART) goals. |
| | Clearly define learning times or minutes within the schedule so that online interventions are a supplement rather than the core curriculum. | Complete classroom walkthroughs during intervention time, and monitor program fidelity during class visits. |
| | Ensure adequate time for training, including teachers, counselors, and response to intervention (RTI) coordinators, so staff use data and reports appropriately. | During campus improvement planning and data team meetings, identify the data points that each team will monitor. |
| Technology | Ensure the campus and classrooms have enough bandwidth to support the technology needs. | During campus improvement planning, include technology needs, sharing academic needs with the district team to ensure enough bandwidth is in place. |
| | Ensure devices purchased are compatible with online interventions. | Ensure prior to purchase that devices are compatible with all interventions or needs for campus by partnering with the technology department and keeping accurate lists of devices and ages of devices. |

| Technology | Collaborate with the school system to ensure online interventions and services are available and accessible at the start of school, with all users—teachers and students—loaded in the system properly. | Coordinate the purchase of services, training, and devices with technology by creating a time line to ensure all systems function at the point of need. |
|---|---|---|
| Online Program or Intervention | Provide access if the program or online intervention has a home-access component. | Partner with local businesses, such as cable companies and local libraries, to ensure families are supported with Internet access at no cost or low cost while informing parents how to access online interventions at home. |
| | Clarify the use of online interventions and programs for engaging practice. | When purchasing online programs and interventions, denote which programs have a universal screener, progress monitoring, and data reports for an instructional response. Some services are good at engaging practice but do not provide data or reports in a manner that would allow a systematic instructional response. |
| | Purchase programs that utilize adaptive learning so that student and teacher dashboards can be used while improving the learning for students. | Complete an extensive review of programs and online interventions to ensure the analytics, reports, and dashboards are there to provide real-time feedback to students, teachers, administrators, and district stakeholders. |
| | Implement online interventions or programs with fidelity. | Collaborate with vendors to ensure the criteria for implementation and utilization of the programs are clear for all users; teach, monitor, and respond to criteria implementation fidelity by including reports in campus communications; celebrate teams that are on target; and coach others in need of assistance. |

Continued on next page →

| Online Program or Intervention | Ensure online interventions or programs provide the needed analytics and reports to all stakeholders in a systematic manner. | When requesting services of companies or vendors for online interventions, review the program analytics (deleted phrase) to ensure the system has the capability of automatically generating reports as needed with data points for all stakeholders—students, teachers, parents, principals, and superintendents.<br><br>If analytics are not available, request the information necessary based on your campus time line for review of data. |
|---|---|---|
| | In a virtual or blended environment, ensure the program or online interventions integrate with the learning-management and student-management systems. | Check the compatibility of interventions with the learning-management system or student-management system to ensure teachers are able to integrate grades across systems to monitor the learning, provide feedback and make data-driven instructional decisions.<br><br>Ensure that there are no hidden costs with systems integrations or plug-ins. |

## Leveraging Time

When considering time as it pertains to online interventions and programs used in blended and virtual environments, the nature of the technology ensures that time for learning and additional support are more readily available. However, like the brick-and-mortar campus, when preparing to work with online interventions—whether blended or virtual—the time investment is made up front to ensure that the intervention advances learning at a higher rate. For example, to ensure that web-based interventions work properly requires a collaborative effort at the district and school levels. This leadership approach fosters autonomy and creativity (loose leadership) within a systematic framework that stipulates clear, nondiscretionary priorities and parameters (tight leadership) (DuFour, 2007). Use of online tools brings new meaning to loose and tight leadership and requires a districtwide time line that speaks to the coordination of departments, such as technology, curriculum, and instruction, as well as student information services.

At our Virtual School and Early College Academy, we had to accept that technology has transformed not only the learning but also how we operate as a school system. Therefore, we made the new components, such as systems integrations, technology, and bandwidth part of the normal processes of change that we manage. In addition, we devised a time line to address the needs of the system, the schools, and the students. Areas that we considered include:

- System integrations

- Technology and bandwidth

- Training

- Master schedule time lines

- Uploading of student rosters and student identification numbers

Thus, we started our time line for master scheduling early enough to ensure we had all the necessary information from our students and moved the collection of the information—the registration process—online as part of our systematic transformation.

Technology and time also affect how we train personnel on the new technologies and on delivering instruction in a blended model. We found it was easier for our school to deliver the staff training and support via an online platform or a blended model as well. This leverages time, as teachers could receive training anytime anywhere.

We also leverage time by recognizing the difference between an engaging program that provides practice and an online intervention. A good online intervention increases our efficiency; thus, we began to seek online interventions with the following characteristics.

- Universal screeners

- Adaptive learning

- Robust reporting systems or dashboards for students, teachers, and administrators

- College- and career-readiness behaviors addressed

- Training videos or modules built in

- Face-to-face or virtual coaching as part of the services

- Real-time progress monitoring for establishing goals, defining interventions, collecting visual data, and responding to the intervention

When we select interventions that have these characteristics, the work of educators is focused on learning and student achievement is increased exponentially. Let's be clear, creating videos for instructional support for students and apps for practice does allow students to have access anytime and anywhere; however, to truly leverage time with interventions and ensure learning, data must fuel the decisions of your professional learning community (PLC).

Engaging programs allow for individual and class practice; however, in a PLC, it is also important for teacher efforts to be interdependent, with shared goals and accountability for reaching those goals. In this age of technology with personalized learning, our students and parents are also an active part of the community.

## Sharing Data

To achieve interdependence, we realized our teams must incorporate the reports from the program into our normal data-meeting protocols, adjust our SMART goals as needed, and continue to work the plan. The data from the online interventions also give our teachers feedback for areas of instruction to improve.

In a virtual school, the processes of data sharing and planning differ from solely brick-and-mortar schools, as the students are in different places in the curriculum, which requires the teachers to set artificial time lines to plan how and when they will respond to the gaps in learning. At our school campus, we offered additional support by doing the following to ensure intervention time occurs within the school day.

- Meeting with intervention providers and campus leadership teams to discuss master schedules and campus needs to ensure each tool met the needs of the students identified as requiring Tier 2 or 3 intervention

- Collaborating with campus staff to define and clarify the use of a blended model for the delivery of effective instruction and interventions

- Coaching staff on how students, teachers, and teams should use data to maximize interventions

We often say that data fuel the team. This is true; however, if used correctly, data also fuel the learning and provide hope to the learner. This is why we expect our students to keep track of their learning outcomes and goals and expect teaching teams to keep data notebooks. Even more important, this belief is why we use online interventions, since they provide and capture the data on individual users in real time.

# Accessing Technology and Interventions

One question many schools on this journey of blended learning through the utilization of online tools for RTI ask is, "What do you do if students do not have the necessary technology or Internet access?" In our school, we found the right question to ask was this: "Would technology afford students the opportunity to learn and function at high levels, and is it something they need?" This question allowed us to work on the right problem.

There are a number of ways in which mobile technology enables educational innovation and makes time for interventions. Based on Project Tomorrow's research, student access has improved across various mobile platforms. Eighty percent of high school students have smartphones, 45 percent have tablet computers, 38 percent have digital readers, and 58 percent have cell phones. These percentages are up from just a few years prior. In 2008, only 28 percent of high schoolers had smartphones. In 2011, only 26 percent of students in grades 6–8 had a tablet computer, compared to 52 percent in 2013 (West, 2013).

These statistics will force schools, leadership, and policies to change. In the words of Jim Shelton, deputy secretary for the U.S. Department of Education, "Students have been locked down by the concept of seat time and locked out of the technological revolution that has transformed nearly every sector of American society, except education" (as cited in Patrick & Sturgis, 2011, p. 7). This is simply not acceptable. It is tremendously apparent that technology makes determining each student's needs easy, because mastery of learning for students and quality teaching for staff are visible. The data and reporting systems allow connections to be realized at a level that traditional systems do not afford. Quality online interventions provide pre- and postassessments for progress monitoring, so teachers can continually group learners as needed while providing students with their own personal playlist for learning.

The adaptability of technology allows teachers to arrange the order of instruction modules based on the learner's need and to provide teacher support and guided lessons. When thinking becomes transparent, teachers are able to see, in real time, which students are learning at a level of mastery and which are struggling on a particular skill. When schools deliver interventions in a blended model, teachers collect multiple data points as well. These data points reveal strengths in teaching that allow the teacher teams to learn from each other and place students with staff members who best understand how to deliver that instruction. This process of monitoring, revising, and extending is powerful for the teacher team and all learners. The team can extend the strength of students while addressing areas of needs. This process also empowers the learner, since students have their own personal dashboards within the technology system.

# Leading and Managing Personalized Online Interventions

The leadership and management of online interventions cannot be outsourced to the companies who provide them. Rather, the principal and leadership team play a critical role in leading the implementation of online interventions. We must remember that technology is only a tool; the principal is responsible for ensuring that high levels of learning are taking place for all students, and he or she must shape the process around guiding questions (see table 12.2).

**Table 12.2: Guiding Questions for Ensuring Learning With Online Interventions**

| Fidelity of Implementation | Who creates the criteria to select and review online tools to ensure campus needs are met? |
|---|---|
| | Who determines if the online intervention meets student needs? |
| | Who monitors and supports teachers with intervention implementation? |
| | Who ensures that fidelity of implementation is understood at all levels on the campus? |
| Utilization of Data | Who determines which data points teacher teams will need to review to improve teaching and learning? |
| | Who determines the time line by which we will communicate data to all stakeholders in the professional learning community as well as what the expected instructional response will be? |
| | How will we make data transparent and utilize them from classroom to classroom to ensure quality learning for all staff and students? |
| | How do we make parents aware of their child's progress with online interventions? How do we teach parents to support their child with any portion of the intervention accessed at home? |
| | How do teams use the data reports in team meetings for learning? |
| | How are students discussing and using the data to ensure they are learning and that their needs are met? |
| | How are we using online interventions to work to the strength of the learner and to ensure college- and career-readiness skills are a part of the learning? |

| Professional Learning | Who determines when to schedule professional development sessions, and what points of fidelity and student achievement will we monitor and improve through professional development? |
|---|---|
| | Will onsite coaches provide implementation and coaching of the tool? |
| | If coaches are supporting the blended intervention, who manages their work, and how is their work used to advance learning? |
| | Which specific administrator is monitoring the learning we expect from these interventions and the support we provide for teachers? |
| Systems Integration | Have we created a time line to denote when systems are checked to ensure computers have appropriate software, icons are pushed out from the district level, and all ports are operational? |
| | Does the online intervention provide a system for managing teachers assigned, students placed in the system, passwords, and the backup of student information and data? If not, who will manage these processes? |
| | Who monitors the bandwidth of the campus to ensure devices and access are adequate for the interventions we use? |
| | Which team is planning to systematically ensure additional devices and bandwidth are in place as needed for classrooms and the school? |

As we move from paralyzing programs to personalized learning with powerful online interventions, we must work to our strengths, grow our global PLC, and provide hope to school leaders, teachers, and students that we can and will provide high levels of learning for all. The strength of our democracy rests on our commitment and will to make this a reality for each and every student.

# References and Resources

Bienkowski, M., Feng, M., & Means, B. (2012). *Enhancing teaching and learning through educational data mining and learning analytics: An issue brief.* Accessed at www.ed.gov /edblogs/technology/files/2012/03/edm-la-brief.pdf on July 7, 2014.

Christensen, C., Horn, M., & Staker, H. (2013). *Is K–12 blended learning disruptive? An introduction of the theory of hybrids.* Accessed at www.christenseninstitute.org/publications /hybrids/ on April 21, 2014.

Conley, D. (2011). *Defining and measuring college and career readiness.* Paper presented at the Educational Policy Improvement Center, Portland, OR.

DuFour, R. (2007). In praise of top-down leadership. *The School Administrator, 64*(10), 38–42.

Fullan, M. (2004). *Systems thinkers in action: Moving beyond the standard plateau.* Accessed at www.michaelfullan.ca/media/13396063090.pdf on April 21, 2014.

Hattie, J. A. C. (2009). *Visible learning: A synthesis of over 800 meta-analyses relating to achievement.* New York: Routledge.

Jackson, Y. (2011). *The pedagogy of confidence: Inspiring high intellectual performance in urban schools.* New York: Teachers College Press.

Patrick, S., & Sturgis, C. (2011). *Cracking the code: Synchronizing policy and practice for performance based learning.* Vienna, VA: International Association for K–12 Online Learning.

Texas Education Agency. (2013). *Early college initiative.* Accessed at www.tea.state.tx.us /index3.aspx?id=4464, July 7, 2014.

U.S. Department of Education. (2010). *Evaluation of evidence-based practices in online learning: A meta-analysis and review of online learning studies.* Accessed at www2.ed.gov/rschstat /eval/tech/evidence-based-practices/finalreport.pdf on March 31, 2014.

U.S. Department of Education. (2012). *Enhancing teaching and learning through educational data mining and learning analytics: An issue brief.* Accessed at www.ed.gov/edblogs/technology /files/2012/03/edm-la-brief.pdf on March 31, 2014.

West, D. M. (2013). *Mobile learning: Transforming education, engaging students, and improving outcomes.* Washington, DC: The Brookings Institute.

Wicks, M. (2010). *A national primer on K–12 online learning: Version 2.* Accessed at http:// files.eric.ed.gov/fulltext/ED514892.pdf on April 21, 2014.

# Epilogue

You have now taken a virtual journey through twelve unique approaches to providing all students with the time and support needed to ensure high levels of learning for all. This journey has included large and small schools, urban and suburban schools, schools that serve a relatively high socioeconomic community, schools that serve a majority of students living at or below the poverty level, schools from the East Coast and the Far East, schools from the middle of America, and schools from the North and South. Undoubtedly, you have seen elements of your school in one or more of these examples. Additionally, almost every example was achieved within the school's existing resources, using its current staff, and in accordance with existing federal, state, and contractual requirements.

We suspect that some educators will read the numerous examples of systematic interventions described in this anthology and claim that providing this level of support might be possible but not desirable, because such actions will result in enabling students and will not properly prepare them for the real world. These critics will instead recommend keeping our traditional approach of offering additional support but allowing students the right to fail, as this will hold students accountable for their actions and teach responsibility.

We absolutely agree that responsibility is a critical life skill. As such, the real question is this: What is the best way to teach students responsibility and ensure high levels of learning? We challenge educators who claim that teaching the traits needed to succeed is best achieved by giving students the option to fail to show evidence that this approach is working at their school. Do the students who decide against getting help benefit from their error in judgment and make better choices due to their failure? Are the students who choose to disregard their homework and miss dead-lines becoming more responsible? Are the students tracked into below-grade-level coursework catching up and succeeding in postsecondary education and beyond?

There is virtually no research or evidence to suggest that higher incidents of failure in secondary school produce higher levels of responsibility, greater academic achieve-ment in college, or a higher likelihood of success meeting the demands of the adult life. Considering that the United States currently has the second-highest collegiate dropout rate in the industrialized world (Porter, 2013), it would be exceedingly hard to argue that the country's traditional secondary "sink or swim" approach is properly preparing students for the rigors of postsecondary education. More likely, these stu-dents are missing assignment after assignment and failing class after class, semester after semester, year after year—all the while showing no newly gained initiative to seek out extra help. Likewise, these students are more likely to live an adult life char-acterized by poverty, government assistance, and incarceration—hardly evidence that our secondary system has properly prepared them for the real world. Based on overwhelming evidence, advocating for our traditional secondary approach to inter-ventions is misguided at the least and downright unethical at the worst.

Even after embracing the need to change our traditional approach and structures of secondary education, a school is still left with the daunting question of how to achieve these outcomes. By providing you with detailed examples from real-life schools, we hope you have a clearer vision of the road that lies ahead. In terms of how you use the information from these schools to impact your own, your journey has only just begun.

We caution you to resist two ways of thinking as you move forward with response to intervention (RTI) at your school. First, please recognize that the culture of ev-ery school is amazingly unique. This means that adopting a bell schedule or any other idea contained in the preceding chapters requires an adaptation to your school culture. In other words, we caution against lifting ideas wholesale and superimpos-ing them on your school. Instead, ask yourself, "What is the thinking behind that schedule, assessment, or intervention practice, and how might that be adapted to fit the unique needs of our school?"

Conversely, we caution against the reaction, "That's a great idea, but it will never work in our building because . . ." Rather than summarily dismissing great ideas too quickly, we recommend focusing on what you can do rather than on what you can't. Do this by asking yourself, "What about that idea resonates with me?" and "Even though we can't implement this idea as stated, how could the thinking behind it be implemented in a way that would work on our campus?" By focusing on the process rather than simply looking at the program, you will move from focusing on the "what" to the "how," and in doing so will discover ways of tweaking the process that might not have been readily apparent as you first considered it.

Finally, we hope that as your journey continues, you will move forward with the realization that it can be done, it is being done, and it must be done for the sake of our students. The schools described in this book did not begin with a perfect plan or possess all the resources required. Surely there were skeptics, and undoubtedly there were missteps along the way. But mistakes were transformed into lessons learned, and stumbling blocks were viewed as stepping-stones. These educators demonstrated the traits they wanted their students to acquire—traits like dedication, perseverance, and compassion. Progress was measured not merely in test scores or credit earned but in the potential success of every student. Ultimately, the educators in this book relied on their most precious resource—each other. Most importantly, they started!

The key to your school's success will begin or end with your willingness to start the journey, for only those willing to take a first step will ever discover what is possible.

# Index

## The Collaborative Administrator: Working Together as a Professional Learning Community
**By Austin Buffum, Cassandra Erkens, Charles Hinman, Susan B. Huff, Lillie G. Jessie, Terri L. Martin, Mike Mattos, Anthony Muhammad, Peter Noonan, Geri Parscale, Eric Twadell, Jay Westover, and Kenneth C. Williams**
**Foreword by Robert Eaker**
**Introduction by Richard DuFour**

How do you maintain the right balance of loose and tight leadership? How do you establish profound, lasting trust with your staff? What principles strengthen principal leadership? This book answers these questions and much more in compelling chapters packed with strategies and inspiration.
**BKF256**

## Simplifying Response to Intervention: Four Essential Guiding Principles
**By Austin Buffum, Mike Mattos, and Chris Weber**

The sequel to *Pyramid Response to Intervention* advocates that effective RTI begins by asking the right questions to create a fundamentally effective learning environment for every student. Understand why paperwork-heavy, compliance-oriented, test-score-driven approaches fail. Then learn how to create an RTI model that works.
**BKF506**

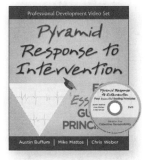

## Pyramid Response to Intervention: Four Essential Guiding Principles
**Featuring Austin Buffum, Mike Mattos, and Chris Weber**

Shift to a culture of collective responsibility, and ensure a path of opportunity and success for your students. Focusing on the four Cs vital to student achievement, this powerful four-part program will help you collect targeted information on each student's individual needs and guide you to build efficient team structures.
**DVF057**

## Making Time at Tier 2: Creating a Supplemental Intervention Period in Secondary Schools
**Featuring Mike Mattos**

Discover practical strategies to build Tier 2 intervention and enrichment periods into the school day, and learn how to work in collaborative teams to create targeted interventions and overcome implementation challenges to ensure all students are successful.
**DVF066**

## Solution Tree | Press
a division of
Solution Tree

Visit solution-tree.com or call 800.733.6786 to order.

**Wait!** Your professional development journey doesn't have to end with the last pages of this book.

We realize improving student learning doesn't happen overnight. And your school or district shouldn't be left to puzzle out all the details of this process alone.

**No matter where you are on the journey, we're committed to helping you get to the next stage.**

Take advantage of everything from **custom workshops** to **keynote presentations** and **interactive web and video conferencing**. We can even help you develop an action plan tailored to fit your specific needs.

*Let's get the conversation started.*

Call 888.763.9045 today.

 solution-tree.com